323.3264 AYRES
Ayres, Ian.
Straightforward :
R0021106104

D0743048

OCT -- 2005

STRAIGHTFORWARD

STRAIGHTFORWARD

How to Mobilize Heterosexual Support for Gay Rights

Ian Ayres and Jennifer Gerarda Brown

PRINCETON UNIVERSITY PRESS

PRINCETON AND OXFORD

Copyright © 2005 by Princeton University Press

Requests for permission to reproduce material
from this work should be sent to Permissions,
Princeton University Press

Published by Princeton University Press,
41 William Street, Princeton, New Jersey 08540

In the United Kingdom: Princeton University Press,
3 Market Place, Woodstock, Oxfordshire OX20 1SY

All Rights Reserved

Library of Congress Cataloging-in-Publication Data

Ayres, Ian.
Straightforward : how to mobilize heterosexual support for
gay rights / Ian Ayres and
Jennifer Gerarda Brown.
p.   cm.
Includes bibliographical references and index.
ISBN 0-691-12134-6 (alk. paper)
1. Gay rights—United States.   2. Heterosexuals—United
States—Attitudes.   3. Homophobia—United States—
Prevention.   I. Title: Straightforward.   II. Brown,
Jennifer Gerarda, 1960–   III. Title.

HQ76.8.U5A97   2005
323.3'264'0973—dc22   2004057504

British Library Cataloging-in-Publication Data is available

This book has been composed in Minion and Futura

Printed on acid-free paper. ∞

pup.princeton.edu

Printed in the United States of America

1   3   5   7   9   10   8   6   4   2

TO OUR CHILDREN

ANTONIA AND HENRY AYRES-BROWN

may you travel all the countries where your hearts lead

and

TO THEIR GODFATHER

AKHIL REED AMAR

you don't need many heroes if you choose carefully

R0021106104

CONTENTS

Straightforward began in a conversation we had with Akhil Amar at our wedding reception in 1993. Akhil, in response to the Hawaii Supreme Court's decision that spring in *Baehr v. Lewin,* wondered about the economic impact of same-sex couples traveling to Hawaii to marry. Shortly thereafter, Jennifer embarked on a project to estimate the impact such marriages might have on Hawaii's economy. She followed with articles exploring the ramifications of a prohibition against judicial bias on the basis of sexual orientation that is on the books in well over half the states. Then she considered how states could pressure private organizations to end their policies of discrimination, even in the wake of the Supreme Court's decision in *Dale v. Boy Scouts of America* to allow the Boy Scouts to discriminate against gays. Her discussion responded to the Supreme Court's emphasis on "expressive association." Jennifer saw that if a state required organizations to inform members about the organization's discriminatory policies, members might exercise their freedom *not* to associate.[1]

For many years Jennifer had been interested in the special opportunities and challenges heterosexual allies face as they voice their support for gay rights. Stepping back to assess the series of articles she had written, she saw a set of strategies to harness or mobilize heterosexual support for gay rights. This book is a working out of this idea, as it applies to discrimination in employment, in private organizations and houses of worship, in marriage and families, and in the military.

Ian considers himself a bit of a Johnny-come-lately to the project, but the truth is that he, too, has long contemplated the dynamics of discrimination. In 1991 he published an article testing for race and gender discrimination in car sales. He moved on to study discrimination in a variety of markets and to support affirmative action as a remedy for that discrimination. These projects have sensitized him to the interplay between economic incentives and moral imperatives. They also fuel a recurring theme you'll find in this book: the analogy between sexual orientation and race.[2]

The issues raised in this book animate both our academic and our personal lives. We feel an abiding disquiet in choosing to marry when same-sex couples cannot, and we have continually struggled with how best to act in a country where the law formally and invidiously discriminates against people we love.

MANY, MANY people have helped us with this book—indeed, so many that if, in expressing our gratitude, we have inadvertently omitted someone, we'll be embarrassed but not surprised. We are particularly thankful to our family and friends, who were driven to distraction by our hectoring questions ("Would you at least cross the street to marry in a nondiscriminatory jurisdiction?"). Many people have helped us through conversations, by reading drafts, or by commenting on papers presenting the book's ideas. Audrey and Ted Brown, Tara Ayres, Mary Coffield, Bo Roth, Jack Hitt, Diane Mazur, Akhil Amar, Kenji Yoshino, Bill Eskridge, Richard Epstein, Janet Halley, Elizabeth Emens, Andrew Koppelman, Robert Morris, Bruce Ackerman, Linda Meyer, Michael Ray, Evan Wolfson, Carlos Ball, William Bratton, Jon Macey, Mary Anne Case, Clark Freshman, Robert Wintemute and David Cruz—these would begin the list, but we could go on. Numerous faculty workshops where we presented chapters or related ideas helped tremendously: participants at Australian National University, UCLA, USC, Colorado, Georgetown, Harvard, Quinnipiac, Toronto, and the University of Virginia were engaged and generous readers. We thank Tim Sullivan, our editor at Princeton University Press, for making this book possible, and Richard Isomaki, whose able editing improved our style and substance. We are grateful to our colleagues at Yale and Quinnipiac (especially our assistants Marge Camera and Sue Passander), and to our deans, Anthony Kronman and Brad Saxton (and before Brad, Neil Cogan and David King), for their continued support throughout this multiple-year project. We have also benefited from the research assistance of Jeanine DeBacker, Todd Cleary, Jessica Ballou, Eric McGrew, Gowri Ramachandran, Richard Gora, Allison Kaye, Steven Wu, Nassir Zakariya, Praveen Krishna, Bijal Shah, Paul Breloff, and Tom Sylvester.

Finally, we thank our gay, lesbian, bisexual, and transgendered friends and family members for sharing their lives and their stories with us. We hope that the book is better for it. We know that we are.

STRAIGHTFORWARD

Heterosexual Allies and the Gay Rights Movement

A first-year law student named Nancy went to her Contracts class with Professor Jay expecting nothing out of the ordinary. But somewhere between sessions on "promise" and "breach," between "expectation" and "reliance," she one day noticed something quite different about Professor Jay. Jay, who combined left-leaning politics and scholarship with a distinctly conservative fashion sense, usually sported short hair, penny loafers, and oxford cloth shirts. But today, Nancy noticed, Professor Jay was also wearing bright green nail polish.

Unable to contain her curiosity, Nancy asked her professor about his new fashion statement. Jay explained that the day before, his young son Ted had come home in tears. On the playground that day, a group of children had encircled him with taunts about his "long messy hair." Noticing Ted's nail polish, they cruelly chided him for being "abnormal." Later, a teacher found Ted hiding under a piece of play equipment, crying because one of his harassers had finally slapped him.

Professor Jay had taken the measures most parents would when faced with a beloved child in this state. He'd reassured Ted in every way possible. He called Ted's teacher as well as the principal of the school and sought assurances that the other children involved would be made to understand that their behavior was unacceptable. But that evening, Professor Jay went one step further: he took his young son in hand and went to the bathroom where the nail polish was stored. Did Professor Jay remove his son's nail polish at that point? No. He asked if Ted would like to paint his father's nails as well. How better, Jay asked, to convey to his son his solidarity and support?

Nancy is bisexual. As she recounted this story to us, her eyes filled with tears. "I know it was just a little, silly thing . . . but I was blown away when my professor told me what he did for his kid," she said. "I mean, when he put on that nail polish he not only told his kid that it's OK to wear what he wants and look the way he chooses; he effectively put himself in something like the same position his son was in. . . . It was as if to say, 'If they go after you, they'll have to go after me too.' All I could think was, what if every gay, lesbian, or bisexual person got this kind of support from the people who loved them? Can you imagine how different our lives would be?"

Let's take this last question seriously. Suppose that every gay man or lesbian in America can call upon at least two heterosexual friends, family members, or coworkers to actively support their struggle for equality. This is not an outlandish possibility—even if the gay community can count just on parents, this would almost produce the level of support we're hypothesizing. Although some parents of gay children do not support their children's struggle, and some parents are no longer alive, we believe that almost every gay or lesbian person in America has at least two supportive nongay friends or family.

If this amount of support currently exists, right now twenty million heterosexual allies stand ready to support gay rights in the United States. Too often, however, those allies have remained silent, leaving gay, lesbian, and bisexual people to struggle alone in their quest for equality. This lack of support stems in part from a sense a helplessness. We sense a palpable anxiety among these allies. "What can I do?" they ask.

This book provides an answer. It gives pragmatic advice to heterosexual allies on what they can do to support their friends. It also suggests how supporters of gay rights (regardless of their sexual orientation) can work to restructure institutions and legal rules to activate heterosexual support. The book thus serves as a guide to action not only in our personal lives and economic activities but in the political sphere as well—suggesting new public policies that are designed to waken this sleeping giant of potential support.

One way to advance gay rights is to recognize instances in which heterosexual people can take action. That is, allies must identify times when they can express their decision to support gay rights; they must recognize the cusps when choice becomes available. Such occasions involve concrete decisions: to speak or remain silent, to act or remain passive. Therefore, the book begins by making visible the existing places in which heterosexual people can act to support gay rights; because these opportunities remain hidden, some people are currently making choices without realizing it.

We also use this book to create new occasions for those who believe in gay rights—especially heterosexuals—to act on their convictions. Finally, the book proposes public policies to create new opportunities for expressing support, suggesting specific legislation that would enable such expression.

Heterosexual allies possess tremendous political and economic clout—should we choose to wield it. Without leveraging this resource, full equality for gay, lesbian, and bisexual people may be difficult or impossible to achieve. So this is a book about when and how to level that influence, in individual choices large and small that in aggregate determine the level of equality in our communities and in our nation. It's also about recognizing when and how to express our preferences.

HETEROSEXUAL PEOPLE who want to engage in the struggle for gay rights must come to terms with an important endowment they bear, an endowment that is both a blessing and a curse. We are referring to what is sometimes called *heterosexual privilege*, "the range of perks and incentives with which heterosexually identified persons are rewarded for conforming to the dominant sexuality."[1] As Jamie Washington and Nancy Evans point out, coming to terms with privilege can be "the most painful part of the process of becoming an ally."[2] Privilege creates certain dilemmas, as Bruce Ryder further explains. "[White heterosexual males] must speak and write with great care, acknowledging our privilege and using it and the authority that comes with it in a manner which is attentive to the limitations of our particular knowledge and experiences."[3] Heterosexual people are endowed with a privilege based upon the social implications of their sexual orientation, and this privilege, if not managed effectively, can create obstacles to their constructive engagement in the struggle for gay rights.

The first obstacle that heterosexual privilege can create is informational. One of its key characteristics is to render itself invisible to the privileged.[4] Those who benefit tend to see their status as a norm. Many progressive, well-intentioned heterosexual people are so used to the advantage their sexual orientation conveys that they are blind to it. Some well-meaning heterosexual people don't know how to support gay rights because they do not see how a *lack* of privilege disadvantages bisexuals, lesbians, and gay men.

For this reason, many heterosexual people are not able to perceive the gay rights issues within their everyday existence. Because they are not personally affected, they do not recognize that a particular policy, rule, or social norm is hurting gay people. For example, many heterosexual people are unaware of the real costs that the prohibition on same-sex marriage im-

3

poses on gay people. Heterosexual employees in a business that lacks health benefits for domestic partners, for example, may be unaware that their gay and lesbian coworkers bear the expense of health benefits for their partners. When a child's high school restricts the types of student groups that can meet on school property to prevent a fledgling gay-straight alliance from forming, many parents do not recognize that the free expression of gay and lesbian people has also been restricted.

Such ignorance isn't surprising. These problems don't affect heterosexuals directly and exist on the perimeter of the public sphere. One of the goals of this book is to highlight issues of gay rights that can play out in heterosexual people's "own backyard" and to suggest ways that they can promote equality by making their voices heard.

Although many heterosexual people are oblivious to privilege and its effect on gay and nongay lives, at times heterosexual people may become acutely aware of it. They may not name privilege as such, but they know that it divides them from the lesbians and gay men they would like to support. Many heterosexual people with progressive attitudes and good intentions feel presumptuous even trying to express support for gay rights. Because they are granted powers and privileges denied to gay people, heterosexuals may feel hesitant—embarrassed, disconcerted, inappropriate—discussing the structures and policies that give them these privileges. Perhaps their experience is similar to that of feminist men or white civil rights workers in the 1960s. Certainly heterosexual people must avoid the temptation to speak *for* gay people (this *would* be presumptuous). The challenge is to find a distinctly heterosexual voice that can constructively speak for gay rights.

This book proposes three distinct general strategies for managing privilege: exercising it, disabling it, and renouncing it. We suggest when it is most appropriate for heterosexual allies to use each strategy—when, for instance, to speak expressly as heterosexuals and when to speak in ways that make their sexual orientation ambiguous. We discuss when heterosexuals should work within institutions to economically support gay-friendly policies, and when they should walk away from institutions, boycott bigoted vendors, and renounce the benefits of privilege.

Exercising Privilege

The first strategy calls on allies to exercise privilege when it will upset conclusions people in power may draw about the views of heterosexual people. Here's a fairly common example. Suppose that a school system is deciding how to cover homosexuality in the standard sexual education curriculum. Conservative organizations may object to any presentation of homosexuality as falling within a "normal" orientation. The school may also hear from gay rights advocacates who support a curriculum that normalizes homosexuality. In the middle are hundreds, even thousands, of parents in the school system who have their own views. Heterosexual parents who support frank, open, and fair discussions about homosexuality in sex ed curricula have a special opportunity, indeed responsibility, to make their views heard. They can work within the system, identifying themselves as heterosexual parents of kids who are going to take sex ed classes. Because heterosexual people are more likely than gay men or lesbians to have children, they gain access and privilege within school systems that gay people lack. It becomes the responsibility of heterosexual people, then, to exploit that privilege to make progress on gay rights within the school system.

Heterosexual allies can also exercise their privilege by supporting gay rights economically. This book will not only make existing choices more visible, it will also create new opportunities to express such support—a chance for allies to "vote with their wallets." *Straightforward* will launch a web site (www.vacationpledge.org) where people can sign a "Vacation Pledge for Equal Marriage Rights." People who sign promise to vacation in the first state that legalizes same-sex marriage within three years of legalization. Many states rely on tourism to support their local economies and generate tax revenue. Through the web site, gay and nongay supporters can make clear that significant rewards await states that innovate on gay rights.

As this book goes to press, the ruling of the Massachusetts Supreme Judicial Court requiring equal marriage rights for same-sex couples in Massachusetts has just gone into effect. The court's action has created pressure for state and federal constitutional amendments restricting marriage to different-sex couples; state civil union may be a compromise position in this battle. At this point, the Vacation Pledge is designed to reward the first state that votes democratically to grant equal marriage rights to same-sex couples—either by legislative action or by the vote of the electorate rejecting constitutional amendments designed to undo judicial action. In the future, a pledge could reward the first state that recognizes a same-sex marriage solemnized in another state. A pledge could reward the first state west of the Mississippi to allow gay marriage. The point is that the pledge can reflect the evolving recognition of same-sex marriage, holding out rewards to the states that propel legal change. More broadly, the pledge demonstrates the economic power of heterosexual allies who act on their privilege.

Another new space for the expression of heterosexual support is the Fair Employment Mark. Launched contemporaneously with the publication of this book, the Fair Employment Mark can be used by licensees to certify that products bearing the mark have been manufactured in compliance with a specified standard of gay friendliness in employment. To start, the mark could be licensed only to employers who voluntarily comply with all that has been proposed in the Employment Non-Discrimination Act (ENDA), the as-yet unsuccessful congressional bill that would protect gay and lesbian workers from discrimination in the workplace.[5] If ENDA eventually passes, the Fair Employment Mark could reflect a yet higher standard of gay friendliness, usable only by employers who offer benefit plans open to employees' same-sex partners, and so on. While the Vacation Pledge calls upon people to express their support in a public, coordinated way, the Fair Employment Mark facilitates individual consumers' private, decentralized choices. These complementary strategies (each embracing a broad range of support levels, and both deploying heterosexual privilege) could maximize the number of people who participate in the gay rights movement. Even as this book encourages gay rights organizations to more effectively deploy heterosexual people in their struggle, it also implements two instruments for doing so.

Small states and small producers have disproportionate incentives to compete for gay-friendly dollars. Even when there are more gay-unfriendly than gay-friendly consumers, some small firms or small states still have strong economic incentives to commit to nondiscrimination policies. In other words, the benefits of "buycotts"—for example, gay-friendly consumers' preference for products bearing the Fair Employment Mark—are likely to outweigh the threat of boycotts by consumers who oppose equality.

Disabling Privilege

The second general strategy (and for some heterosexual people, the most difficult) is to disable one's own heterosexual privilege by making one's sexual orientation ambiguous. You cannot claim the perquisites of heterosexual status if others can't discern your sexual orientation. Making sexual orientation ambiguous requires a tolerance—perhaps even enjoyment—of uncertainty. While exercising privilege involves acting explicitly *as a hetero-*

sexual person, heterosexual allies who "ambiguate" serve the cause of gay rights by *forgoing* opportunities to identify as heterosexual. In some contexts, we'll make progress only when heterosexual people are willing to be "mistaken" for bisexuals or as gay.[6] Heterosexual people's willingness to present themselves ambiguously is, in some ways, a test of their support for gay rights and a prerequisite to making a real difference in some areas of public policy.

This strategy requires heterosexual allies not to be so quick to clarify their sexual orientation, to resist the urge to say, "Well, I'm heterosexual, but I support gay rights." From time to time, heterosexual people should merely state their support for gay rights—and let the audience draw whatever conclusions it likes about their sexual orientation. Creating ambiguity can be as simple as a choice of words. A woman can refer to her husband not as her husband but as her "spouse" ("My spouse and I are academics"). She might leave open the question of whether her spouse is a man or a woman.[7] Perhaps use of the word *spouse* rather than *partner* already identifies her as legally married and therefore involved with a member of the "opposite" sex. But as increasing numbers of same-sex couples participate in religious and civil wedding ceremonies and thereafter refer to each other as "spouses," the mere avoidance of gender specificity can create ambiguity. All of this is to suggest that when a woman uses the word *husband*, she marks herself as part of a heterosexual couple, ridding her description of even the hint of ambiguity.

As with the strategies of exploiting and renouncing heterosexual privilege, the book will approach ambiguation from the collective as well as from the individual perspective. For example, we propose a form of ambiguation that would promote the integration of sexual minorities in the military, disabling heterosexual privilege in a venue that has enshrined discrimination.

Straightforward proposes that the Department of Defense, with congressional support, could create "inclusive commands" to which recruits could be assigned when they indicate a willingness to serve with fellow service members who are openly gay or lesbian. This idea relies upon the notion that the best way to integrate sexual minorities into the U.S. military may be through a voluntary system. By asking all recruits whether they are willing to serve with openly gay or lesbian service members, the inclusive command would force recruits to express and perhaps confront their own prejudices. Even more importantly, the question permits willing recruits (gay and nongay) to express their support for an integrated military. The inclusive command thus creates a special role for heterosexuals in the process of integration, shifting the focus away from gay service members (who, as even opponents of integration concede, are not the problem) to the heterosexual soldiers working beside and responding to them.

For the inclusive command to work, progressive heterosexual service members must be willing to serve with openly gay and lesbian soldiers in a unit characterized by its inclusive nature—even if a consequence is that some people assume that members of the inclusive command are gay or lesbian. Like strategies that harness privilege, disabling privilege through ambiguation relies upon individual choices, but it also stems from a structure put in place to coordinate individual decision-making (the inclusive command itself, as well as the statutory or regulatory reform necessary to implement it).

Despite its usefulness in some contexts, ambiguation isn't appropriate in every situation. Ambiguity can cause problems that have rarely arisen in other civil rights struggles. When white people supported civil rights for African-Americans in the 1960s, they were clearly members of the majority who supported the rights of the minority. The same may be said about gender, age, and (sometimes, not always) disability. In these contexts, people outside the minority can speak without implying that they personally gain from the changes they advocate—their altruism is clear. A white man will not be mistaken for black, nor will an activist standing at a microphone be mistaken for a quadriplegic. But sexual orientation doesn't work this way. Those who speak for gay rights are often assumed to be gay or lesbian themselves. Perhaps this is a sad commentary on a lack of empathy in our culture; perhaps this is just a reflection of the hatred that has been directed toward gay people for so long (the assumption being that only someone personally harmed by discrimination on the basis of sexual orientation would object to it). Either way, the problem of ambiguity creates tensions for heterosexuals who support gay rights.

Ambiguation thus creates a dilemma for heterosexual allies. If a heterosexual supporter who is assumed to be gay too quickly clarifies her sexual orientation, her flight from a lesbian identity stigmatizes gay people.[8] If being gay isn't so bad, an observer might ask, why are you so quick to make clear that you are *not*? On the other hand, if heterosexual supporters cultivate ambiguity, they engage in a kind of reverse passing, pretending to status and experience they lack. Moreover, if *everyone* were to "pass" as gay or lesbian, an odd sort of recloseting could occur, hiding the "truly" gay or lesbian among a sea of pretenders.[9] This strategy was powerful—if only in legend—when gentiles in Denmark wore the yellow Star of David on their lapels during the occupation of Denmark by the Nazis during World War II.[10] At that time, some gentiles felt that the only thing they could do to help Jews was literally to hide them.[11] Most gay men and lesbians no longer need literally to hide. Some must remain closeted to keep their jobs—especially members of the armed forces—and others come out only selectively to maintain social or family relationships. Generally, however, the shared goal is to have the option to be open about sexual orientation. The world for which most gay rights activists strive is one in which people can be open about their lives and loves without fear of violence or condemnation. The task of heterosexual supporters therefore becomes not to hide gay people but to work to create a world that is safe—one in which gay, lesbian, bisexual, and straight people can live with love, respect, and integrity.

We propose guidelines for nongay allies that may help them determine when ambiguation is a useful strategy. We encourage allies to ask themselves several questions.

- *Would creating or tolerating ambiguity trivialize sexual orientation?* Nongay allies should take care lest they suggest that homosexuality is a game or a costume to be taken off and on at whim.
- *Will my audience think less of me if they perceive me to be gay, lesbian, or bisexual?* Ambiguation is useful in upsetting the assumptions of antigay audiences, and in aligning the nongay ally with a group the antigay audience seeks to harm.
- *Can I entertain internal ambiguity about my sexual orientation?* The closet and the deception it requires have done a lot of damage. Nongay allies should be careful not to compound the lies by reversing them; ambiguation makes more sense if a nongay ally can acknowledge and appreciate the fluidity of sexual orientation.
- *Should sexual orientation be irrelevant to the discussion or transaction at issue?* Ambiguation can be a good strategy for diluting the prejudicial effect of homosexuality in contexts where sexual orientation ought to be irrelevant. In some cases, however, a person can speak with greater authority if he or she has the lived experience of a gay, lesbian, or bisexual person. To ambiguate in this latter group of cases—where the sexual orientation of the speaker is relevant—would effect an unseemly misappropriation of gay identity; nongay allies should make clear their privileged location in such situations.

How might we apply this theory to ourselves as we write this book? In some ways, we are reluctant to "come out" about our sexual orientations because we believe that sexual orientation is far too complex and fluid to be cabined into the narrow categories that most political discourse permits. On the other hand, it is important to be clear about the perspectives and experiences from which we address the subject of this book. We are privileged: husband and wife, a happily married couple and the parents of two wonderful children. To the wider world, we would be identified as heterosexual.[12] That might lead some readers to give what we say greater credence, and others to dismiss it out of hand. To the extent anyone gives us greater deference based on our heterosexuality, we are inclined to ambiguate and tell you we are bisexual. Certainly we both acknowledge and appreciate the indeterminacy of sexual orientation and can honestly say we perceive some bisexuality in our own identities and desires. But that is not our lived experience—we've not had the relationships and experiences that subject so many LGBT people to discrimination. And because those experiences and histories are relevant—our position as privileged people limits our perspectives in ways that are important here—we think it best to disambiguate. At least right now and for this purpose, we speak to you as heterosexuals.

Renouncing Privilege

The third strategy is to renounce heterosexual privilege, explicitly separating oneself from an institution that ordinarily grants or enhances heterosexual privilege. Rather than calling on allies to work for change from within a system, this strategy encourages us to abandon some systems altogether. For example, if a private association makes clear that it reserves the right to discriminate on the basis of sexual orientation, then a member (perhaps after making some attempts to change the policy) can support gay rights by quitting the organization. The key is to renounce this membership in the institution and the privilege that accompanies it in a public way so that the action can have the desired symbolic or political effects.

The arc of the book, from strategies of exercising, to disabling, and then to renouncing privilege, roughly tracks the distinction between strategies of "voice" and "exit."[13] This arc also corresponds to a shift from opportunities many heterosexual supporters would welcome, to choices that may seem difficult and unwanted. It is almost certainly easier for allies to exercise privilege than to ambiguate or renounce privilege.

Many of the ideas in the first part of this book will seem pretty sensible. Although it takes strength, speaking up in our communities will appeal to most readers—the challenge is to identify issues and resources in ways that enable such courageous speech. Some of our proposed strategies will even seem pleasant: taking vacations and purchasing products are things most people like to do, and many already exercise their social conscience in making such choices (animal testing in cosmetics being but one example). *Straightforward* suggests ways to make these choices in the service of human equality.

In contrast, ambiguation—particularly the proposal for an inclusive command—may make some people uncomfortable. They might prefer not to answer the inclusive command question ("Are you comfortable serving with openly gay and lesbian soldiers?"), or they may dislike any suggestion that they should closet their own heterosexual orientation ("This is my partner").

And finally, renouncing privilege—the third general strategy—may require divisive and therefore potentially counterproductive choices. Any discussion to exit perforce cuts off voice—when we disassociate, we remove ourselves from difficult but often constructive conversations. Asking heterosexuals to renounce marriage or to boycott the Boy Scouts may exacerbate the backlash against gays and alienate potential supporters. Some of these choices to renounce privilege will be rejected by readers. We believe, however, that it is good to be honest with oneself and others about the way we benefit from, and thus participate in, discrimination. And if such reflection leads us to change our lives or our laws, so much the better.

Thus, we will provide guidance on when renouncing strategies may be productive. And as before, we will suggest not only guides to personal action but also types of public policy that might facilitate the choice of renunciation. In particular, we propose a specific statute to respond to the discrimination practiced by private organizations such as the Boy Scouts of America.

In the wake of the U.S. Supreme Court's decision permitting the Boy Scouts to discriminate against James Dale on the basis of his sexual orientation, this book proposes legislation, the Informed Association Statute, that gay rights organizations can pursue at the state level.[14] This legislation would require any organization wishing to discriminate on the basis of sexual orientation to obtain the written consent of its members, certifying that the discriminatory policy of the organization has been disclosed to, and ratified by, each member. Members, then, would have to acknowledge and thus implicitly support discriminatory policies. This strategy would harness heterosexual support as people declined to join such organizations or rallied to repeal their discriminatory policies. The Informed Association Statute would force heterosexual people to decide whether they are willing to signal their support for discrimination against gays. For many, this would be uncomfortable, as it would force them to confront the discriminatory nature of their associations and to choose whether to affiliate with such discrimination.

While it is useful from time to time to think about the "forest" of choice, this book is more interested in the "trees"—the specific choices that confront real people in their real lives.

The rest of the book traces these ideas in greater detail. Part I develops various strategies for selectively exercising heterosexual privilege. Chapter 2 aims to make more visible the existing spaces in which heterosexual people can support gay rights. It suggests that heterosexual allies can work for gay rights by exploiting the privilege and access they possess in their own parishes, PTAs, parenting, and workplaces.

Chapter 3 offers a new strategy for heterosexual allies troubled by marriage laws that discriminate on the basis of sexual orientation. The Vacation Pledge for Equal Marriage Rights, launched with the publication of this book, uses a web site to collect promises from individuals that they will reward progressive legislation on marriage rights by spending tourism dollars in states that extend marriage rights to same-sex couples. This strategy harnesses the economic and political clout of gay and nongay consumers collectively.

Chapter 4 presents the Fair Employment Mark, a strategy that would allow supporters of gay rights to exercise their economic clout individually, as they choose to purchase products bearing a mark that signals gay-friendly employment policies on the part of the manufacturer. As it does with the Vacation Pledge, with the Fair Employment Mark *Straightforward* is working to create and publicize a space in which heterosexual people can express their support for gay rights.

Part II turns from strategies in which supporters act *as heterosexuals* (exercising privilege) to strategies of ambiguation. Chapter 5 provides a theory of ambiguation, including examples of ambiguation in other contexts, and then provides guidance about when it is appropriate.

Chapter 6 presents a legislative strategy that rests, in part, upon heterosexuals' tolerance for ambiguation. The inclusive command as a means to integrate sexual minorities into the U.S. military relies to some extent upon ambiguation because it calls into question the assumption that discipline and good order can be maintained only if we pretend that all service members are heterosexual. By permitting gay and lesbian members to be open about their sexual orientation, the inclusive command simultaneously ambiguates and clarifies.

Finally, Part III turns to the strategy of renouncing privilege through boycotts of discriminatory organizations. Chapter 7 provides a general theory of when renouncing privilege (including boycotts and public shaming) is likely to be productive and when counterproductive. The chapter considers a public policy that would apply the renunciation strategy to discriminatory organizations. Using the Supreme Court's decision in *Dale v. Boy Scouts of America* as a springboard, this chapter proposes the Informed Association Statute, legislation that would facilitate more informed and therefore more principled decision-making on the part of heterosexual people contemplating membership in discriminatory organizations. Some people put to the hard choice might not be willing to sign a private acknowledgment that they are associating with an organization that retains the right to discriminate on the basis of sexual orientation.

Chapter 8 explores the possibility that "renouncing marriage" could be a powerful way for heterosexual people to express their support for gay rights.

The book concludes in chapter 9 with a discussion of the relationship between heterosexual allies and the major organizations advocating gay rights. This chapter answers the question: How much are heterosexual people morally obliged to sacrifice for the cause of gay rights? Various approaches are possible. Supporters could give up some pro rata share of the societal benefits they receive by virtue of their heterosexuality, or simply follow instructions from a credible gay rights organization. Who should select the optimal strategy, and if heterosexual supporters retain the authority to decide, how should they exercise that decision-making power? This final chapter will make clear that the theory of advocacy propounded by this book is not one that requires self-abnegation by heterosexuals. Instead the book will present a pragmatic approach to help heterosexual allies determine how much of their resources they are morally obligated to devote to the cause.

Straightforward is deeply concerned with affecting change. The goal is to provide a concrete guide to action. We hope to mobilize heterosexual allies with a mixture of welcome (and perhaps not-so-welcome) opportunities. The collective impact of our individual choices can help dismantle a status quo in which gay and lesbian people are subject to overt discrimination in marriage, in the military, and in employment. We aim for a world that is more joyful and more just.

Part I

Exercising Privilege

In some of her earlier work, Jennifer focused on same-sex couples as sources of tourism revenue following a state's recognition of same-sex marriage. In this book, we're shifting focus to another group: allies who can deploy voices, access, influence, *and wallets* to support gay rights. Our goal here is to describe strategies for deploying both political and purchasing power of allies in ways that promote gay rights.

Chapter 2 focuses on the ways heterosexuals can use their positions as coworkers, parents, and parishioners to support gay rights. Chapter 3 then turns to financial matters, arguing that heterosexuals can powerfully promote gay-friendly public policy by "voting with their wallets." Even though the phenomenon of the "gay dollar" is widely recognized and marketing agencies increasingly focus campaigns on gay consumers, little is said about nongay consumers who support gay rights. And while many businesses have begun to market their products and services directly to lesbian and gay consumers, few boast of their gay friendliness outside the gay community. Thus, a discrete group of consumers has been largely ignored. These consumers are heterosexual allies, people whose decisions about how and where to spend money could be influenced by companies' employment and marketing policies with respect to sexual orientation.

Perhaps it is rational for sellers to ignore heterosexual allies as a group of consumers to be identified and courted. It may be difficult to prove that nongay people would base buying decisions on a seller's policies and practices regarding sexual orientation—so difficult that no producers deem it worth the investment to attract this illusive set of consumers.

But identifying untapped consumer groups and dissecting their preferences minutely is, after all, what marketing is all about. Polls, surveys, focus
groups, and other empirical methods could quickly tell a producer whether
nongay consumers would react positively to gay-friendly policies or marketing. It may be that producers have failed to do this sort of study because
marketers don't think that consumers would spend money in ways that are,
in some sense, altruistic. Unless consumers have something personally to
gain or lose, the thinking might go, they will not consider social policy in
their buying choices.

And yet we have plenty of evidence to counter just this assumption. Individuals and consumer groups have in several contexts demanded social
policies on behalf of interests and concerns that are not directly their own.
From the environment to child labor to health crises in developing nations,
issues that do not directly impact consumers have often influenced their
spending decisions. The trouble is that no one, so far as we're aware, has
ever suggested to heterosexual people that they *should* pay attention to the
way a company treats gay consumers or employees. Heterosexual consumers have never been asked to buy from gay-friendly businesses or travel
to gay-friendly cities and states. The time may be right to start asking.

Rather than threatening to boycott, we should promise to patronize. This
is where both the Vacation Pledge for Equal Marriage Rights (chapter 3) and
the Fair Employment Mark (chapter 4) enter. By promising to vacation in the
first state that democratically embraces equal marriage rights, supporters of
gay rights project their political voice beyond the borders of their home
states. They also demonstrate their willingness to spend money to reward
states and businesses that support fairness. Correspondingly, through the Fair
Employment Mark, employers signal their "gay friendliness" to the consumers who would make choices based on such criteria. Both strategies provide cover for elected representatives, employers, and consumers who support gay rights on the merits, but value monetary rationales for their actions.

These chapters have performative as well as explanatory goals, which
means that we aim not only to *describe* economic strategy, but also to *take
action* consistent with that strategy. In tandem with this book, we have created public space—accessible at www.vacationpledge.com—where supporters of gay rights can pursue a portion of the economic strategy set forth
in chapter 3. We are also launching the Fair Employment Mark, which can
be used by any company that promises not to discriminate on the basis of
sexual orientation.

Parenting, Parishes, PTAs, and Places of Employment

Where after all do universal human rights begin? In small places, closest to home—so close and so small that they cannot be seen on any map of the world. Yet they are the world of the individual person: The neighborhood he lives in; the school or college he attends; the factory, farm or office where he works. Such are the places where every man, woman, and child seeks equal justice, equal opportunity, equal dignity without discrimination. Unless these rights have meaning there, they have little meaning anywhere. Without concerted citizen action to uphold them close to home, we shall look in vain for progress in the larger world.

Eleanor Roosevelt

When Jon was a senior in college, he took his girlfriend home to meet his parents. He knew that his old-fashioned father would not let them sleep in the same room during the visit. And in fact, when they were standing at the airport's luggage carousel, Jon's dad said words so familiar that Jon could recite them word for word.

"I don't care what you two do off at school, but you can't sleep together while you're under our roof."

Jon wasn't upset or surprised by this injunction, but he was very surprised by what his dad said next about Jon's sister, Jane, who is a lesbian.

"Jane is coming to visit from school next month with her girlfriend, and your momma and I have decided that they can sleep together in the same room."

Jon's jaw dropped. "What? Why can Jane sleep over with her girlfriend when I can't? Why the double standard?"

But the biggest surprise was his dad's explanation:

"You have the ability to marry your girlfriend and start sleeping together at our house. But society doesn't give your sister that right. It wouldn't be fair to your sister to treat you the same."

The father's position is remarkable for several reasons. First, it demonstrates how the equal protection principle demands disparate treatment for dissimilarly situated people. The law's discriminatory bar against same-sex marriage led Jon's father to treat his children differently—but fairly. Second, it shows the possibility of innovative empathy. At a time when many parents struggle to see beyond the rigid rules of the past, Jon's parents strive to see things from their lesbian daughter's perspective. Finally, the story shows how people can use their privilege as heterosexuals to foster gay rights. Jon's parents were using their power as heterosexual parents to remedy the state's discrimination—if only in a small way.

A central theme of this book may be difficult for some heterosexual people to hear: nongay allies of gay rights must manage the difficult tension created by our privilege as heterosexuals. This tension arises because even as heterosexuals work to dismantle the structures and belief systems that endow them with privilege, they may find it tempting to exploit the access and influence their privilege creates. Knowing when and how to speak *as a heterosexual* and thus self-consciously from a position of privilege is an important skill for heterosexual gay-rights activists.

Acknowledging the existence and power of heterosexual privilege is an essential first step to learning this skill. Without it, heterosexual people, living within the shelter of privilege, will miss important facts about the lives and desires of the gay and lesbian people with whom they are working. And although heterosexual people cannot step out of their privileged status entirely, we must be conscious of the ways this privilege affects judgments about where and how to devote our energies.

Because privilege is by its nature invisible to those endowed with it, many heterosexual people find it difficult to acknowledge their status.[1] Of course people can hold hands or kiss their significant other without being beaten or fired! But the simple fact is that heterosexuals can do many things in our society that gay and lesbian people cannot. This is true not only because of de jure and de facto state discrimination but because of powerful social discrimination as well.

To help make heterosexual privilege visible, Professor Devon Carbado has helpfully cataloged dozens of ways in which heterosexual privilege can manifest itself.[2] Rights to marry or to serve in the military without concealing one's sexual orientation are two of the more readily apparent features of heterosexual privilege. Other, subtler evidence of privilege emerges in the way heterosexual couples are received by employers, coworkers, family, and friends. Representation of heterosexuality in popular media[3] or school curricula also reflect its privileged status, but few heterosexuals recognize their advantages without prompting.[4]

Professor Carbado's list is particularly helpful in that it recasts discrimination *against* gay people as privilege *advantageous to* heterosexual people. This helps to bring into relief the zero-sum nature of privilege and social hierarchy.[5] What gay people lose with respect to rights or status, heterosexual people gain in special regard or respect.[6] But not all situations give rise to this zero-sum dynamic.[7] Granted, if heterosexual privilege determines who will receive a finite resource, such as a job or a tax benefit, extending rights to gays may cause some corresponding loss for heterosexuals. But several items on Carbado's list do not have this quality. Many of the "privileges" he lists could be extended to gays with no loss in value for heterosexuals. For example, walking safely as a couple, expressing affection in public, and meeting with ready acceptance from friends and coworkers have inherent value that would not deteriorate if gay people were included in the zone of safety.[8]

While recognizing privilege is a crucial (and often untaken) first step, the more difficult question is what can be done to dismantle these systems of discriminatory privilege.

One reasonable approach for straight allies is to renounce heterosexual privilege altogether. With increasing sensitivity to privilege, and helped by instruments like Carbado's list, heterosexual people could systematically set out to give up all the benefits flowing to them based upon their sexual orientation. This would include, for example, staying unmarried, staying out of the military and discriminatory private organizations such as the Boy Scouts of America, and (as existing or potential couples) forgoing any behavior in public that would identify them as heterosexual (flirting, touching, kissing, holding hands, etc.). It would also require heterosexuals to refrain from public references to their significant others, since this is something heterosexuals are privileged to do but many gay and lesbian people must suppress.[9] The most dramatic and in some ways problematic form of privilege renunciation could require heterosexual people to cover their heterosexuality or even "pass" as gay, lesbian, or bisexual.[10]

Some heterosexuals might want to forgo the benefits of their sexual orientation, regardless of the consequences, because these benefits are invidiously denied others. Giving up some of the goodies they receive as heterosexuals might give them a greater sense of solidarity with their fellow citizens who are gay or lesbian. Or allies may choose to repudiate privilege because they believe such action will weaken the system that produces it. Privilege would then become like an unused muscle—reduced to a shadow of its former self.

But such an approach assumes heterosexual people are able to step out of their privileged status—a doubtful proposition in many contexts. Moreover, attempting to forgo the benefits of privilege at all times, in all contexts, means that heterosexual people would sacrifice the opportunities their privileged status provides to change the system. The truth is that in some contexts, identifying and speaking *as a heterosexual* will contribute in special ways to the struggle for gay rights and to the eventual dismantling of heterosexual privilege. Instead of renouncing privilege, sometimes it will be more efficacious for heterosexuals to exercise their privileged status to support gay rights.

Advocates could embrace their identity as heterosexual people only "in directions that reverse and displace" the heterosexism that imbues that identity with such power.[11] While this strategy of exercising privilege may sound abstract, what we have in mind is far from it. For example, a school board is more likely to listen to the views of presumptively heterosexual parents than the claims of presumptively childless gay activists. The goal of this chapter in fact is to cash out the potential benefits of speaking as heterosexuals.

To adopt this more pragmatic, results-oriented approach is not to abandon a moral stance. It does not mean that heterosexuals accept their privileged status. Representative Barney Frank, who has worked many years in the trenches of Congress, a deeply heterosexist institution, has articulated clearly the moral power of "pragmatic incrementalism."

> The notion that being concerned about implementation somehow means you don't care about your ideals is the single stupidest sentence I hear uttered by otherwise intelligent people. What that says is I care so much about these values, they are so important to me, that I will be absolutely indifferent to whether or not I make any progress in accomplishing them. You, I think, have a right to be totally nonpragmatic about your favorite color, about what season of the year you like. Things that are of relative triviality, fine, don't be pragmatic. Who

cares whether they happen or not? But when you're talking about the most fundamental human values, how dare you say, "Well, I care about these, and I will therefore pay no attention to whether or not they get advanced." We can argue about what's the best way to advance them, but it simply cannot be rationally said that the depth of your concern is shown by the shallowness of your effort to implement what it is you're concerned about.[12]

A pragmatic, incremental approach may be most useful, then, in managing the tensions created by heterosexual privilege. The approach is incremental because it looks for small footholds by which the larger goal of equality might be achieved, and pragmatic because it focuses on function, consequences, and results. Pragmatic incrementalism takes into account the political, social, and economic reality to wrest benefits from the social landscape, however small, whenever and wherever they are achievable. Sometimes, this pragmatic approach would call for heterosexual people to work within heterosexist structures and institutions, exploiting the access and influence their heterosexuality gives them—but only when the ultimate goal is to dilute or destroy the privilege that gives them a voice.

An example from the writings of Cornell West illustrates the power of privilege and suggests responsibilities on the part of privileged people to put their power to good use.[13] West, an African-American man, writes about an incident that occurred one rainy day when his efforts to hail a cab were unsuccessful. He believed that cab drivers were passing him by because of his race. When a white woman nearby was able to hail a cab, she said to him, apologetically but nonetheless as she stepped in the cab, "This is really ridiculous, is it not?"

West includes the woman's statement to validate his own perception that taxi drivers passed him by because of his race. Carbado interprets this as West's invocation of a trustworthy witness.[14] But Carbado wants to make clear that people endowed with white, male, or heterosexual privilege should not "create the (mis)impression that, because they do not experience the subordinating effects of patriarchy and heterosexism, their critiques of patriarchy and/or heterosexism are more valid and less suspect than the critiques propounded by lesbians, straight women, and gay men."[15]

But what both West and Carbado do not say (what may seem so obvious to them that it need not be stated) is that the white woman bypassed an opportunity not only to acknowledge the injustice but to do something about it. She might have seized the power given her by the cab driver and turned it in the direction of equality. Having secured the cab, she might have said to the driver, "I believe this gentleman was ahead of me," using her privilege—her ability to get the cab to stop—to shame the cab driver and enable West to get the cab he deserved. Such action might have had not only a salutary short-term, *ex post* effect (West would have been drier and less inconvenienced) but also potentially a long-term, *ex ante* effect (the cab driver would have been brought into greater awareness of his actions, and through interaction with an African-American man who defied the driver's stereotypes, might have revised his worldview ever so slightly). Through such action, the white woman would have partially forgone her privilege; she would have been forced to wait for the next available cab instead of taking the one that should have picked up West, exploiting her privilege long enough to get the driver to stop for her.

Pragmatic incrementalism cannot work without integrity and candor. Although a complete renunciation of privilege might prove politically ineffective, it does have the virtues of principle and purity. The question for pragmatic incrementalism becomes, can one retain the questioning, at times self-critical perspective of renunciation but apply it to discipline actions that might seem both overly expedient and insufficiently principled?

If so, a more nuanced approach might emerge. This approach would not give carte blanche to heterosexuals who would unthinkingly take advantage of their privilege, in something akin to paternalism. It would instead challenge them to consider, first, whether engagement with a heterosexist institution is a necessary step toward achieving the desired goal of equality. It would also push heterosexual activists to consider carefully the most effective way to exploit their institutional privilege. Should they take a cooperative or combative stance? Should they speak explicitly as heterosexual people, or make their orientation ambiguous and thereby challenge listeners to question the relevance of the speaker's sexual orientation? Pragmatism tempered by reflection would also help ensure that heterosexual activists do not purport to *speak for* gay people, unless some specific individual or group of people has authorized them in this way. But this approach also has the added advantage of getting people in out of the rain even as we work for change.

With this as an introduction, let us turn to specific contexts in which heterosexual people might speak up in support of gay rights, and the ways they might manage heterosexual privilege in each situation. The rest of this chapter is devoted to suggesting ways that heterosexual people can seize their comparative advantage and advocate gay rights in their jobs, schools, houses of worship, and everyday family life. Because we believe that such advocacy calls for a kind of politics that truly begins at home, this chapter starts with very private realms, especially parenting, and then works outward in ever-broadening circles of public life.

Making Gay Rights Advocacy a Part of Everyday Life

Straight allies of gay rights don't have to go out of their way to find opportunities to advocate gay rights; chances arise along the ordinary paths and routines of our lives. When discussions within families, schools, houses of worship, or places of employment implicate sexual orientation or gender stereotyping, heterosexual people who speak in support of gay rights accomplish two things: they change the discourse and they stand in solidarity.

First, no matter what the outcome of the discussion, when heterosexual allies speak, a new perspective can enter the discussion: that of a traditional "insider" to the organization advocating equality for traditional "outsiders." Simply by raising the points from this new perspective, heterosexual supporters change the discourse.

Second, when heterosexual people speak for gay rights, they stand in solidarity with gay and lesbian people inside and outside those institutions. Whatever the outcome of the discussion, this sort of solidarity signals a shift, however slight, in the organization's center of gravity and may help other gay rights advocates—gay or straight—to feel less marginalized. Within established, traditional institutions, heterosexual supporters can find opportunities to work—with sensitivity and care—for some measure of social change.

Parenting

In 1972, Morton Manford was physically attacked at a New York protest and demonstration for gay rights. Morton's parents learned of the attack on the local news. Outraged at the failure of police to intervene, Morton's mother, Jeanne Manford, responded by marching with her son in the next New York Pride Day parade. After many gay and lesbian people approached Jeanne during the parade and begged her to talk to their parents, she decided to begin a support group—Parents and Friends of Lesbians and Gays. The first formal meeting took place in March 1973 at a local church. Approximately twenty people attended. Today PFLAG has more than two hundred thousand members and local affiliates in almost five hundred communities across the United States and abroad.

PFLAG has changed the lives of many parents and gay or lesbian children by helping parents come to terms with their children's homosexuality. The work of this organization is unquestionably constructive and important. But PFLAG underscores the extent to which heterosexual parents—even those who consciously support gay rights—often wait until their own sons or daughters come out to them before they actively express their support. What if heterosexual parents began their support for gay rights at an earlier stage?

Parents usually treat their children as presumptively heterosexual. If this presumption is rebutted, many parents find a way to accept and even to find happiness in their child's relationships and life choices.[16] Parents who support gay rights might consider a more radical and proactive approach. They could let go of the heterosexual presumption from the start, raising their children in a way that would leave open a full range of sexual identities for their children. To put this approach in more concrete terms, parents could raise their children with the assumption that they *might*, in fact, be gay. In what ways would such an assumption affect parenting?

In a provocative essay, Eve Kosovsky Sedgwick explains "How to Bring Up Your Kid Gay." Sedgwick's radical proposition in this essay is that parenting could be a site for the *production* of homosexuality. To introduce this notion, Sedgwick observes that the first edition of the American Psychiatric Association's diagnostic manual (the DSM-III, in 1973) to eliminate homosexuality as a mental disorder was also the first to *include* a new diagnosable, treatable disorder: "numbered (for insurance purposes) 302.60: 'Gender Identity Disorder of Childhood.'"[17] Sedgwick points out that although the diagnosis is "nominally gender-neutral," the threshold for pathologizing boys is much lower than for girls: the label applies to a girl "only in the rare case of asserting that she actually is anatomically male," but a boy can be treated for the disorder "if he merely . . . displays a 'preoccupation with female stereotypical activities as manifested by a preference for either crossdressing or simulating female attire, or by a compelling desire to participate in the games and pastimes of girls.'"[18]

Sedgwick's concern is that the APA may have delisted homosexuality as a mental illness but limited its approval to gay men and lesbians who conform to gender stereotypes. Thus, gender stereotyping and homophobia in psychology and psychiatry find legitimacy through the back door. The gay rights movement has ignored this development, Sedgwick argues, because the movement must de-emphasize "the links between gay adults and gender-nonconforming children."

The core paragraph of Sedgwick's essay bears repeating.

The naturalization and enforcement of gender assignment is not the worst news about the new psychiatry of gay acceptance, however. The worst is that it not only fails to offer, but seems conceptually incapable of offering, even the slightest resistance to the wish endemic in the culture surrounding and supporting it: the wish that gay people *not exist.* There are many people in the worlds we inhabit, and these psychiatrists are unmistakably among them, who have a strong interest in the dignified treatment of any gay people who may happen already to exist. But the number of persons or institutions by whom the existence of gay people is treated as a precious desideratum, a needed condition of life, is small. The presiding asymmetry of value assignment between hetero and homo goes unchallenged everywhere: advice on how to help your kids turn out gay, not to mention your students, your parishioners, your therapy clients, or your military subordinates, is less ubiquitous than you might think. On the other hand, the scope of institutions whose programmatic undertaking is to prevent the development of gay people is unimaginably large.

Sedgwick's essay invites us to consider the possibility that parenting could resist that "programmatic undertaking." Her most interesting suggestion is that homosexuality ought to be treated not as an unfortunate occurrence to be tolerated or accepted once formed in adults but something to be *celebrated* as uniquely and specially a part of people.

To implement this radical suggestion, parents might begin by conducting a thought experiment. They could assume that they might be raising what Sedgwick has called "proto-gay" children (children who are or will become gay). Such an assumption could increase parents' sensitivity to the ways their own words and actions are part of the "undertaking . . . to prevent the development of gay people." Considering the possibility that a child might become a gay adult when he or she *is still a child* could help parents see the ways they suggest, perhaps subtly, that homosexuality in their children would be tolerated but not celebrated. Consider, for example, how easy it is to assume that our daughters will love and marry men, that our boys will love and marry women.[19] How often do we stop, even when our children are very small, to hold open—and articulate—the possibility that they will love or marry (or both!) members of their own sex? Consider how easy it would be to speak to our children in gender- neutral ways: "Some day, if you love someone deeply you might decide to make a lifelong home with that

25

person." Hearing us speak in ways that are more open to nontraditional relationships could help not only the children who eventually do turn out to be gay or lesbian; it would also help our "proto-straight" children to be more accepting of and comfortable with their gay and lesbian peers. These conversations do not need to be clinical or loaded with abstract jargon. Parents could tell their child, "I think it would be fine for you to go out with either a man or a woman. There's nothing wrong about that."

A woman we know named Donna once told us that this is precisely the approach she has adopted in raising her son and daughter. Because Donna holds open the possibility that her children are or will be gay, she wants to speak to them about homosexuality in ways that are affirming—or at least neutral. "Becoming a parent has increased my support for gay rights," she said, "because I am so aware that my own children could be affected. I want the world to treat them fairly, whatever their sexual orientation might be."

Once the "die is cast," so to speak, it becomes evident to some parents that they should support, love, and nurture their adult offspring who come out as gay or lesbian. But for many heterosexual people, translating their political support for gay and lesbian causes into the way they raise their own children may be difficult. Few heterosexual parents think about child rearing as a site for the *production* of homosexuality; few of us consider that our behavior and our rhetoric could permit or suppress the natural growth of our children as gay, lesbian, or bisexual people, even in their youth.

We recognize that we tread on controversial ground here. We do not mean to align with a strong position on either side of the "nature versus nurture" debate about the "causes" of homosexuality. This debate is largely irrelevant to the argument we're making about parenting. Whether homosexuality is a choice or not, whether its roots are in genetics, hormones, or socialization (at home or elsewhere), the job of parents is to convey to their children that homosexual and heterosexual relationships possess equal potential to be good, loving, legitimate, and worthy ways of living.

Perhaps the best analogy here is "handedness." The majority of people are right-handed, which is to say they prefer to do certain tasks (writing, swinging a baseball bat, using scissors) with their right hands. As recently as the mid–twentieth century, however, left-handed people were not only in the minority, they were also seen as transgressive, even sinister. Even after moral condemnation faded, left-handedness was considered less convenient than right-handedness, as "lefties" struggled with customs and instruments designed with right-handedness in mind. This condemnation (at worst) or desire to avoid inconvenience (at best) led some parents and educators not so long ago to expend some effort to reorient left-handed children.

Few if any parents or teachers today would think it appropriate to force right-handedness, for whatever reason. The hand with which one writes is considered (outside of baseball pitching) a neutral characteristic. And even if left-handed people must adapt somewhat to operate in a world often designed for right-handedness, parents and teachers count these costs as minute compared to the burdens imposed on children required to switch. In this way, parents have learned to stay out of the way of their children's development of handedness. If a child naturally picks up a spoon or pencil with his left hand, parents are no longer encouraged to switch it.

What if parents similarly approached their children's developing sexuality? This would, first of all, make clear that the homo or hetero distinction is as morally neutral as left- or right-handedness. Second, parents wouldn't steer children's developing sexual and affectional orientation toward heterosexuality. Thus, if a child were to express feelings of romantic attraction or affection for someone ("I love Sandy so much I want us to get married!"), parents would react to this declaration without regard to the genders of the speaker and the object.[20] Just as we care less about the hand a child writes with than about *what* they write, we might focus less on the gender of a child's potential mate and more on ensuring the quality of the *content* of that child's friendships and relationships—respect, affection, kindness, love. This is just an example. In some cases, more active intervention might be appropriate to point out alternatives to children when society explicitly or implicitly normalizes heterosexuality.

The point of this analogy is obviously not to suggest that sexuality is just like handedness. The hostility and discrimination visited upon gay, lesbian, and bisexual people in our society provides many otherwise progressive parents reason enough to steer their children away from homosexuality; a lefty's difficulty with scissors bears no comparison. Nonetheless, the analogy does suggest the ways parents might leave open the possibility *and thereby maintain the legitimacy* of different ways of growing and living, simply by maintaining some neutrality.

Why do so many parents who (consciously, anyway) have neutral or even positive views of homosexuality unconsciously work to suppress homosexuality in their own children? The answers to this difficult question are no doubt complex. Most people if forced to be candid would admit that they aspire for children who will in many ways resemble themselves. When children choose paths that diverge from their parents' in significant ways, this can cause negative feelings that range from minor annoyance to deep disappointment. Heterosexuality is one of many characteristics that nongay parents might hope to instill in their children, not out of any conscious homophobia, but simply out of a more general effort to replicate themselves.[21]

A second reason even progressive parents might suppress their children's homosexuality has already been alluded to: parents love their children and want to protect them from hostility and discrimination—harms that many gay people face every day. Few parents would *wish* such challenges upon their children. To the extent that they could, through their parenting, reduce the likelihood of their children having to deal with these challenges, many parents would choose to do so. Parents who nurture an identity or set of behaviors that will make a child's life more difficult often *share* the characteristic that might subject the child to hostility or discrimination. Thus, Jewish parents will raise their children within their religious tradition despite anti-Semitism. African-American parents will raise their children with pride in their heritage and identity notwithstanding racism. It is much more difficult for parents who do not face the challenges themselves to deliberately subject their children to those potential obstacles.

Finally, parents do not generally think about their children—especially young children—as *having* a sexuality.[22] When children's sexuality starts to manifest itself in adolescence, it is probably difficult for parents to connect that emerging sexuality to things the parents said or did earlier in the child's life.[23] This disconnect between early childhood and subsequent sexuality is perhaps exacerbated in the case of "proto-gay" children because many parents misunderstand homosexual identity to involve primarily or exclusively sexual activity.

Increasingly, people are beginning to understand that homosexuality, like heterosexuality, is not only about sexual activity. As Fern Kupfer has ably noted, it is about "who sits across from you at dinner, whom you take your walks around the block with, whom you send valentines to."[24] On these matters, we are very comfortable conversing with our children. And on these matters, consider how much we *do* convey heterosexist assumptions about love and romance, even to very young children. Thus, the narrative of playing house must always include a mommy and a daddy and children. Do we leave our children's imaginations open to playing house with two mommies or daddies? Must the fairy tale always focus on a prince and princess? Do we tell our children stories of same-sex affiliation and love in terms equally positive?[25] These are small but potentially significant changes that can alter children's views, significantly broadening or narrowing the life paths that appear accessible to them.

These questions lead to another strategy parents might use to broaden the life paths of their children: thinking more carefully about the ways we socialize our children to certain gender roles. Parents largely determine their children's latitude for behaviors and preferences that do not conform to society's gender norms. Even when the children spend significant amounts of time in the care of others, parents can express and to some extent enforce their own standards for gender-appropriate behavior. If a boy were to request a doll for his birthday, for example, his parents hold the power to give him a doll or permit him to receive a doll from someone else. If the boy spends time at day care or preschool, his parents can ask that he be free to play with dolls or dress up without harassment from teachers, peers, or parents of other children. And when a boy or girl engages in gender-nonconforming behavior, parents can suppress their own impulse to treat the child's behavior as a sort of drag performance—as something funny or unusually amusing. If we take seriously a little girl's attraction to what is beautiful, graceful, or glamorous, why not also take a boy seriously when he is drawn to those things? And if a girl is active, loves trucks and construction vehicles, or prefers Batman to Barbie, those preferences, too, should be handled in a neutral, matter-of-fact way (rather than the cause for concern that she is insufficiently nurturing or gentle).

The relationship between gender nonconformity and homosexuality, or gay rights for that matter, is a difficult and complex one. We would reinforce stereotypes if we were to suggest that gay men generally spend their boyhoods wearing tutus or playing with Barbies (some do; some don't), or that lesbians were all great softball players as girls (some were; some weren't). One needn't extend the argument to such ridiculous conclusions, however, to see that suppressing homosexuality in our children may be part of a larger dynamic that makes parenting a process of preparing our children to do and be "what is expected" of them—and what is expected of them *as boys* or *as girls* can be a part of the process, too.

Professor William Eskridge, who has studied the history of gender and sexuality in the United States, connects current-day homophobia to late-nineteenth-century efforts to enforce clear gender roles for men and women.

> Setting up the effeminate man as a degeneration of masculinity, men were reassured of their own manhood. Setting up the lesbian as an object to be feared,

men asserted their central role in women's lives. The creation of homosexuals as a despised class reinforced the gender norms of male superiority and control. In short, there is a historical as well as logical connection between *compulsory gender binarism*, the idea that men must be masculine and women must be feminine, and *compulsory heterosexuality*, the idea that sexuality must consist of a man having sex with a woman.[26]

Indeed, according to Professor Eskridge, "the idea of rigid gender lines historically preceded the idea of compulsory heterosexuality." Thus, legislators passed laws against cross-dressing and prostitution at about the same time they enacted abortion and contraception laws—all with the design "to shore up procreative marriage." Gender role was the focus of the initial attacks on homosexuality: "women and men who departed from their biological gender roles (passive/nurturing and aggressive/entrepreneurial, respectively) were deemed 'inverts' by the sexologists and then by regulators."

This history suggests that although homosexuality and gender nonconformity do not always come together (which is to say, many gay men and lesbians may generally meet the surface requirements of their respective genders), at a deeper level, all gay people are defying the demand that is perhaps central to their gender roles: that they desire members of the "opposite," rather than their own, sex. By suppressing more surface manifestations of gender nonconformity, society (and, crucial to our argument, parents) seek to prevent or correct the central, nonconforming desire of homosexuality. This could be deliberate or inadvertent. We're appealing here to the parents who would not reject a gay or lesbian child and who, in the abstract, profess to "have no problem" with homosexuality. For these parents, the challenge arises to translate more global philosophies into the daily practicalities of parenting.

"How to Bring Up Your Kid Bisexual"

In *Vice Versa*, her brilliant book on bisexuality, Marjorie Garber tells the story of Elizabeth, a Chicago woman in her thirties who "found herself in deep erotic conversation" via the Internet with James, a Washington, D.C., architect. After three weeks of daily electronic contact, James suggested that they meet in person. He booked a hotel room for them in Los Angeles, where they agreed to meet at the hotel bar. But when Elizabeth arrived, she was met with a bit of a shock: James turned out to be a woman named Jessica. Jessica and Elizabeth talked for an hour about what had happened. They decided to go through with their romantic rendezvous, despite the change in circumstances. Elizabeth explains, "Our intimacy was real . . . I couldn't suddenly pretend just because of gender that it never existed." For Elizabeth, "gender is just a label," and "who I have sex with doesn't define me. It's how well I can connect with another person that does."[27]

To push our argument even further regarding parents' role in the moral and sexual formation of their children, consider the possibility that parents might try to promote a bisexual orientation in their children. The idea here would be to suggest to children that bisexuality might be morally preferred to either heterosexuality or homosexuality. Again, this type of parenting would not require abstract or clinical speech. A parent may simply say to a child, "I hope you will not choose whom to love because of their race or sex. I think it would be wrong for you to not love someone because of his or her gender."

This is a position that is currently embraced by virtually no one. Why would anyone hold this outrageous view? Here's why: bisexuals don't discriminate on the basis of sex. Of course, there are many types of bisexuality, and many if not most bisexuals may discriminate in various ways that relate to sex—for example, only preferring women with certain attributes and men with others. But here we have in mind the moral superiority of "sex-blind" bisexuals—who don't take sex into account in choosing their partner. This is a thought experiment, but it's more than that. It's also a way to think critically about sex and sexual orientation in a way that can help our kids. So bear with us for a bit.

Because our society generally views sex discrimination as morally wrong, preferring to assess people on their merits, one could argue that the romantic realm should be no different. Both heterosexuals and homosexuals "discriminate"—preemptively excluding from contention for their most intimate relationships one half of the population. Such discrimination should impose heavy burdens on us to explain why the disqualifying characteristic is relevant to our decision. If we seek to form and maintain other relationships without regard to sex (relationships between employers and employees, clergy and congregation members, commercial proprietors and their customers, teachers and students, and friends, to give just a few examples), why should it be that the realm of sexual and romantic relationships is unapologetically carved out as safe space for sex discrimination? The norm against sex discrimination should not be a rule that applies only to the "other guy," such as government or employers. And there is no reason that it should apply to us only with regard to relatively unimportant decisions. One could argue, in fact, that the norm against sex discrimination should apply all the more strictly as the importance of decisions increases.

Asking yourself how you would respond to a parallel question of race discrimination often clarifies how you should respond to a question of sexual orientation discrimination. When someone arbitrarily writes off a group of people on the basis of race, we have little trouble calling that person a bigot. Imagine a famously single, handsome, young white actor—a real "ladies man"—unabashedly proclaiming in an interview, "I'm not attracted to black women; they just don't get me excited." Many people would doubtless consider such statements not only tasteless but racist as well. Although we might view his preference as equally fixed and unchangeable, it would nonetheless be embarrassing for many parents if their heterosexual white son were to declare: "I feel attracted only to white women."[28] Interestingly, it could also be embarrassing if he were to say that he feels attracted only to African-American or Asian-American women, troubling both in the historical context of oppression and in the social context of exoticization.[29] Here, the preference becomes something akin to fetish. Even if we accept the fact that race plays a powerful role in sexual attraction, it would seem morally preferable for a man to seek a mate according to her character and personality without making race a disqualifying or essential characteristic.[30]

From this perspective, then, we might pose the rather provocative question: Why don't we think of heterosexuals and homosexuals as sexual bigots, unabashedly discriminating on the basis of sex? Can we defend such discrimination, and if not, how can we raise children to have as little regard for sexual preference as they do for handedness?

One potential defense starts from the premise that sexual desire is the result of chemistry, not conscious choice; it is nonsensical to apply moral standards to processes that take place at this primitive level. Hunger, for example, isn't a moral choice. If hormonal, genetic, and evolutionary forces all conspire to create a strong sexual desire for members of a particular sex to the exclusion of the other,[31] who are we to question nature's call?

If we invoke nature this way in other contexts, however, the inadequacy of the response becomes clear. Generally, we do not accept biological drive as exempting behavior from moral scrutiny. So while hunger itself is not a moral choice, eating meat can be construed as such. As parents, we would be devastated if our children turned out to be Ted Bundy–like serial killers—even if this compulsion were somehow hard-wired biologically.

And we would not hesitate to condemn such killers. Likewise, we would also be disappointed if our children discriminated on the basis of race—even if their racialized attraction were somehow biologically based.

A second sort of response comes from people who would justify sex discrimination by their children to facilitate procreation. Parents who otherwise consider themselves "progressives" have reported a sense of loss when they realize that their child's bisexuality or homosexuality reduces their own chance for grandchildren.

Although heterosexual people are more likely to bear and raise children than gay, lesbian, or bisexual people are (and, indeed, this chapter argues that it is just this statistical likelihood that imposes certain responsibilities on nongay people to use wisely the increased access and influence attending their role as parents), it is by no means the case that homosexuality or bisexuality makes it impossible for a person to become a parent.[32] Reproductive technologies as well as adoption law reform are permitting more and more people to become parents outside of heterosexual unions.

What is left of the procreation argument in the face of ever-improving reproductive technology and chances for adoption? If, in fact, it is no longer necessary to pair by male and female in order to procreate—if eggs, sperm, and women's uteruses can be purchased, rented, or donated in the quest to create children outside traditional heterosexual pairings—then something other than procreation must drive the preference for coupling one man with one woman. While one can raise concerns about and even bemoan the "commodification" of reproduction, these concerns—though serious—are not insurmountable through careful thought and regulation.

But in fact the procreation justification for mixed-sex pairs—that is, discrimination favoring heterosexuals—has flipped and become the reverse: a mixed-sex pair justification for traditional methods of procreation. In other words, traditionalists object that certain reproductive technologies may undermine the traditional, "natural" way to make babies. This accounts for the long-standing struggle within the leadership of the Roman Catholic Church to work against contraception, artificial insemination, and in vitro fertilization because these methods circumvent the heterosexual reproductive process. Procreation per se does not justify heterosexuality; heterosexuality is the measure by which the propriety of procreation is judged.

So the argument that procreation justifies discriminating *for* heterosexuality is specious, and so are views of morality arguing for and based on "procreation" as a central human good. In the face of reproductive technologies and wider opportunities for adoption, these arguments rest on a deeper foundation: a bedrock layer of bias for heterosexuality, resting on a still deeper set of values based on a specific reading of the Bible.

The invocation of Scripture or theology can be a bit of a conversation stopper when it comes to gay rights. One might engage in some rigorous debate about the accuracy of translations or the larger significance of biblical passages quoted out of context, but the discussion often spirals to points of such fundamental value that trade-offs and compromises can seem impossible. Perhaps it is fortunate that the separation of church and state enshrined in the U.S. Constitution seems to deter many lawmakers from offering religious rationales for public policy.

But in *private* debates of morality there's no denying that religion can provide a coherent and sometimes powerful rationale for moral preferences. For example, a religious perspective may offer a coherent response to our question about personal sexual "bigotry." The response is to say that, yes, heterosexuality and homosexuality do require a certain discrimination on the basis of sex, but the preemptive value given to "God's design" for human beings transforms what might at first appear to be gender-based bigotry into religious duty. Still, one might push back to ask how far religious justifications can go in excusing gender-based discrimination.

A final ideological response to the question about bigotry could come from the opposite end of the political spectrum. Some theorists might argue that categorical homosexuality must be insulated from moral criticism of any sort as part of a larger liberationist impulse. Sexual orientation, in this view, is a political and aesthetic choice deserving protection and support—no matter what form it takes. To find aspects of it that create uneasiness, to problematize a particular form of sexuality, can make it even more deserving of protection. The very strong liberationist impulse would protect almost all explorations of sexual identity in order to promote a respect for diversity in desire. Like the traditionalist response outlined above, the queer theorist might retreat to an overarching principle that trumps the nondiscrimination norm. In this case, however, that overarching principle is liberation. What would otherwise be seen as an unfortunate or even immoral act—discriminating on the basis of sex—is transformed: for the traditionalist, discrimination becomes religious duty; for the radical theorist, discrimination becomes sexual liberty. Thus, very few people seem to believe that sexual orientation is sufficiently a matter of choice that it should be subject to moral judgment *and* that the moral good points to *bisexuality*.

While the analogy to race may highlight the discrimination inherent in heterosexuality and homosexuality, it also illuminates the strongest defense of desire for one gender over the other, one rooted in the theory of *antisub-ordination*. Antisubordination norms give priority to correcting historic oppression—in this case, subordination of minorities and women. A focus on antisubordination would require that any rule or practice be viewed in the historic context of oppression, and its validity be judged according to this standard: does this rule or practice tend to supplant or perpetuate that subordination? Granted, in some ways the antisubordination response sounds a little like the traditionalist and queer theorist responses: it acknowledges the disparate treatment on the basis of gender, but argues that a higher good will excuse or even require some forms of discrimination. The antisubordination norm is particularly interesting, though, because it allows for more nuanced judgment of the various possible orientations than do other ideologically based responses.

Consider how an antisubordination response would play out in the context of race-based sexual preferences. To simplify matters extremely, assume that people fall into one of two groups racially—black or white—and one of two groups sexually—homoracial (attracted only to people of their "own" race) or heteroracial (attracted only to people of the "other" race). Thus, four groups of people emerge:

> Black homoracial
> White homoracial
> Black heteroracial
> White heteroracial

In assessing the moral justification for each orientation, we would take into account the historic subordination of African-Americans.

For example, we might find much stronger moral justification for a black homoracial orientation than a white homoracial one. A white homoracial orientation could easily stem from unconscious prejudices or belief in white superiority. Of course, a black homoracial orientation could also stem from the same impulse (belief in black superiority). But in the historical context of oppression of and discrimination against blacks in America, an African-American person's preference for relationships with members of her own race could also be explained by a desire to avoid the vestiges of racism and race-based disparities that could make an interracial relationship especially difficult. Thus, while an antisubordination defense could respond to any allegation of bigotry that might be lodged against the black homoracial orientation, it would not justify the white homoracial orientation.

Assessing the morality of heteroracial orientations (attraction only to people of the "other" race) might yield different results depending upon whether the subject of the examination was white or black. But how these preferences fare under our antisubordination framework is unclear. If an African-American person feels romantic or sexual attraction only to white people, does this perpetuate or undermine the subordination of African-Americans?[33] Conversely, if a white person desires only black partners, is that an inclination that pushes toward liberation or is it an objectifying, exoticizing move that further entrenches black people's subordination? Compared to the white homoracial, black heteroracial, and white heteroracial orientations, an orientation that holds attraction and attachment possible without regard to race—or, perhaps, with either race depending on the individual involved—seems morally preferable. In this approach, sex and romance are possible with white or black partners. Such an approach would seem generally superior. The only possible exception would be for black homoracials who, in order to avoid racism and racial power plays, might prefer in their most intimate relationships to connect with others who share their experience and perspective as members of a historically oppressed minority group.

And now back to gender. Here, orientations could break down into four groups.

> Female homosexual
> Male homosexual
> Male heterosexual
> Female heterosexual

Just as racism served as a backdrop for examining justifications for the four race-based sexual orientations, so too a history of oppression and discrimination against women—and lingering bias or belief in male superiority—could illuminate our consideration of the gender-based sexual orientations.

Just as black homoracial preferences fared best, so lesbians might find that their elimination of men as partners is justified in ways that no other sexual orientation group can claim, because lesbians can claim to be avoiding subordination by men. Women may need "the room of one's own" that same sex relationships provide. Male and female heterosexuals cannot justify their preference for one sex to the total exclusion of the other as having any basis in the subverting of male supremacy. Instead, as Sylvia Law and Andrew Koppelman have argued, an insistence on heterosexual pairing reinforces traditional gender roles and hierarchy within our most intimate relationships.[34] Gay men might argue that their preference for men has liberating effects because it works against the assignment of roles based on gender within marriage or other intimate relationships. Still, the rejection of a historically oppressed group (women) out of preference for a historically empowered group (men) appears inconsistent with an antisubordination norm. Lesbians alone could justify their desire for women to the exclusion of men as a liberating move; women in relationships with other women might expect to experience less gender stereotyping than they would get in a heterosexual pairing. By refusing to participate in relationships that might perpetuate the subordination of women to men, lesbians might argue, they demonstrate that male supremacy (and resulting subordination of women) is not necessary for the operation of healthy, loving relationships, and thus potentially weaken the grip of male-supremacist thinking in *all* relationships. Because the antisubordination norm carries great weight, it might give lesbians a strong, coherent response to the provocative question posed above: the disqualification of men as potential intimates is based not on bigotry, but on a desire to *free* women from gender-based expectations about their role in relationships.

At the end of the day, we see some power to the antisubordination justification for same-sex preferences as an alternative to bisexuality. And we are under no illusions that this thought experiment is likely to convince many readers. Still we are concerned that so many progressives are unselfconscious in even asking the question whether their own sex discrimination is moral. At least asking this question with regard to the next generation—where the die may not yet be cast—is a good place to start.

Concrete Steps to Take at Home

1. Remember that your child might be gay, and nurture your child's growth as a potentially heterosexual, bisexual, or homosexual person.
2. Talk to your child about love and marriage in gender-neutral ways.
3. Read aloud children's books that present positive images of gay couples and families headed by same-sex couples. We've included some suggestions at the end of this chapter.
4. Give older children high-quality chapter books that include characters who are gay, lesbian, or bisexual. Again, see our suggestions at the end of the chapter.

5. Give your child a variety of toys and encourage play without regard to gender.

6. Dress your child in clothing that is relatively unisex, giving due regard to your child's taste and preferences.

7. Provided they are "out," talk openly about LGBT friends and family members. Make sure your child understands that the same-sex partner of a friend or family member is not just a "friend," but a spouse or significant other, similar to boyfriends or girlfriends, husbands and wives in heterosexual couples they know.

8. If your child wants to join an organization that discriminates on the basis of gender or sexual orientation, discuss the reasons why that organization has this policy (a soccer team limited only to girls or even a boys' choir is almost certainly more justified in its gender discrimination than the Boy Scouts of America is in its sexual orientation discrimination). If you do not support the form of discrimination practiced by that organization, make sure that your child understands this. You might decide, after discussion with your child, that you will not permit him or her to join the organization.

Heterosexual Supporters in the Schools

Parenthood confers special access to a battleground for gay rights that has at times proven controversial and especially wrenching: the schools. Society sees parents as having more at stake in the debate than nonparents. At the same time, people who are uncomfortable with homosexuality may consider heterosexual people to be more credible than gays.[35] This second basis for heterosexuals' comparative advantage creates some real dangers; if heterosexual advocates for gay rights explicitly exercise this privilege (if they claim to be more credible than gay and lesbian parents, or presume to speak for them), they run the risk of ratifying the beliefs they seek to overturn. But even in the face of such danger, heterosexual people must stand and be heard.

Because children are involved, passions and protective instincts are quickly aroused. Unfortunately, many people feel protective for the wrong reasons: oftentimes, school officials think they are protecting children from a nefarious influence when the subject is homosexuality. When this happens, parents whose children will be affected by an antigay policy have special standing to voice their support for gay teachers, gay students, and a curriculum on sexuality that is balanced and fair.

Although gay and lesbian teachers probably enjoy more job security today than they did twenty years ago, in many schools and school districts, openly gay or lesbian teachers are vulnerable. Many gay and lesbian teachers remain closeted at work, fearing discovery and the consequences that could follow. Teachers have been fired or reassigned because principals or parents believe that homosexuality leads to sexual predation or that gay and lesbian teachers may be seeking to "recruit" vulnerable students. In such cases, reality doesn't matter. Perception does, and it is this perception that gay and lesbian teachers must face. This is where heterosexual parents of schoolchildren come in.

In her exhaustive study of developing employment protections for gay and lesbian teachers, Karen Harbeck repeatedly argues that "many more GLBT people *and our heterosexual allies must come out of the closet* so all of us can enjoy our civil rights and protect ourselves and GLBT youth from hardship."[36] Although Harbeck does not suggest that the consequences of "coming out" will be the same for both groups, she nonetheless acknowledges that many heterosexual allies fear that supporting gay rights will lead to reprisals, including, if they are teachers, "compromise" of their own employment.

Sadly, some heterosexual teachers have been punished for speaking out in support of LGBT colleagues or encouraging their colleagues to create safer environments for gay students. Don Bergman, a history teacher at Kalamazoo Christian High School, had an epiphany when his son, Brad, came out. Don realized that his school was not dealing with homosexuality in a constructive way: "If it was talked about at all, teachers said it was sinful, or students reviled it as disgusting, weird, perverted, or simply 'nasty.'" Don set out to change this. He requested a policy for students and staff that would curtail negative, harassing discourse and foster a more supportive environment for gay teens in the school. His colleagues shunned him, refused to discuss his concerns, and complained to the school principal that Don was "obsessed with homosexuality and promot[ing] unbiblical views." Eventually, as pressure for his resignation mounted, Don quit his job. Notwithstanding this loss, Don stands by his actions: "If I made an error in some way, I'm glad I erred the way I did. Silence is complicity."[37] Heterosexual school employees and parents of children in schools should follow Bergman's example, supporting LGBT students and teachers.

The first step for heterosexual parents is simply speaking out. They can make clear that the equation of homosexuality with predation is a destructive myth and that gay and lesbian teachers do not "recruit" young people to become gay. Moreover, in junior high and high schools, supportive heterosexual parents can emphasize that many gay and lesbian teenagers are coming to terms with their sexual orientation in an extremely hostile environment,[38] which leads to an alarmingly high suicide rate among gay, lesbian, and bisexual kids. Rather than presenting a problem, openly gay and lesbian teachers can serve as a crucial resource for parents, children, and school administrators in reversing this trend.

Interestingly, growing concerns about gay and lesbian youth may be making life better for gay and lesbian teachers. As educators and administrators come to terms with the terrible toll homophobia takes on LGBT youth, many schools and school districts are working affirmatively to make their schools physically and emotionally safer places. One such school district has expressly acknowledged that hiring and retaining gay and lesbian teachers is one good way to improve school days for gay and lesbian teenagers.

Unfortunately, this well-intentioned policy led to a lawsuit. In *Irizarry v. Board of Education*,[39] a woman involved in a long-term cohabiting relationship with a man challenged a Chicago Board of Education policy that extended spousal health benefits to domestic partners of school employees only if the partner was of the same sex as the employee. The board of education justified this disparate treatment on two grounds. First, it argued that because marriage is not available to two people of the same sex, the recognition of a domestic-partnership surrogate is more important for homosexual than for heterosexual couples (who could obtain the benefits by marrying). This argument echoes the story at the beginning of the chapter, where Jon's father allowed his daughter to sleep with her girlfriend during a visit home. Second, and for our purposes more interestingly, the board claimed that the health benefits were offered to same-sex domestic partners of employees to attract gay and lesbian teachers, who would in turn provide support for homosexual students. The board's brief explained,

> lesbian and gay male school personnel who have a healthy acceptance of their own sexuality can act as role models and provide emotional support for lesbian and gay students. . . . They can support students who are questioning their sexual identities or who are feeling alienated due to their minority sexual orientation. They can also encourage all students to be tolerant and accepting of lesbians and gay males, and discourage violence directed at these groups.

40

The irony of this position was not lost on Judge Richard Posner writing for the court: "This line of argument will shock many people even today; it was not that long ago when homosexual teachers were almost universally considered a public menace likely to seduce or recruit their students into homosexuality, then regarded with unmitigated horror." Judge Posner acknowledges that some doubt exists as to whether good health benefits actually attract potential employees. But what seems unquestionable is that the board's desire to attract gay and lesbian teachers is entitled to deference, at least on a review for rationality.

> It is not for a federal court to decide whether a local government agency's policy of tolerating or even endorsing homosexuality is sound. Even if the judges consider such a policy morally repugnant—even dangerous—they may not interfere with it unless convinced that it lacks even minimum rationality, which is a permissive standard. It is a fact that some school children are homosexual, and the responsibility for dealing with that fact is lodged in the school authorities, and (if they are public schools) ultimately in the taxpaying public, rather than in the federal courts.

Chicago is a huge school system, with some forty-five thousand employees. It is encouraging to think that a school system of this size and potential influence not only recognizes the needs of gay and lesbian students but also sees that gay and lesbian teachers are an important part of any effort to educate and mentor those students.

In more than two thousand schools nationwide, students have formed "gay-straight alliances," student-led clubs that "aim to create a safe, welcoming and accepting school environment for all youth, regardless of sexual orientation or gender identity/expression."[40] In such clubs, LGBT youth and supportive nongay peers can meet to discuss issues and plan activities designed to combat prejudice and discrimination in their school. Gay-straight alliances in some schools find their attempts to meet on school property or engage in meaningful activity thwarted by school administrators, often in response to protests from the community. In the face of such opposition, members of the community who wish to support gay and lesbian youth must speak up. This is particularly true of people whose children attend the schools in question—whether or not the children want to join the gay-straight alliance. All children at the school benefit from such organizations, because they help to create more welcoming and accepting environments.

But the uphill battle facing all gay-straight alliances will be especially steep if administrators and parents do not work together to insure a safe, supportive environment in the school generally. School administrators, gay rights advocacy organizations, and even a federal judge have noted the difficulty of this task.[41] In 2001, the parents of a Woodbury, Minnesota, high school student named Elliott Chambers requested and obtained a preliminary injunction permitting the boy to wear to school a sweatshirt emblazoned with the words, "Straight Pride." The principal of the school had forbidden him to wear the shirt "in light of offense taken by other students and the Principal's safety concerns for Elliott and other Woodbury students."

The principal was responding to two incidents in the 2000–2001 school year, one involving vandalism to a car driven by a student whom other students saw as homosexual, another involving a fight between a black student and a white student who was wearing a bandana bearing the Confederate flag. The principal was aware of two things: ambient hostility toward homosexuality among the students of the school, and the likelihood that violence could erupt over articles of clothing bearing racist messages. The principal apparently put these two pieces of information together and concluded that a "Straight Pride" sweatshirt might be seen as analogous to the Confederate flag, creating a "disruption to the educational process." The principal banned the shirt and suppressed Elliott's speech to protect both Elliott and other students (especially gay and lesbian students offended by the phrase "Straight Pride," which they took to be an antigay message).

The judge held that Elliott demonstrated a "strong likelihood of success in establishing that" the principal's decision was unreasonable and therefore violated Elliott's First Amendment rights of free expression. The judge issued an injunction permitting Elliott to wear the "Straight Pride" sweatshirt to school. Judge Frank included in his opinion several statements about the difficult balance principals must strike between nurturing diversity, respecting freedom of expression, and maintaining an intellectually and emotionally safe environment in which all students can learn:

> While the sentiment behind the "Straight Pride" message appears to be one of intolerance, the responsibility remains with the school and its community to maintain an environment open to diversity and to educate and support its students as they confront ideas different from their own. The Court does not disregard the laudable intention of Principal Babbitt to create a positive social and learning environment by his decision, however, the constitutional implications and the difficult but rewarding educational opportunity created by such

diversity of view point are equally as important and must prevail under the circumstances.

Judge Frank delivered his most powerful message at the end of his opinion, where he outlined more explicitly the task of all community members as they balance the values of diversity and free expression. It's worth quoting at length.

> Finally, it is difficult for this Court to understand why all parties to this lawsuit and the members of the Woodbury community, including its parents, schools, student councils, and community leaders, have relinquished their responsibility to a federal court to create parameters of behavior for its schools and its youth. . . . [I]t will always remain the privilege and responsibility of the parents and citizens of Woodbury to raise and nurture its children into decent and caring human beings who treat people with dignity, respect, kindness, and equality. Messages of hatred, bias, and intolerance should not be a part of any child's up-bringing. The great men and women who have brought this country to where it is, while having a vision of the constitutional vigilance that must be maintained to preserve a civilized and democratic society, have always valued, first and fore-most, kindness and compassion and a keen understanding that all people are considered equal under the law regardless of their race, religion, culture, sexual orientation, or gender.
>
> Students at Woodbury High School, and in every school in this country, de-serve a safe, secure, and robust learning environment, free from disruption and violence. The Court would suggest that it is now the responsibility of the par-ties and all members of the Woodbury community to resolve these issues within their community, rather than the Court, if the best interests of all stu-dents and children in Woodbury are to be served. Perhaps then, something truly good could result from the unfortunate circumstances surrounding some of the events that led to this case. The students of Woodbury High School de-serve no less.

As Judge Frank so ably explains, the community as a whole must determine the best way to educate its children in a safe environment. This makes clear the responsibility of heterosexual people supportive of gay rights to make their views clear, lest the misapprehension develop that it is *only* gay and lesbian teens and adults who hold these views.

Another issue that parents can address within the schools is the curricu-lum, particularly regarding the teaching of health or sex education. How homosexuality is to be treated in such courses has been the subject of much debate in some school districts. Accurate and relatively neutral presentation of information about sexuality and health benefits all students—this is, after all, the premise behind these classes. Gay and lesbian teens have expressed how beneficial it can be to get information about homosexuality in sex ed courses. The alternative source of information, for many children, would be the playground or the locker room—and most adults can testify to the accuracy of these sources.

Even in lower grades, some books or other materials have entered the canon that reflect shifting views of family composition, and this has troubled people who disapprove of homosexuality. Of course, many would claim that a value-neutral presentation of homosexuality does not exist: to present it within the range of "normal" sexual behaviors or family life is to adopt an approving normative stance.[42] On the other hand, to delete any mention of homosexuality in a health class, or to ignore families headed by two people of the same sex, is to treat homosexuality as marginal, "other," even pathological. If the controversy is inescapably political, then nongay allies need to make a political statement. If describing homosexuality or intimacy between people of the same sex imparts a message of approval, parents whose children will use these course materials must make clear that they will tolerate—indeed, that they embrace—this message. School officials need to know where community sentiment falls, even if it is not determinative, and in the course of debate, some who are skeptical of the course material might just be persuaded.

Concrete Steps to Take at School

1. Read all of your school's sex education materials to monitor the treatment, if any, given to homosexuality, bisexuality, and gender identity (whether or not your child is in the grade that uses the materials).
   a. If these topics are ignored, suggest a switch to materials that discuss sexuality and gender identity in an affirming or at least neutral way.
   b. If the materials condemn or pathologize sexual minorities, insist that the materials be changed. For a list of materials that you might suggest, check the resource guide at the end of this chapter.
   c. If the sex ed curriculum covers sexuality and gender identity in an affirming or neutral way, be sure to tell teachers and administrators that

you approve, and offer to speak to any parents who might from time to time express concerns or reservations about the materials.

2. Find out whether your child's middle school or high school has a gay-straight alliance group. If it does, volunteer to be a resource, supportive parent, or chaperone for meetings and field trips. If it does not have such a group, work with supportive teachers or administrators in the school to start one, appropriate for the age of the children and the location and type of school. You can find a sample letter urging the creation of such a group at the American Civil Liberties Union web site.[43] In many schools, students might be reluctant to join such a group—especially when it is getting off the ground. Although it would be unlawful for a school to require a GSA to remove the word *gay* from its name, some students might prefer more ambiguous names. Calling it the "Diversity Discussion Group" or "Civil Rights Club" might be a start, but be open about the fact that the group will discuss sexual orientation among a list of other characteristics. Parents will want to know what their children are involved with, and LGBT kids who are looking for support will need to know that this is a group addressing some of their concerns (even if those concerns are raised in the context of a larger discussion).

3. Find out whether your school district has a written nondiscrimination policy that includes sexual orientation. Simply by asking, you will convey your interest and let administrators know that someone is paying attention.
   a. If your district has a nondiscrimination policy that includes sexual orientation,
      i. Express your approval.
      ii. Ask whether a teacher or student has ever invoked that policy against official action.
      iii. Ask what the performance record of each principal in the district has been with respect to the nondiscrimination policy.
   b. If the school district lacks a nondiscrimination policy or if it has a policy that omits sexual orientation from the protected characteristics,
      i. Work to put a policy in place that includes sexual orientation. For a sample letter requesting such a policy, check the ACLU web site.[44] Some school districts have faced resistance when they've amended policies to include sexual orientation. The ACLU devotes a section of its web site to resources parents can use to urge the adoption of nondiscrimination and safe schools policies.[45]

ii. If your school is private and nonsectarian, this process should be even easier to complete, because you'll have much less bureaucratic red tape to work through.

c. If your school is religious, you can still ask about nondiscrimination and insist that sexual orientation be included in the policy. Even if the denomination continues to condemn homosexual "conduct," most do not condemn homosexual status or identity. It is often easier for an employer to prove an employee's gay identity than to prove his or her "conduct." Policies that protect identity, therefore, will in practice offer some protection, though the protection is far from complete.

4. Check your school's library to make sure that students can find information about homosexuality there. This should include a variety of materials, such as science and health, history, law, sociology, fiction, and poetry. Ask librarians to compile bibliographies they can share with students who are interested in learning more about homosexuality and bisexuality, gender identity, and LGBT families, and make sure that the books are available within your school's library or easily accessible through an interlibrary loan system. In addition, librarians can compile a list of works by LGBT authors. For some ideas, see the resource guide at the end of this chapter.

5. Ask whether your school sponsors a Boy Scout troop. If Boy Scouts are permitted to use space on the same basis as other outside organizations, then your school is merely complying with current law. If, on the other hand, your school gives additional support to the Boy Scouts by aiding in recruiting, publicizing events or activities, or giving any sort of financial support, ask that such sponsorship be discontinued. Point out that the Boy Scouts of America discriminate on the basis of sexual orientation in membership. Express your desire not to associate with them, even indirectly through your school's sponsorship. See chapter 7 in this book for some stories of churches, corporations, and schools that have discontinued their support of the Boy Scouts because of the BSA's discriminatory policy.

6. Join the PTA. Run for office if you are so inclined, or simply attend meetings whenever you can. In addition to the big topics highlighted in this chapter—curricula, employment practices, and student groups, look for opportunities to raise issues of diversity, orientation, and identity as seemingly unrelated topics arise. As topics come up for discussion, ask yourself, "How, if at all, would this affect LGBT teachers or students? How

would this affect heterosexual teachers' or students' understanding of sexuality and gender identity?"

Houses of Worship

Gay rights advocacy in a religious setting faces special challenges. The organization may be very hierarchical. Or the religious faith in question may adhere strictly to tradition or doctrine that condemns homosexuality. Even in religious traditions that are conservative, dogmatic, or hierarchical, however, heterosexual supporters of gay rights may find opportunities to speak their conscience. Because opponents of gay rights often use history, tradition, and religion, it may be especially important to show that sincere people of faith can hold differing views on homosexuality. In this context, as in others, an additional benefit of speaking up is that gay and lesbian members of that house of worship may appreciate knowing that at least a few heterosexual members stand in solidarity with them, and that they are not completely isolated within that religious body.

The issues likely to give rise to such discussion are varied. Many religious organizations have openly discussed equal marriage rights (or rites). Some denominations—as well as individual congregations acting (some quietly, some openly) in defiance of their larger church hierarchy—have been celebrating marriage or commitment ceremonies for same-sex couples. Some clergy members—with or without the blessing of their congregations or denominations—have been celebrating commitment or holy union ceremonies. Some have been punished. Many individuals, gay and straight, have signed the Petition for Equal Marriage Rights created by Lambda Legal Defense and Education Fund, a document expressing support for the legalization of same-sex marriage. A few congregations have signed this petition as a body. In very different religious bodies, courageous allies have opposed attempts to garner signatures for petitions opposing equal marriage rights.

A second set of issues revolves around the employment of gay or lesbian clergy. Just as many denominations have struggled with the issue of marriage for same-sex couples, so have many dealt with clergy members coming out. Some denominations have made clear that they deem openly gay or lesbian people to be not qualified to serve as clergy and church leaders. Others have encouraged and accepted openly gay people in their vocations.[46] As with marriage, the issue is often handled at the congregational level, with individual parishes, temples, or church communities deciding to hire or retain a clergy member, despite (or even because of) his or her open homosexuality.

While such issues remain unresolved within a religious body, gay clergy face the very real possibility of losing their jobs and their ministry if they speak about the issue. In such situations, the responsibility may fall with particular weight on heterosexual clergy and laypeople to be a voice for equality within their institutions. They are empowered to speak—either by rule of the religious body or simply by political reality. In some denominations and religious traditions, if a gay clergy member came out and spoke to an issue from personal experience, official procedures to fire him would begin. Gay perspective on an issue could be suppressed (or retroactively discredited, which could render it ineffective). If gay people cannot speak within the church *as gay people*, heterosexual people bear particular responsibility to speak, both for gay and lesbian clergy and on their own behalf. Here is a case in which it may be possible—even necessary—for advocates to exploit the privilege and access given them as heterosexuals to move in liberating directions.

Some denominations are so hierarchical, and so strongly opposed to gay rights, that allies can only resist antigay initiatives—actually promoting progressive measures may seem impossible. In such contexts, advocacy may be more subtle but no less courageous. Consider the case of Father Henry C. Frascadore of St. Dominic's in Southington, Connecticut. The Knights of Columbus and the Family Institute of Connecticut were promoting a petition drive against civil marriage for same-sex couples. Father Frascadore had received a letter from his archbishop endorsing the petition. The archbishop further suggested that his endorsement be read to the congregation on a Sunday marked for gaining signatures at Roman Catholic parishes throughout Connecticut. Not only did Frascadore decline to promote the petition from the pulpit or read the archbishop's endorsement, he preached a homily about acceptance and inclusion.[47]

Mission statements and membership policies can give rise to another sort of discussion about homosexuality. Some denominations have permitted individual congregations to denote themselves "open and affirming," "embracing," or "inclusive" communities—terms used to signal a strong value placed on diversity, sometimes euphemistic labels that are meant to welcome sexual minorities into the faith community. Many Christian denominations accommodate a wide diversity of views on homosexuality. In the Presbyterian Church and the United Church of Christ, to cite two examples, communities have been riven by debates about homosexuality and whether a particular congregation should be designated an "open" or "embracing" one. In some cases, the debates that precede a decision to be "open" or "inclusive" can be heated; members who support gay rights can lend their voices in ways both calming and constructive.

In summer 2003, Episcopalians meeting in general convention voted to ratify the election of an openly gay man, Gene Robinson, as bishop coadjutor of New Hampshire. The vote followed days of discussion, debate, and prayer among the participants of the convention. Reaction to the ratification was swift and strong. By the autumn 2003, the Episcopal Church USA was facing criticism from around the globe and threats of schism within its own ranks. Parishes and dioceses opposed to Bishop Robinson's election have created a national organization called the Network of Anglican Communion Dioceses and Parishes (NAC).[48] Some parishes and dioceses within NAC are withholding parish pledges and other giving from the Episcopal Church USA. Some are instead redirecting the money to NAC itself.[49] In an attempt to keep these breakaway parishes and dioceses within the Episcopal Church USA, the church has devised a Delegated Episcopal Pastoral Oversight (DEPO) plan, which permits conservative parishes to request supervision by more orthodox bishops when they disagree with the positions taken by their own bishop, particularly with respect to homosexuality and the church. St. Anthony of Padua parish in Hackensack, New Jersey, is an example of one conservative church that has already asked its bishop to surrender pastoral oversight pursuant to the DEPO plan and instead appoint a retired bishop from Wisconsin to visit the parish, celebrate Eucharist, and preside at confirmation. They have also asked to designate the ways in which their contribution to the diocese should be spent, to avoid supporting projects with which they disagree.

Other Episcopal parishes and dioceses are elated with the decision of the 2003 general convention. Some are pushing their bishops to approve marriage rites for same-sex couples so that these couples can receive the blessing of their faith community just as marrying heterosexual couples do. But these supportive individuals, parishes, and dioceses have been slow to organize. As this book goes to press, it is not at all clear that the Episcopal Church USA or the global Anglican Union, for that matter, will hold together. In the months and years to come, church members with multiple perspectives on homosexuality will have to find ways to talk to one another about the issues, and heterosexual supporters of gay rights will play a key role in these conversations.

A few individuals within a house of worship could have an even greater impact than in other contexts. Often, in religious contexts, it is taken as an article of faith that homosexual activity is sinful or contrary to religious teachings. Yet, in some cases, little real analysis or scholarship informs such views. Heterosexual members of congregations can powerfully affect a discussion if they are ready to advocate for gay rights not only in terms of equity or social policy, but also on grounds of theology, scriptural interpretation, spiritual growth, and conscience. In many faith communities, individual members may have a greater opportunity to influence their community's policies than a lone parent could have in a large school bureaucracy. As in educational contexts, moreover, some people will be unwilling to speak until they know that at least a few others share their view. Though it is never easy to be the first mover, the payoffs can be tremendous when momentum develops.

Because churches operate on limited budgets, individuals or small groups of people can also have a big impact on the financial life of a religious community if they reduce or withhold their annual donations. This financial dimension can enhance the impact of a few in ways that would not so easily occur with educational institutions (which often operate under state supervision or with larger enrollments and budgets, diluting the impact of a few supporters).

Mel White is the director of Soulforce, a self-described "national network of people of faith committed to applying the principles of relentless non-violent resistance . . . to the liberation of sexual and gender minorities from religious policies that exclude and discriminate against God's GLBT people." In 2001, Soulforce proposed a "Faithful Dissenter's Campaign" encouraging "gay, lesbian, bisexual, transgender (GLBT) people and allies to withhold all or a percentage of their usual contribution to denominations that discriminate against them." Mel White explained, "For thirty years, GLBT people and their allies have been supporting oppression with every dollar we donate and every special talent/gift we volunteer to our local churches. . . . This campaign by Faithful Dissenters to Withhold Tithes and Offerings is designed to empower and give voice to our oppressed sisters and brothers and to 'step up' the level of spiritual resistance against local congregations and/or denominations that discriminate."[50]

Getting the financial attention of religious leaders is sometimes a good way to gain access on policy matters. There is power in a threat to withhold money (or in a promise to pay it, as we'll argue in chapters to come). Before gay rights supporters adopt this tactic, it is important to remember that both supporters and opponents of gay rights can exert financial leverage—as the NAC has been demonstrating in the Episcopal Church USA. We generally favor "voice" over "exit" as the more effective strategy in working for change.

In response to the NAC's withholding of hundreds of thousands of dollars from the diocese of Connecticut, for example, the vestry of St. Thomas's in New Haven voted in the summer of 2004 to create a fund specifically designed to counter the NAC's action. With a working title of Faith United: The Bishop's Fund for Humanity, the fund will "accept contributions from people dedicated to promoting policies and practices of inclusion in the Connecticut Diocese of the Episcopal Church."[51] The fund is discretionary: the contributors will be gay rights supporters, but the bishop is not required to spend the money on LGBT-related projects. This is because the fund creators believe "we achieve the greatest gain by presenting Fund contributions as an initiative driven by our ideals and given in a spirit of Christian faith 'without strings attached.'"[52] Simply stated, then, the fund is designed to counter a conservative boycott with a progressive "buycott" (we'll discuss buycotts in greater detail in chapters 3 and 4).

After some amount of time, effort, and process, such constructive efforts may prove fruitless. Gay rights supporters may look for new congregations or denominations when policies of exclusion appear intractable. If you don't see this point with respect to sexual orientation, consider other characteristics: If your house of worship refused to marry racial minorities or interracial couples, would you be willing to continue to worship there?[53] If you remain in a church that discriminates on the basis of sexual orientation but resolve to work for change, how long do you stay? And how do you discharge the duty you feel to change the institution and its policies?

The strategy of working within the system has a certain stationary quality: at any given moment, it seems the easier and more appropriate course in the short run to give the group just a little more time to change. But it might be useful to step outside of the moment and announce a point in the future at which you would refuse to associate any longer—when you would walk away from a discriminatory house of worship. If you choose, as we do, to exercise "voice" over "exit" for the short or intermediate term, it becomes incumbent upon you actually to speak—to agitate actively for reform. Silence (ongoing, passive association with a discriminatory house of worship) is not an acceptable alternative to "exit" for faithful people of conscience who support gay rights.

Concrete Steps to Take in Your House of Worship

1. Make sure you know and understand thoroughly your church's official teachings on homosexuality. If they are not clear to you, propose that your congregation form a study group focusing on them, and that a member of the clergy help to lead the group. What elements of sacred scripture, theology, tradition, or history inform your faith community's position on homosexuality? What alternative readings of scripture might be legitimate?

2. Learn about LGBT groups within your denomination (LGBT groups can be found in almost every major faith community, if not on a local level, then certainly at the regional or national level). Access information via the Internet or subscribe to listservs or mailing lists maintained by the group. Consider joining or volunteering for the LGBT organization. Propose that your own congregation become a partner or affiliated congregation with the national LGBT group, if this is a possibility.

3. Learn about Soulforce events or activities directed toward your religious denomination, and support them, either financially or with your presence.

4. Ask how your congregation approaches issues of sexuality and sexual orientation with respect to the religious formation of youth. Just as you ask for materials that are respectful of LGBT people in school sex ed curricula, ask that materials presented to youth approach homosexuality in a way that does not condemn (many LGBT youth have been badly damaged by negative messages from their faith communities).

5. If you belong to an "open and affirming" congregation, develop a network with other "open and affirming" congregations in your area, including those from other religious faiths or denominations. Supporting LGBT people in their faith could be a point of interdenominational cooperation.

6. Learn about the "Madison Affirmation" organized by Soulforce. This statement affirms the goodness and legitimacy of all of "God's lesbian, gay, bisexual, and transgendered children" and calls for an end to all "policies and practices which create barriers and restrictions to the full participation of gay and lesbian Christians in all of the privileges and responsibilities of church membership." It has been signed by more than ninety clergy and lay professionals, and was reprinted in a local Madison, Wisconsin, newspaper.

Heterosexual Supporters on the Job

The final arena we address here is the workplace. Support can begin with as basic an idea as familiarity. Getting to know fellow employees who are gay, lesbian, bisexual, or transgendered can be the single greatest opportunity heterosexual people have to learn about homosexuality and its impact on people's lives. As in other cases, such friendships may dismantle some of the prejudices people carry all their lives,[54] helping many nongay people to address some of their own homophobia. Understanding the concerns of LGBT friends at work and supporting their requests for fair treatment on the job are important tasks for some heterosexual allies. It is at work that many LGBT people suffer the greatest discrimination. Economist M. V. Lee Badgett has found evidence that discrimination against gay, lesbian, and bisexual workers "reduces their incomes relative to heterosexuals with the same education, experience, and other important characteristics."[55]

Support can be displayed in small ways, such as speaking up when other employees make antigay remarks or tell offensive "gay jokes." It could include the display of supportive posters, cards, buttons, or signs in and around your office, classroom, or cubicle. Bonnie Leckie, a high school teacher in Chesterton, Indiana, hung a poster in her senior literature classroom featuring ten famous people, including Walt Whitman, Cole Porter, and Eleanor Roosevelt, along with the following text: "Unfortunately, history has set the record a little *too* straight . . . Sexual orientation does not determine a person's ability to make a contribution, let alone history." When a parent complained about the poster, Leckie refused to remove it. The parent submitted a written complaint, and school officials convened a committee to determine whether the poster was objectionable. At two public hearings, many people spoke in support of Leckie and the poster. Ultimately, the committee took no action and the poster remained. Leckie downplays her role, claiming that she is "not much of an activist or hero— an accidental one at best. The situation stumbled upon me, with no intent on my part." Still, her case suggests the small but powerful ways that ordinary people can support gay rights in the everyday course of employment.[56]

Recognizing this, Lucent Technologies and its employees have developed the Safe Space Program. A brochure suggests the following list of practices and behaviors for employees who want to support the program:

> Display a Safe Space emblem in your office (for Lucent Technologies, the logo is a pink triangle within a green circle).

Do not permit homophobic comments or jokes.

Do not assume everyone is heterosexual.

Use inclusive language.

Include domestic partners.

Treat the subject of sexual orientation in a positive manner.

Respect the privacy of the individual.[57]

These individual actions can help to change the culture of a workplace. Their impact is enhanced if a company personnel officer supports and helps to organize them.

A different sort of program fosters open communication at work between LGBT and nongay employees. At Eastman Kodak, some employees are invited to participate in a program called Can We Talk. At Can We Talk meetings, volunteers disclose their biggest fears and preconceptions about LGBT people. LGBT employees in the group then address those issues. The program started with managers, but is now offered to employees at the shop-floor level as well.[58]

In some cases, supporting gay rights in the workplace calls for more formal, organized activity. For example, heterosexual and LGBT employees could band together to request a company nondiscrimination policy that includes sexual orientation. If the workplace lacks a nondiscrimination policy of any kind, employees might organize a coalition to propose a policy that includes multiple characteristics. Finding common ground between groups of historic "outsiders" in the workplace can bring LGBT employees' issues into a larger circle of concerns and help nongay people see the analogies between sexual orientation and gender or race.

About 23 percent of companies surveyed in 2003 offer domestic partner benefits to same-sex couples, according to the Society for Human Resource Management.[59] If LGBT employees are asking an employer to include same-sex domestic partners in the package of employment benefits— including health care, family and medical leave, bereavement leave, access to a partner's pension, the ability to name a partner as a beneficiary for retirement and life insurance benefits, company scholarships for children and adoption benefits—supportive heterosexual coworkers can let the employer know that they fully support the change. A heterosexual supporter could organize meetings to explain the proposed change in benefits policy to all employees, or encourage the company's human resources officer to hold the meetings. These sorts of meetings could quell the fears of employees who might object because they worry the change will cost them money.

The meetings could also provide an opportunity to tell the stories that show the similarities between same-sex domestic partners and heterosexual spouses, thus raising employees' understanding and empathy.

The stories could come from people like sixty-one-year-old Bud Peterson of Houston, Texas. His partner, Miles Glaspy, fifty-seven, receives health coverage through a domestic partner benefits program at Bud's job. But the value of that coverage, about thirty-five hundred dollars, is added to Bud's W-2 statements and taxed. As a result, Bud pays about eight hundred dollars more in income tax each year to get health coverage for Miles than his married heterosexual coworkers pay to cover their spouses. "Most people absolutely have no idea this goes on," Peterson says. "There are people who work with me and value me as a gay person. It's not apparent to them that I'm discriminated against."[60]

This is not the only sort of inequality suffered by LGBT employees, even at companies that cover domestic partners. Companies often require same-sex partners to prove that they have been a couple for some specified period of time, or they require the LGBT employee to provide more than 50 percent of the family income to cover the same-sex domestic partner. Even very committed couples may not be able to meet such standards, while many married heterosexual couples receive unquestioned coverage despite their inability to meet the same standards.

What if you work in a place that has no openly gay employees? Do heterosexual supporters have nothing to do at work in this case? Even if (perhaps especially if) you work in such a place, you can provide important support for gay rights. What policies or practices, formal or informal, might keep LGBT employees from coming out at work? What characteristics of your workplace might project an unfriendly face to LGBT applicants or prospective applicants? These are the questions to ask yourself and your coworkers. One advantage of a "safe space" program, like the one at Lucent Technologies, is that it does not put the onus on LGBT employees to come out and lead the group. Indeed, even in the absence of openly gay employees, a workplace could start the sort of safe space program that might facilitate recruitment of openly gay employees or encourage existing employees to come out at work.

A final strategy to promote employment fairness for LGBT people is political, and it is one that heterosexual allies could do much to support. One state and at least nine city or county governments have enacted "equal benefits ordinances," which require companies contracting with the state or locality to offer employees equal benefits regardless of sexual orientation. For example, a contractor bound by an equal benefits law would be required to offer equivalent coverage to employees' domestic partners if the contractor offers health insurance and other benefits to employees' spouses. Encouraging your state or local government to enact an equal benefits law could be an important step on the large scale that would promote equality in sweeping ways.

Similar laws can promote equality in the workplace in other ways. For example, the city of Portland, Maine, requires any organization that receives funds from the city's Housing and Community Development Program to provide equal benefits to employees' domestic partners and legal spouses.[61] Similarly, Broward County, Florida, creates incentives for employers to offer equal benefits by extending a bidding preference of 1 percent of the bid or proposal price to a contractor that provides equal benefits to employees' domestic partners.[62] These approaches are less sweeping than equal benefits ordinances, but may prove more politically feasible in some localities.

Concrete Steps on the Job

1. If your workplace has a personnel officer or human resources professional, ask him or her whether the company has and supports an LGBT employee group. If such a group exists, contact a member of the group, offer your support, and ask what actions you can take to be of help.
2. Start a safe space program or ally group at your workplace.
3. When coworkers socialize, try to insure that LGBT employees are encouraged to bring their partners or significant others whenever spouses are invited (but also respect people's privacy: do not assume that an LGBT friend or her partner is "out" to everyone).
4. Ask whether health care coverage and other employee benefits are available for employees' same-sex partners. If not, write a letter to your company head and personnel officer suggesting that such benefits become available. Show the letter to fellow employees and try to get as many signatures as possible.

Conclusion

Some of the strategies for gay rights advocacy considered in this chapter are radical—everything from raising your kids to be bisexuals to walking away from discriminatory churches. But others are quite traditional. There is nothing new in the notion that we should assert our values within the communities we inhabit (families, schools, jobs, or houses of worship), and that our access or privilege within a community can enhance the *obligation* to speak. What may be new here is a prescription for a certain self-consciousness as we speak. Heterosexual advocates for gay rights need to be conscious of their own situation in the debate, the fact that they derive benefits from their sexual orientation denied to LGBT people. Particularly at the personal, local level contemplated in this chapter, such sensitivity is crucial.

As we move out of the intimacy of family, school, or religious body, it may be less important for heterosexual supporters to be conscious of privilege. Strategies may change. Commercial and political realms may call for different approaches—ones that are less personal. As we shall see in the chapter that concludes this book, however, a consciousness of privilege will always be helpful for heterosexual allies because it will influence how they work within organizations that advocate gay rights.

A final word is in order about the transition into the chapters that follow. We hope that the chapter you've just read has inspired you to take action for gay rights and given you new ideas about how you might accomplish positive change. We begin with parenting, PTAs, parishes, and places of employment because some of the most effective gay rights activism can take place on a very small scale, along the daily paths we all tread.

That said, for many of us activism should take place on a larger scale as well. "Write a letter to your senator or representative" is the first and most obvious response when people ask how they can support civil rights. Yet the civil rights issues that confront us continue to call for concerted political action—and yes, writing a letter to your state or federal representatives can help with a myriad of issues. Consider the actions Congress *could* take:

> Repeal the military's "don't ask don't tell" policy and with it the Solomon Amendment that pulls federal funding from academic institutions that bar military recruiters from campus
> Pass the Employment Non-Discrimination Act covering sexual orientation
> Reject the proposed Federal Marriage Amendment
> Amend the marriage law in the District of Columbia to include same-sex couples
> Repeal the federal Defense of Marriage Act and pass a statute requiring states to recognize same-sex marriages celebrated in other states and the District of Columbia

Make clear that tax, immigration, and other advantages flowing to married
people under federal law will be granted to same-sex couples who are
validly married under the laws of any state or the District of Columbia
Withhold federal funding from a state's agencies or divisions if that state's
law discriminates on the basis of sexual orientation; similarly withhold
federal funding from private organizations that discriminate on the basis
of sexual orientation

As this list suggests, Congress has the power to improve the lives of LGBT
people tremendously, and heterosexual people who support such measures
should join their voices with LGBT citizens and advocacy groups.

Similarly, state and local governments can pass statutes requiring equal
rights for LGBT people in a variety of important settings: marriage, divorce,
custody, adoption, employment, housing, and public accommodations, to
name but a few. These strategies are crucial to the battle for gay rights, and
they continue to require committed, direct political action. Of course heterosexual allies should write letters, make phone calls, attend rallies and
public hearings, and host parties and meetings in their homes for grassroots organizing. Nothing that follows in this book should dissuade you
from such activism.

We do recognize, however, that not all gay rights supporters (gay or nongay) are ready, willing, or able to take part in direct political action. Or they
are interested in other tactics they can pursue along with traditional political activism. Therefore, in the chapters that follow you will find proposals
that explore supplemental, even ancillary approaches. We offer these not as
a global substitute for the direct tactics outlined in this chapter, but instead
as a challenge to remain open to new counterintuitive strategies in the quest
for equality.

Resource Guide

Children's Books

Wendy E. Betts. "Gay and Lesbian Characters and Themes in Children's Books."
1995. http://www.armory.com/~web/gaybooks.html.
RainbowSauce.com. *Gay, Lesbian, Bisexual, and Transgender—Young Adult Fiction.*
http://www.rainbowsauce.com/glbtfic/glbtteen.html.
RainbowSauce.com. *Children's Books for Gay and Lesbian Parents.* http://www
.rainbowsauce.com/glbtfic/glbtkids.html.

One Parent Families Scotland. *Children's Books: Gay and Lesbian Families*. http://www.opfs.org.uk/helpdesk/infopool/childbks/gaylesb.html.

Sex Education

Robie H. Harris & Michael Emberley, *It's Perfectly Normal: Changing Bodies, Growing Up, Sex, and Sexual Health* (1996).

Elizabeth Casparian, Eva Goldfarb, Richard Kimball, Barbara Spring, and Pamela Wilson. *Our Whole Lives*. A series of sex ed curricula designed for children grades K–12, distributed by the Unitarian Universalist Church, emphasizing "self worth, sexual health, responsibility, and justice & inclusivity,". See *What Is Our Whole Lives?* http://www.uua.org/owl/what.html (last visited June 26, 2004).

School Nondiscrimination Policies

Gay, Lesbian and Straight Education Network. http://www.glsen.org.

American Civil Liberties Union. Model Anti-harassment and Discrimination Policies for Schools. http://www.aclu.org/LesbianGayRights/LesbianGayRights.cfm?ID=9214&c=106.

Boulder Valley School District. http://www.bvsd.k12.co.us/sb/policies/AC-R.htm.

The Vacation Pledge for Equal Marriage Rights

In May 1993, the Hawaii Supreme Court ruled in the case of *Baehr v. Lewin* that denying same-sex couples the right to marry may be gender discrimination.[1] The case was remanded to the trial court, which held that the state had failed to present a compelling state interest justifying the discrimination inherent in the marriage law. In response, the legislature approved and the voters ratified, by overwhelming majority, a constitutional amendment exempting the state's marriage law from the usual requirements of its equal rights amendment. In light of the constitutional amendment, the Hawaii Supreme Court dismissed the case. Although the legislature and many voters in Hawaii preferred to amend the constitution rather than extend equal marriage rights to same-sex couples, the state did extend some rights by creating a new legal status: "reciprocal beneficiaries." This status does not confer the same rights as marriage and has no effect outside the state's borders. Similarly, the Vermont legislature, following a state supreme court mandate, made civil unions legal in 2000. California established a statewide domestic partnership registry in 1999, gradually expanding the rights conferred by registration; by 2003, California domestic partnership had evolved to be nearly coextensive with marriage. Civil unions and domestic partnerships duplicate rights and responsibilities of marriage but stop short of applying the marriage label to same-sex couples. Determining the effect of these legal relationships outside the states' borders will require some time and litigation.

Although support for marriage is not universal in the gay community, recent years have seen a growing momentum in the struggle for equal marriage rights, and the pace of change has accelerated. In 2003 the Supreme Judicial Court of Massachusetts held in *Goodridge v. Department of Public Health* that the commonwealth could not constitutionally deny same-sex couples the right to marry.[2] The court gave the legislature until mid-May 2004 to extend full, equal marriage rights to same-sex couples. As we go to press, hundreds of same-sex couples have married in Massachusetts and will soon begin to test the effect of those marriages outside the commonwealth.

Thousands of couples in San Francisco; New Paltz, New York; Sandoval County, New Mexico; and Portland, Oregon have received licenses and been married by local officials who interpret their state laws (including their state's constitutional requirement of equal protection) to require equal marriage rights for same-sex couples.[3] The attorney general of New York, Eliot Spitzer, has opined that New York law "presumptively requires" the state to recognize same-sex marriages "validly performed under the law of other jurisdictions."[4] Meanwhile, President George W. Bush has endorsed "an amendment to our Constitution defining and protecting marriage as a union of man and woman as husband and wife."[5]

One of the difficulties in writing about same-sex marriage is that events are unfolding so quickly that it is difficult to predict the state of play by the time this book finds its way into your hands. But as we write this chapter, no state legislature has voluntarily extended full and equal marriage rights to same-sex couples. Massachusetts has legalized same-sex marriage by court order (pursuant to the court's interpretation of the commonwealth's constitution), but a majority of the commonwealth's legislature seems to object, and has initiated a three-year process to amend the Massachusetts constitution. Thus, in November 2006, Massachusetts voters may be asked whether they want to amend the state's constitution to ban same-sex marriage and instead grant same-sex couples the option of Vermont-like civil unions.

This failure of state legislatures to adopt equal marriage rights for same-sex couples is not for lack of economic incentives. The first state that gives same-sex couples equal marriage rights may dramatically increase its tourism. Same-sex couples from across the United States would travel to the first-mover state, perhaps bringing friends and family with them. Once there, they would marry and—if the state is attractive enough—honeymoon. In the process, they would spend money. In 1995, one of us (Jennifer Brown) estimated that the present value of a change in marriage law for the first-mover state could reach three or four billion dollars.[6]

The key to this analysis is that tourism revenue is not an end in itself. State tourism boards have developed multipliers to show that each dollar tourists spend generates additional private income, tax revenue, and jobs. For example, using the multipliers developed by Hawaii's Department of Business, Economic Development and Tourism in 1994, Jennifer estimated that increased tourism following an expansion of marriage rights in the state could raise the present value of Hawaii household wealth by $6,700 on average, and reduce unemployment by 13.5 percent.

Lest you think these numbers might be inflated by our partisan leanings, *Forbes* magazine in April 2004 estimated that if same-sex couples currently living together were permitted to marry, they would spend a whopping $16.8 billion in the first several years following legalization.[7] This spending would be spread over various sectors of the so-called wedding industry, which includes jewelry, housewares, apparel, photography and video, catering, and travel, to name a few. The Forbes researchers relied upon U.S. census data showing that roughly 92 percent of heterosexual couples living together in 2000 were married; they assumed the same percentage of same-sex couples who live together would get married if given the chance, yielding a group of 546,000 same-sex couples ready to marry (not immediately, but within several years). Since 85 percent of heterosexual couples have wedding receptions, the authors assumed that 464,000 same-sex couples would do the same, and that each couple would spend $22,000, the national average according to The-Knot.com, the country's "largest online wedding site." This adds up to $16.8 billion dollars in wedding-related spending, much of which is spent in the state that actually celebrates the marriage. You might think that the researcher's assumptions are insufficiently conservative. Suppose, however, that only 46 percent of same-sex couples would choose to wed rather than the 92 percent the researchers assumed. All you need do is half their final estimate—and $8.4 billions dollars still looks like a substantial bit of revenue.

Despite these potential economic benefits, no state has taken this step. So why haven't state legislatures gone after these "gay marriage" dollars? The reasons are of course more political and social than economic. In many states, significant constituencies are aligned against equal marriage rights— and they can make things ugly for gay-friendly politicians. What allies have to do is make clear to legislators that they can count on our support— material and moral—when they face such challenges. Antigay groups have not only blocked equal marriage rights in their own states; they've also sought to insure that their state denies recognition to marriages celebrated by same-sex couples in other states. After the Hawaii Supreme Court ruled in the *Baehr* case, some of these states began to pass antirecognition statutes making clear that they would refuse to recognize a marriage between people of the same sex celebrated in any other state. As of 2004, thirty-eight states have passed these antirecognition (or "mini-DOMA") statutes.[8]

The Commonwealth of Virginia has gone the furthest. It recently passed a statute that not only denies recognition to same-sex marriages and civil unions celebrated in other states, it even purports to make "void and unenforceable" any "partnership contract or other arrangement between persons of the same sex purporting to bestow the privileges or obligations of marriage."[9] By its terms, such a statute could make it difficult or impossible for same-sex couples to protect themselves and their families through private ordering in wills, powers of attorney, and other legal arrangements. Legal challenges are inevitable.

Antirecognition statutes depress the hopes of same-sex couples that their marriages would be recognized in their home states, and might accordingly dampen their willingness to travel to the first-mover state for weddings. This in turn would reduce the first mover's expected revenue from the legal change. But the demand for Vermont civil unions (generally acknowledged to have little more than symbolic value outside the state) has been high, even among couples who live outside Vermont. Indeed, the lion's share (over 75 percent) of Vermont civil unions have been contracted by out-of-state couples. And journalists have noted the impact on the Vermont tourism industry.[10]

A similar phenomenon is playing out now in Massachusetts. Soon after the Supreme Judicial Court decision required same-sex marriages by May 2004, we received a "save the date" invitation to attend a wedding of two women friends, to be held on Cape Cod. Since legalization on May 17, 2004, hundreds of couples have already traveled to Massachusetts to marry. Massachusetts has no residency requirement and only a three-day waiting period between the date of application and the date the license is issued. This should make it relatively easy for nonresidents to come to Massachusetts for their weddings.

But life is not always so simple. State officials opposed to equal marriage rights have cited a 1913 "reverse evasion" statute that denies the right to marry in Massachusetts to any out-of-state couple whose marriage would not be valid in their home state. This statute was originally enacted when Massachusetts permitted interracial marriage but the majority of states did not. The effect of the statute, if strictly enforced, would have been to prevent Massachusetts from becoming a haven for interracial couples fleeing the discriminatory laws of their home states. It is sad and strange that the governor and attorney general of Massachusetts now resurrect this dusty statute, again to limit the reach of Massachusetts's nondiscrimination in marriage. If they succeed in their efforts to keep same-sex couples away, Massachusetts will be the poorer for it—literally.

Don't Boycott—Buycott!

Chapter 8 will consider (but ultimately reject) a marriage boycott as a means to promote equal marriage rights. Boycotts withhold economic or other benefits in order to punish bad behavior. This chapter considers and ultimately advocates the flip side of boycotts. What if, instead of punishing bad guys, we sought to *reward* good guys? A "buycott" aims to do just that, as it bestows economic or other benefits in order to reward positive action.

One might object that the distinction is merely rhetorical: it surely sounds more positive and optimistic to talk about rewarding gay-friendly institutions than to talk about punishing antigay ones. But in a world of finite resources, rewarding good guys will also punish bad guys—implicit in every buycott is the reality that institutions that are not gay-friendly could lose business. To the extent a buycott directs the flow of consumer dollars to one set of actors, it inevitably directs dollars *away* from another set. As we'll explain in greater detail below, however, a one-to-one ratio is often lacking between the good guy's gain from the buycott and the competitor's loss, because the chance that either would capture the business, absent the buycott, may have been very slim.

Somewhere between boycott and buycott lies an offer of patronage. Here, consumers seek to induce or elicit positive behavior by offering or promising a reward. This doesn't mean that the consumer will necessarily withhold that reward until the positive action occurs; it only means that the first entity to take that positive action is guaranteed to receive the reward.

This chapter proposes a Vacation Pledge for Equal Marriage Rights, through which people would promise to vacation in the first state where either the *legislature* or the *electorate* itself votes to extend marriage rights to same-sex couples. The promise would be to vacation in this first-mover state within three years of the legislative or referendum vote. In subsequent sections, we'll discuss the details of the pledge and why we think it might be especially effective in fending off both the Massachusetts and federal constitutional amendments that would ban same-sex marriage (as well as preventing the end-run invocation of desultory statutes like the Massachusetts reverse evasion statute). But before going into these details, we step back to introduce the rationales for buycott strategies more generally.

COMPETITIVE FEDERALISM refers to the way states can compete with each other for revenue by passing particular kinds of legislation and regulation. For example, competitive federalism leads states to compete for tax and other revenues generated by certain business activities within their borders.[11] Competitive federalism could also lead states to compete for the tourism revenue from solemnizing same-sex marriages. As Connecticut is to insurance, Delaware is to corporate law, and Nevada is to gambling, marriage, and divorce, so Massachusetts (or some similarly situated state) could become to same-sex marriage. The history of competitive federalism suggests that first movers often generate disproportionate and long-lived benefits, as demonstrated by the ongoing dominance of Delaware in the provision of corporate law.[12] States have competed for the sorts of individual and collective benefits sketched here, and same-sex marriage could provide another opportunity for such competition.

Not all states would have equally strong incentives to seize this first-mover advantage. Powerful interest groups within every state are almost certain to oppose legislation that authorizes same-sex marriage. But in some states there may be a sufficient coalition of supporters to pass such legislation. A state that has relied heavily upon tourism but currently suffers excess capacity in that industry could welcome the influx of new customers. A state that is politically progressive is more likely to welcome LGBT tourists, friends, and families. In light of these factors, Jennifer has argued elsewhere that Hawaii, New Mexico, and Vermont are three states that might seriously consider legalizing same-sex marriage.[13]

A state with a small population will enjoy more dramatic per capita benefits from the increased tourism revenue, so ideally the first-mover state should be relatively small. Legislators are most likely to vote in favor of recognizing same-sex marriage if they can persuade skeptical constituents that the legal change means money in their pockets. For example, in 1993, Apple Computer sought to build an eighty-million-dollar customer support center in Williamson County, Texas. The county commission initially voted three to two to deny Apple's request for a tax abatement, motivated by opposition to Apple's gay-friendly employment policies. This decision placed in jeopardy the fifteen hundred high-wage jobs and three hundred million dollars in local economic benefits that Apple could bring to the county. Commissioner David Hays reversed his vote a week later, and the commission approved an alternative tax package that contained the financial inducements Apple wanted most. "The bottom line," according to David M. Smith, director of public education for the National Gay and Lesbian Task Force, was that "jobs triumphed over prejudice."[14] An additional four billion dollars in tourism revenue obviously has greater per capita impact in a state with three million residents than it has in one with twenty-three million residents. This is consistent with the larger pattern of competitive federalism, in which smaller states have been the specialists in other areas of the law (such as Delaware with corporate law, South Dakota with banking, and Nevada with gambling).[15]

ON THE DEMAND SIDE, the "gay dollar" is already a recognized phenomenon. In recent years, gay rights advocates have taken stock of the community's economic clout. Gay dollars, which have the words *gay dollars* stamped or written on their face, are meant to demonstrate the spending power of the gay community. The gay community and its supporters have sought to exercise that spending power positively. For example, when voters in Tampa, Florida, enacted an antigay rights ordinance, the Human Rights Task Force of Florida responded by instituting a buycott rather than a boycott. The group published a directory of businesses that have "policies in support of gays and lesbians."[16] In the first five months of the directory's publication, the list grew from 105 to 430 entries.[17] Todd Simmons, spokesperson for the Human Rights Task Force of Florida, explained, "We decided on an approach that would empower us economically and politically. The buycott has improved our standing in the community. Businesses and other institutions have changed their policies to get in our book."

Large companies have launched advertising campaigns targeted to gay consumers, including AT&T, Anheuser-Busch, Apple Computer, Benetton, Philip Morris, Seagram, Sony, and Absolut.[18] The story of Absolut vodka illustrates the way gay and lesbian consumers demonstrate loyalty to supportive manufacturers and other businesses. Absolut, it seems, was one of the first major labels to advertise in gay publications. According to Rick Dean, vice president of Overlooked Opinions, "The gay community tied it back—Absolut was there on the back cover of gay publications before the others, and Absolut vodka is poured at gay bars."[19] George Slowik, publisher of *Out* magazine, notes that gay men and lesbians are "an audience not accustomed to being courted, so they're more apt to notice who's supportive and who's not, particularly at this point. The first ones in will reap extra benefits in each category."[20] The same sort of loyalty that allows Absolut to "reap extra benefits" as the "first one in" could allow the first state that legalizes same-sex marriage to reap extra revenue from tourists wishing to show their support for the legal change.

This brand loyalty is also evident in the travel industry. According to one marketing executive, "All a mainstream company has to do is show up at a gay travel expo and because of brand loyalty, gay and gay-friendly travelers will use them and their business will increase."[21]

Data about brand loyalty among LGBT consumers suggest that the first state to extend marriage rights to same-sex couples could expect to enjoy the benefits of increased tourism even after it loses its first-mover monopoly. Additional states might begin to extend marriage rights to same-sex couples, but lesbian and gay tourists and their friends would remember that the first-mover state was the groundbreaker. Loyalty to that state could continue to generate substantial tourism revenue even after same-sex couples start to celebrate their marriages in other states.

Designing the Pledge

A first step is to decide the substance of the pledge itself. What should be the event that triggers the duty to vacation? And what should be the duty that is triggered? At the web site we've created (www.vacationpledge.org), the pledge appears this way:

> WE, the undersigned, promise to vacation in the first state that democratically chooses (by either legislation or voter referendum) to legalize same-sex marriage, within three years of the effective date of the legalization.

Note that by signing the pledge, people promise to vacation in any state, so long as it is the first to democratically legalize marriages between people of the same sex. Pledge signers might find themselves, therefore, vacationing in a state they would not otherwise have planned to visit. This only means that states with a very low probability of attracting tourists have even more to gain from the pledge and less to lose from a boycott.

We also give pledgers a three-year period to visit the first-mover state. This time frame should be long enough so that people do not feel unduly constrained when signing the pledge, and so that the potential first mover does not fear an overwhelming influx of visitors following the recognition of marriage for same-sex couples. If the time frame is too great, on the other hand, signators may be less likely to remember and honor their pledge and the state will discount future revenue increases to account for the time value of money.

The design of the substantive trigger is of particular importance. There are several alternative triggers that are worthy of consideration. For instance, the pledge could extend an offer to a specific state (such as Massachusetts, Vermont, or New Mexico). This approach might attract a larger number of signers, because people could assess ahead of time the attractions of the states they would be promising to visit. On the other hand, even a state with a low tourism profile could be a pleasant place to visit, and a vacation—even in a state one might not otherwise choose to visit—seems a small "sacrifice" to make for the cause of gay rights.[22] We choose a first-mover trigger instead of a state-specific trigger as a way of harnessing the full effects of competitive federalism. This is a race that any of the fifty states is free to join.

Democratizing Legalization

Finally, the pledge as we've worded it requires democratic action—the obligation to visit the state is triggered by the effective date of a statute or referendum vote extending marriage rights to same-sex couples. Massachusetts' Supreme Judicial Court has already interpreted its constitution to require equal marriage rights. But judicial legalization is not sufficient to trigger the rewards of the pledge vacation dollars. The pledge is designed to create a democratic incentive for the electorate or the legislature itself—so it is action by the legislature or the voters themselves that triggers the pay-off. This democratic trigger might be particularly relevant to the coming battle in Massachusetts.

The judicial victory in Massachusetts is not the end of the struggle for equal marriage rights. The Massachusetts House and Senate, meeting in a constitutional convention, narrowly approved a resolution to amend the Massachusetts constitution to ban same-sex marriage. To become law, the amendment must be approved by both the state House and Senate by a simple majority in 2005, and a majority of voters must then approve the amendment in a 2006 public referendum.[23] The Vacation Pledge, though not state specific, is crafted to apply to the coming Massachusetts amendment fight. Either a legislative or electoral rejection of the state constitutional amendment to ban same-sex marriage would trigger the vacation duty.

These coming votes in the Massachusetts House and Senate and the November 2006 referendum are fixed, specific events around which to mobilize support. To most people, these votes appear to create an opportunity for conservative legislators to roll back the progress made by the court. It looks like a set of votes *against* equal marriage rights. But that's seeing the glass half empty. Another perspective sees that the Massachusetts Supreme Judicial Court has established a default of full and equal marriage rights for same-sex couples, which makes these legislative and referendum votes on the proposed constitutional amendment an opportunity to vote *for* equal marriage rights. In this way, the court's decision in *Goodridge* and the subsequent legislative activity have set the stage for our nation's first major democratic embrace of same-sex marriage. All the legislators and voters of Massachusetts need do is defeat the proposed constitutional amendment.

Victory is hardly assured. But if it comes, it will be a moment that progressives should celebrate both as a victory in and of itself and because it is likely to undermine some of the rhetoric around the proposed federal constitutional amendment banning same-sex marriage. It will show that through direct action or the actions of their duly elected representatives, the people can accept and support equal marriage rights for same-sex couples. The pledge then gives the signatories an opportunity to collectively celebrate this victory and simultaneously reward the people who made it possible.

The fact that Massachusetts has up to now been a *judicial* legalization—forced by the Supreme Judicial Court's interpretation of the state's constitution—has provoked outrage from opponents, like President Bush, who claim that "activist judges" are thwarting the will of the people. Indeed, opponents disingenuously warn that, because of the "full faith and credit" clause of the federal constitution, as few as five justices in a single state could force the entire country to recognize same-sex marriages. Proponents claim justification for a federal constitutional amendment exclusively defining marriage "as a union of man and woman" in the need to rein in these nonrepresentative judges.

A state legislature or a referendum of the general electorate that voluntarily extends equal rights powerfully undermines the current calls for a federal constitutional ban. The democratic embrace of same-sex marriage reveals the non sequitur in opponents' argument for a federal constitutional ban. The federal amendment claims to be driven by a concern with the anti-democratic manipulations of unrepresentative judges, but the ban itself preempts the right of individual state legislatures to decide this issue for themselves. The existence of a state where democratically elected officials or the electorate itself affirmatively opted for same-sex marriage would make it impossible for opponents to play the "activist judges" card. It is for this reason that we propose a vacation pledge to reward *legislative* or *electorate* legalization (as opposed to *judicial* legalization)—notwithstanding the existence on the ground of same-sex marriages in Massachusetts.[24]

Let us be clear: we believe that the judicial legalization of same-sex marriage in Massachusetts was a major victory. For the first time, the highest court in a state has unequivocally said that the state will solemnize same-sex marriages. Massachusetts has already shown that same-sex marriages do not undermine civilization. Life goes on. But a vacation pledge for a more democratic legalization is an important additional step that places the court's action on a firmer foundation and is likely to fend off the current calls for a federal marriage ban.

Are there any other state actions that are ripe for a first-mover pledge? You bet. The impetus for democratizing legalization could also be applied to the question of whether same-sex marriages of one state will be recognized in other jurisdictions. Accordingly, once same-sex marriage is legalized in some first-mover state, we could imagine creating a competition over which of the other forty-nine states will be the first to recognize these marriages. At first, this seems to implicate not legislative incentives, but merely federal constitutional requirements that "[f]ull faith and credit shall be given in each state to the public acts . . . of every other state."

But it turns out that the legislative behavior of a particular state can importantly determine whether or not it has to recognize the same-sex marriages of another state. This is true both because courts have found a "public policy exception" to the general recognition requirement and because the constitution gives Congress the power by general laws to define "the effect" of states' public acts. The federal DOMA attempts to do just this—giving individual state legislatures the option of not recognizing same-sex marriages performed in other jurisdictions. Commentators have questioned whether Congress, when acting pursuant to the full faith and credit clause, can actually give states the power of nonrecognition.[25]

What is important for these purposes is that in the shadow of the federal DOMA and the full faith and credit clause, a state's legislative activity is likely to impact (and may decisively determine) whether the state will have to recognize same-sex marriages of another jurisdiction. For example, New Mexico currently has on its books a statute that reads:

All marriages celebrated beyond the limits of this state, which are valid according to the laws of the country wherein they were celebrated or contracted, shall be likewise valid in this state, and shall have the same force as if they had been celebrated in accordance with the laws in force in this state.[26]

On its face this statute suggests that New Mexico waives any public policy exception or DOMA-based right of nonrecognition. If a same-sex couple's marriage is valid in Massachusetts, it "shall be likewise valid in [New Mexico]."[27] Conversely, the thirty-eight states that have adopted antirecognition statutes are more likely to succeed in court challenges to nonrecognition.[28]

This democratization of foreign recognition was underscored in 2003 by a letter opinion of New York attorney general Eliot Spitzer. Spitzer opined that while same-sex couples did not have a right to civil marriage in New York, New York had a duty to recognize same-sex marriages that were valid where performed. Lest one conclude that Spitzer, like Massachusetts' "activist judges," was speaking unilaterally and without any basis in the democratic process, one should remember two things. First, Spitzer was himself elected and reelected by the people of the state of New York in 1998 and 2002, respectively.[29] Second, antirecognition statutes have been proposed and defeated in the New York state legislature in the past several years.[30] And in those same legislative sessions, New York has passed several statutes creating rights and protections on the basis of sexual orientation.[31]

There may come a time when it is appropriate to launch another vacation pledge for the first state that democratically chooses to recognize another jurisdiction's same-sex unions. In one sense, this race may already be over—because New Mexico's unusual statute on its face does just this. But New Mexico's statute may not survive Massachusetts legalization. Or it might be appropriate to reward the first state to democratically enact legislation requiring recognition *after* same-sex marriage becomes a reality.

Of course, it may be harder to organize a vacation pledge that focuses on "recognition." The coming Massachusetts referendum on marriage itself is a definitive, high-profile event that will generate lots of Kodak moments— one way or the other. Recognition of same-sex marriage, in contrast, is a drama normally played out by smaller, decentralized groups of litigants on the courthouse steps. For these reasons, the current Vacation Pledge is focused on encouraging a first state to democratically legalize equal marriage rights. First things first. One step at a time.

Marketing the Pledge

The mechanics of collecting signatures are greatly simplified by the Internet. The pledge is housed at a web site, which people can easily visit to sign the pledge. In this way, the pledge is mechanically similar to a petition drive, except that rather than merely exhorting as a petition does, the language of the pledge includes the element of a promise or offer. In conjunction with the publication of this book, we have created a site for the Vacation Pledge for Equal Marriage Rights (www.vacationpledge.org). Institutions and organizations can promote the pledge through various media, including print, broadcast, web sites with links to the pledge, and "push" technology—e-mails to their members that include a link back to the official pledge web site. You can also find a link to the pledge at the web site for this book, www.straightforwardbook.com.

We are setting an admittedly ambitious goal of one million signatures. Instead of a million-man march, we seek to dangle the carrot of a million signatures to encourage Massachusetts to do the right thing. While the task of generating a million signatures seems daunting, we hope to recruit supporters in college LGBT groups as well as PFLAG organizations. A million signatures means that roughly a half of 1 percent of the U.S. adult population needs to sign. Obviously, the signatures of the LGBT community itself would be sufficient to meet this amount. But the task will be all the easier if the community reaches out to friends and family. At the grassroots level, a million-signature goal would mean that our home state of Connecticut would need to generate about twelve thousand signatures. A petition drive at local colleges and universities, where five hundred gay rights supporters each sought twenty-five signatures, would more than reach this goal.

Of course, it is difficult to predict how many people would sign the pledge—especially now that Massachusetts has judicially required equal marriage rights. Same-sex couples who have already traveled to be married in Massachusetts and who want to make sure that the validity of their marriages is not called into question by the subsequent referendum are natural people to organize a pledge drive. This will especially be the case if we are right in guessing that Massachusetts' 2006 referendum—or even the 2005 legislative vote that precedes it—is likely to be the first electoral or legislative vote that could potentially trigger the pledge's vacationing duty.[32] Similarly, unattached gay men and lesbians (as well as couples with no interest in marrying) might sign the pledge in order to signal their support for an equality-enhancing legal change. Members of, or contributors to, the na-

tional Freedom to Marry coalition, New England Gay and Lesbian Advocates and Defenders (GLAD), Human Rights Campaign, Lambda Legal Defense and Education Fund, the National Center for Lesbian Rights, GLAAD
(Gay and Lesbian Alliance Against Defamation), and the National Gay and
Lesbian Task Force might be likely participants in the pledge.

Finally, and perhaps most important for this book's analysis, heterosexual allies might sign the pledge. Who are the people likely to fall into this
group? Parents, sisters, brothers, friends, and coworkers of lesbian and gay
people, members of PFLAG, contributors to other progressive policy organizations, such as People for the American Way, Moveon.org, the ACLU,
and the National Organization for Women. Just as conservative or funda-
mentalist churches might serve as organizers for a boycott, so "open" or "affirming" churches might promote the pledge among their members.[33] One
could also look to circulation numbers for progressive publications such as
Ms. magazine or *The Nation*.[34] This is not to assume that all readers of these
publications support gay rights, but the bulk of subscribers do lean left on
these issues. In any case, through aggressive promotion in a variety of
media, it should be possible to secure the signatures of a million people taking the pledge.

But before the pledge is implemented, it is useful to take on two potential
criticisms of the strategy, which we will refer to as a boycott concern and a
commodification concern. The next sections take up each of these points.

The Boycott Concern

An important drawback to a buycott strategy such as the Vacation Pledge is
that it might trigger a retaliatory boycott. This possibility of antigay organizing is not mere paranoia. In several settings, boycotts have been announced to punish organizations that promote gay rights.[35] But there are
strong structural reasons to be confident that the buycott effect on tourism
is likely to be much more powerful than any boycott.

Indeed, the most important impact of the Vacation Pledge may be not to
convince legislators or electors that the state will reap an economic benefit
from legalization, but rather to allay their fears of economic loss. Some
states might fear economic harm from extending equal marriage rights to
same-sex couples. They might worry that disapproving consumers and religious organizations would punish the state through an organized boycott.
In addition, they could fear a "tipping" dynamic, through which consumers

who were not boycotting might make individual decisions to avoid the state, thinking it had become a sort of "gay mecca."[36] Indeed, one wonders whether Massachusetts governor Mitt Romney is concerned about just this sort of result when he protests that "Massachusetts should not become the Las Vegas of same-sex marriage."[37] But for every expected dollar lost to boycotting or tipping, many more expected dollars could be promised to the state through the pledge.

Consider the following hypothetical. Imagine a fictional state—we'll call it the state of Grace—which is deliberating a change in the marriage law to include same-sex couples. In the course of legislative hearings, let us suppose, opponents of equal marriage rights argue that if it were to extend marriage rights to same-sex couples, the state would suffer grave economic harm—particularly in its tourism sector—because millions of Americans would boycott the state. To determine its expected loss from boycott, the state would first need to estimate the number of people expected to participate in a boycott. The target group of consumers for a boycott related to same-sex marriage would probably be a combination of social conservatives, conservative Christian church members, and members of organizations that fall to the far right on the political spectrum (such as the organizations that spearheaded Colorado's Amendment 2, which would have amended the state constitution to prohibit local governments from passing human rights ordinances or other laws protecting LGBT people—had the U.S. Supreme Court not struck it down as an equal protection violation).[38] Of course, some overlap exists in the membership of these groups. Even so, this could be a very large group of consumers, perhaps as many as ten million.[39]

Next, the state of Grace would consider the average revenue generated by each person who visits the state. Let us assume that each visitor to the state spends $500 on average, a figure that includes things like food, lodging, entertainment, and retail shopping.[40] But note: even if the state assumes strong compliance with the boycott, the expected loss from a boycott would *not* be $5 billion (ten million boycotters multiplied by $500). The state of Grace would have to adopt a more subtle analysis in order to reach an accurate calculation of the real cost of equal marriage rights.

The state would also have to factor in the *probability* that, absent a boycott, these ten million people would have visited the state in a given year. States know how many American visitors they receive each year. In Hawaii, for example—a popular tourist destination—the state welcomes nearly four million American visitors each year (out of a total U.S. population of 285 million).[41] This gives the average American only a .0136 chance of visiting Hawaii in any given year.[42] Since Hawaii is remote and expensive to reach, let us suppose that the state of Grace assumes a greater likelihood that the average American will visit Grace in any given year. Indeed, assume it is more than twice as likely that people will visit Grace. If Grace therefore assumes a .03 chance of welcoming any individual American to the state in a given year, that probability must be factored into the total loss due to the boycott. Multiplying $5 billion by .03 renders an expected loss from the boycott of $150 million per year. A boycott therefore brings one group of Americans from a .03 probability of visiting Grace down to a zero probability. This is not a huge change in the chance than any given individual will visit Grace, but if the group is large enough, the boycott can constitute a serious threat to the state's tourism economy.

Suppose, however, that supporters of gay rights have been able to promote a credible Vacation Pledge. Then the state of Grace could balance the expected loss of boycotters' business against the expected *gain* of business from the signers of the pledge. Suppose that we are successful and one million people have signed the pledge, promising to vacation within three years in the first state to democratically extend marriage rights to same-sex couples.

Before the pledge was instituted, the state of Grace would have calculated the expected revenue generated by this group of one million people at about $15 million per year.[43] But if the pledge signers have made a credible promise, Grace can count on a visit from them; the probability of gaining their business moves from .03 all the way to 1.00. Assuming that pledge signers honor their promise, the expected revenue attributable to this group of one million people becomes $500 million, which, divided over three years, comes to $167 million per year, $152 million more than they would have been expected to generate in the absence of the pledge.[44]

The expected gain from even a relatively small group of pledge signers, who raise their probability of visiting Grace from .03 to 1.00, can offset or even outweigh the expected loss from a much larger group of boycotters who reduce their probability of visiting Grace from .03 to zero. This is because Grace's expected revenue changes much more dramatically for each person who promises to visit than it does for each person who threatens to stay away. Indeed, because of the importance of probability in calculating expected tourist revenue, boycotters would have to outnumber pledge signers by more than ten to one in order to make Grace's expected loss from a boycott exceed the expected gain from a pledge.

Promises to visit from a group of people who have signed their names and provided their addresses can be more persuasive than blanket boycott threats by leaders of even large organizations, because the individual members of those organizations have not spoken for themselves in the same way the pledge signers have. Moreover, in the tourism industry, names and addresses of possible tourists could be very useful to the first-mover state.[45] In the wake of a legal change conferring equal marriage rights, the state could extend special promotions to the pledge signers, reminding them of their commitment. This could increase their incentives to visit the state or extend their stay on a trip they already plan to make.

Organizers of the pledge might disclose names but keep addresses of signatories confidential until a state actually fulfills the conditions of the pledge by granting same-sex couples equal marriage rights. Simply giving a state one million "leads"—the names and addresses of potential travelers—could confer a huge asset.

The Commodification Concern

There is, however, another set of concerns with the buycott strategy. Is it appropriate to monetize the case for human rights? To some, there is something distasteful about an appeal for support on this basis when right-minded lawmakers should support same-sex marriage simply because it is a basic human right. To commodify the value of same-sex marriage is to suggest an invidious economic calculus that—notwithstanding the previous section's discussion of boycotts and buycotts—might be contingent on future events.

To these concerns, we plead guilty. To some extent, we are commodifiers. But we are pragmatic commodifiers. We have the strong sense that discrimination in marriage laws is a dam that is about to burst. Like reproductive freedom, equal marriage rights will be very hard to take away. Once people see that same-sex marriage does not "undermine" the institution of marriage, it will remain with us. To our minds, securing this basic right a fewer years earlier is worth the cost of commodification.

Finally, some people have questioned the buycott strategy not because it is commodifying gay rights particularly but because it is commodifying law generally. If creating legislative incentives through the Vacation Pledge is legitimate, why not just have people pledge to send the first-mover state a check if it legalizes same-sex marriage? Or why not have someone like George Soros offer to pay Massachusetts a billion dollars if it does (or does not) legalize?

This concern with commodifying law more generally is a difficult issue. But in some ways the ship has sailed. Corporations promise to locate manufacturing plants if special laws are passed giving them tax abatements (sports teams too!). And the offer of payment by Soros (or same-sex marriage petitioners) to the state is much more defensible than another common method of creating legislative incentives: contributions to legislators' campaign funds. When the promised payments go to the state, the elected officials of the state are well placed to decide whether accepting the offer is in the state's best interest—and they will need to defend their decision at the next election.

Indeed, there is a way in which commodifying law enhances democracy in our federal system of competing jurisdiction. Recent years have seen a surge of state legislative activity to avoid recognizing marriages between people of the same sex.[46] The U.S. Congress in 1996 passed the so-called Defense of Marriage Act, which defines marriage for federal purposes as being between one man and one woman only, and makes clear that states are free to refuse to recognize marriages between people of the same sex celebrated in sibling states. When gay men and lesbians become convenient scapegoats in political contests to appear most committed to "traditional family values," advocates for gay rights can find it harder and harder to be heard in political discourse. The pledge expands the political power of gay rights supporters beyond the boundaries of their home states and lets the voice of trapped minorities find voice in other jurisdictions. Just as cumulative voting in corporate law ensures minority shareholders a few seats on a corporate board, interjurisdictional buycott pledges might allow minority preferences to be expressed in at least a few states.[47] A pledge can give people a voice in political arenas—on economic terms—where they might actually be *heard*, without the background buzz of competing moral views drowning out the message.

Conclusion

The pledge is part social organizing, part academic inquiry. It moves the theoretical notion that states will compete for revenues into the political and social spheres. The pledge could uncover what people would be willing to pay, how much they would sacrifice economically, to know that at least one state in the United States has eliminated a particular kind of de jure discrimination on the basis of gender and sexual orientation. But the beauty of the pledge also lies in this: it does not call for a great sacrifice. By signing the pledge, supporters of gay rights promise to do something they would likely do anyway—take a vacation. *Where* they take that vacation, however, is determined by the fact that they have signed the pledge. Sometimes people like to have a noble excuse for doing something pleasurable. The Vacation Pledge for Equal Marriage Rights provides just this sort of opportunity.

The Fair Employment Mark

This chapter follows closely on the heels of the preceding chapter by proposing yet another way supporters of gay rights can vote with their wallets, rewarding progressive policies and institutions. Just as consumers can travel and spend tourism dollars to support progressive state and local governments, so, too, they can reward companies that treat gay employees fairly, by purchasing their products and services. To facilitate such progressive purchasing decisions, this chapter describes a coordinating mechanism, the Fair Employment Mark. The Fair Employment Mark does not currently exist, but if launched and monitored, it would advance the practice of gay rights advocacy on the ground, in the workplace—where it matters most for many lesbians and gay men.

The idea is simple, really. The Fair Employment Mark would be an innocuous symbol, such as *FE* inside a circle, that would signal to knowing consumers that the company manufacturing the product has officially instituted and complied with a given set of employment policies. This chapter will propose one potential set of policies as a standard for licensing the mark. Others are possible.

The Fair Employment Mark would operate as a "certification mark." Certification marks are used to signal that a product or service bearing the mark has met a specific standard set forth by the certifying entity. Groups or individuals can register certification marks with the federal government much as we do trademarks. The difference is that a trademark owner must be involved in producing the item or service bearing the mark,[1] while a certification mark owner must remain independent and may not produce any of the goods or services to which the mark applies.[2] Certification marks are not common. Owners of certification marks are held to high standards of conduct: decisions about whether or not to certify a product or service must be based exclusively upon the criteria the owner has set for the mark. In other words, certification cannot be based on a user's willingness to pay a fee to the owner of the mark (other than a minimal fee covering administrative costs). In effect, the certifying entity must operate as a nonprofit. It takes a special sort of organization or individual to institute a certification mark—one committed to the values reflected in the mark.

Seen in this light, the Fair Employment Mark is an idea that is both simple and traditional. Commerce in the United States has nurtured a venerable tradition of labeling products to improve work conditions for groups of oppressed people. Trade union labels first came into circulation as a way of promoting shorter workdays. In 1869, the Carpenter's Eight-Hour League of San Francisco created a stamp that permitted lumber mills to signal that they ran on an eight-hour schedule rather than a ten-hour schedule.[3] This was typical of most union labels that followed, as they were generally used to promote better working standards and to guard against the use of tenement-house, sweatshop, and prison labor.[4] By the turn of the century, union labels were used by printers, bakers, woodworkers, harness makers, iron molders, broom makers, coopers, photographers, shoemakers, custom tailors, mattress makers, blacksmiths, brewers, egg inspectors, barbers, and coal distributors.[5]

Although some early labeling schemes attempted to promote the quality or healthfulness of the product, the union label stood primarily for "better pay and improved work conditions."[6] Before legislation was passed outlawing child labor, for example, private organizations devised and administered labeling programs to promote products manufactured without the use of child labor.[7] Now U.S. consumers are faced with a growing number of products manufactured in countries where employment laws are lax or nonexistent.[8] Some consumers want to buy products that protect the environment or animal rights. Today, many products in the United States bear marks relating to issues of moral import to consumers: environmental impact, animal testing, fair trade, sweatshops, and child labor. The Fair Employment Mark would similarly permit consumers who care about gay rights to spend their money in ways more consistent with their values.

To stand the best chance of success, the symbol should aspire to these goals:

1. *Progress:* It should symbolize a set of policies that represent a *real advance in employment protections* for gay men and lesbians.
2. *Efficient enforcement:* Those policies should be *enforceable* by a broad spectrum of actors with incentives to monitor the behavior of companies using the mark.
3. *Targeted transparency:* The symbol should be *recognizable* to knowing consumers, but *not so explicit* that it causes uninformed consumers with antigay feelings to avoid the product or service.

The rest of the chapter discusses each of these goals in greater detail.

Promoting a Real Advance in Employment Protections for Gay Men and Lesbians

Various standards are possible to set qualifications for use of the mark. The simplest and most straightforward standard (and the one that we will ultimately adopt) borrows directly from the Employment Non-Discrimination Act (ENDA), a bill that has been proposed repeatedly since 1993 but not yet enacted by Congress.[9] ENDA would, in effect, include sexual orientation in the group of characteristics that Title VII already makes off-limits as the basis for the terms and conditions of employment.[10] More specifically, ENDA would forbid employers from discriminating on the basis of sexual orientation with regard to hiring, firing, or terms of employment; forbid retaliatory conduct; and be enforced by the Equal Employment Opportunity Commission.[11] ENDA would adopt the basic disparate treatment framework developed under Title VII, but would exclude religious organizations and the military from its coverage. It would not allow disparate impact claims, and would not require affirmative action or the provision of employee benefits to domestic partners.[12]

It is this last characteristic of ENDA that might cause it to fall short as a standard for the Fair Employment Mark. While ENDA clearly represents a major advance in employment protections for gay men and lesbians, members of Congress who are pushing it have had to limit its reach in order to make it more politically palatable. The statute has an understandably modest goal: to prohibit disparate treatment—that is, employment discrimination on the basis of sexual orientation.

The Fair Employment Mark, in contrast to ENDA, would be part of a voluntary system. Companies would be opting into the Fair Employment Mark and its requirements rather than having those requirements imposed by statute. The voluntary nature of the program might lead companies to commit to standards more exacting than ENDA requires.

A more ambitious standard for the mark would go beyond ENDA and also mandate the provision of health care and other benefits for employees' same-sex domestic partners.[13] To extend health benefits to employees' same-sex domestic partners could be seen as a form of affirmative action. The mark might require this as a way of responding to the state's own discrimination against same-sex marriage. In jurisdictions where same-sex couples cannot signal their commitment through civil marriage, they are unfairly harmed by employment policies that condition certain benefits upon civil marriage.

Employers who refuse to extend health benefits in this way could argue, however, that they are treating all employees equally: gay or straight, employees receive family health benefits, but only if they are married. But such a response misses the point. This is not a case in which the harm arises from treating similarly situated people differently. Instead, the harm results from treating differently situated people the same, without regard for the background conditions of inequality that cause this treatment to affect them in different ways.

By removing the requirement of civil marriage with respect to same-sex couples (but not with respect to different-sex couples, who have the option of marriage to signal their commitment), an employment policy granting health benefits to employees' same-sex domestic partners could remedy disparate impact discrimination. The trouble is that an employment policy extending health benefits to same-sex domestic partners but not different-sex domestic partners could be seen as discriminating against heterosexuals, thus violating the nondiscrimination policy that forbids discrimination on the basis of sexual orientation. Therefore, the Fair Employment Mark could require licensees to offer health benefits to employees' domestic partners, regardless of gender.

Many companies have voluntarily achieved this standard already. Whether out of a corporate ethic of fairness to all employees or a recognition that gay men and lesbians can be valuable employees worth recruiting, more and more companies are including domestic partners in employee benefits packages. In fact, recent studies show that more than four thousand U.S. companies offer their employees domestic partner health benefits. Nearly half of the Fortune 500 companies do so.[14] Thus, while domestic partner health benefits might go beyond ENDA's basic requirements, thousands of profitable companies are already meeting that standard, suggesting that many more could do so as well.

Other possible standards are suggested by the Human Rights Campaign (HRC) Corporate Equality Index, a one-hundred-point system that rates corporate policies and actions toward the lesbian, gay, bisexual, and transgender community.[15] The HRC Corporate Equality Index rates several hundred of the country's largest corporations on the following criteria:

1. The company has adopted a written nondiscrimination policy that includes the words *sexual orientation.*
2. The company has adopted a written nondiscrimination policy that includes the words *gender identity* or *gender expression.*
3. The company offers same-sex domestic partner health insurance benefits.
4. The company supports an LGBT employee or resource group.
5. The company offers diversity training that includes discussion of sexual orientation or gender expression in the workplace.
6. The company advertises to the LGBT community, sponsors LGBT events, or makes charitable gifts to an LGBT or HIV/AIDS-related community organization.
7. The company does not actively engage in actions that would undermine the dignity and worth of lesbian, gay, bisexual, and transgender employees.[16]

Here we see a rating system already in place that applies a broad array of criteria. HRC also subscribes to incrementalism. It has announced that index criteria in 2006 will give increased weight to equal benefits, workplace policies for transgender employees, and diversity training.

HRC uses its criteria to rate the companies on a 100-point scale, so that a company can achieve a relatively high score even if it cannot certify that it complies with all of the seven standards. Companies that achieve a 100 percent score can use an HRC "Corporate Equality Index 100 Percent" service mark. Several companies—including American Airlines, Ford Motor, and Pepsico—are HRC mark licensees.

The Fair Employment mark might set a lower bar to increase the number of qualifying companies. The HRC criterion referring to "gender identity," for example, effectively requires employers to refrain from discriminating against transgendered people. Only fifty companies responding to HRC's Corporate Equality Index survey "include gender identity, characteristics or expression in their non-discrimination policy."[17] For many employers, inclusion of gender identity in the company's written nondiscrimination policy would be seen as too radical a move to be attempted, and they would opt out of using the mark despite their willingness to include sexual orientation in the policy.

Gender identity illustrates well the difficult choices that an incremental approach requires. In the interests of gay, lesbian, and bisexual employees, the licensing agreement for the Fair Employment Mark might emphasize sexual orientation, even though such a system would leave transgendered people out of the calculus. Incrementalism works on the assumption (or, at least, the hope) that fair treatment on the basis of sexual orientation is a step in the right direction, a step that brings us closer to fair treatment on the basis of gender identity at some point in the not-too-distant future. Such pragmatic choices, though difficult, are not unique to this book: ENDA as proposed would forbid employment discrimination on the basis of sexual orientation but not extend to gender identity.[18] If the next version of ENDA proposed in Congress includes gender identity, the argument for covering gender identity in the Fair Employment Mark would strengthen.

Another criterion on the HRC scale that might be difficult for some employers to meet is the one requiring that the company support an LGBT employee group. The HRC criteria do not explain how an employer would "support" an LGBT employee group. Is it enough if the company can certify that such a group exists, and can provide one contact person involved in the group? Some employers may be too small to support such a group, lacking a critical mass of openly LGBT employees. The HRC standards recognize this fact when they provide, as an alternative to support for an LGBT employee group, that a company could establish a senior level diversity council. Even the smallest company could fulfill this requirement. Note, however, that such criteria go beyond tracking civil rights laws, or bringing sexual orientation more on par with race and gender in employment protections. LGBT employee groups and diversity councils are forms of affirmative action, as they represent affirmative steps to recruit gay and lesbian employees and make the workplace more comfortable for them.

Some might criticize this approach as going too far, taking on the character of a "shakedown" that demands concessions in exchange for a certification of fairness. The Reverend Jesse Jackson and his civil rights organization, PUSH, have been subject to this critique. Some observers have accused them of giving companies charged with racial discrimination a sort of absolution in exchange for large donations to PUSH.[19] In the case of the Fair

Employment Mark, however, the requirements for certification should escape such criticism. If companies using the mark must pay a licensing fee, the certifying entity should be careful to set that fee at a level that covers administrative costs but does not generate profits. The list of requirements cannot be endless; at some point, the factors might appear to impose an unreasonable burden, one companies should not have to bear in order to be characterized as "gay friendly" or "fair" to lesbian, gay, and bisexual employees. The certifying entity would be imposing the Fair Employment Mark standards not for its own benefit, but for the good of licensees' employees, and would thus avoid the appearance of self-dealing that has at times brought PUSH under fire.

To encourage adoption and send a clear message to targeted consumers, the mark should rest on objective criteria. Some of the factors in the HRC index are potentially problematic on this score. Consider how subjective and difficult to police the following criteria could be:

> The company advertises to the LGBT community, sponsors LGBT events, or makes charitable gifts to an LGBT community organization.
> The company does not actively engage in actions that would undermine the dignity and worth of lesbian, gay, bisexual, and transgender employees.

Actions that undermine the dignity and worth of LGBT employees could be difficult to define and observe. Companies might wonder if this standard exceeds the requirements ENDA would impose.

Similarly, it might be difficult to assess the importance of a company's sponsorship of LGBT activities and events. A company that directs significant resources to an event and becomes closely identified with it should get more credit than one that merely takes out a small ad in a print program. Such distinctions may be difficult and time-consuming to detect, however, and even more difficult to convey under the rubric of the Fair Employment Mark. This is not to say that charitable giving and support for LGBT events are unimportant, but only that the Fair Employment Mark might not be the best vehicle for promoting these activities.

One response to these difficulties would be to permit the mark itself to signal varying levels of company compliance. The mark might include a numeral signaling the company's rating on an index similar to that used by the HRC. Thus, for example, cereals made by General Mills might bear a label reading "FE = 9", while cereals made by Kellogg would rate only "FE = 7". General Mills could boast its higher number because it has included sexual orientation in its nondiscrimination policy, offers domestic partner health insurance benefits, and has an LGBT employee group.[20] These three factors—a nondiscrimination policy that covers sexual orientation, health benefits for domestic partners, and an LGBT employee group—are the easiest, most objective criteria to monitor, and General Mills has fulfilled all of them. Kellogg does not offer domestic partner health benefits, which suppresses its score.[21] This difference might provide some consumers a reason to buy Cheerios rather than Rice Krispies. But the example of General Mills and Kellogg suggest a reason *not* to combine the mark with a numerical rating. The difference between offering or withholding health benefits for domestic partners is significant, but the difference between a score of 9 and a score of 7 may be insufficiently transparent to convey this difference to consumers.

For pragmatic reasons, we reject these subjective and varying signals. Companies might worry that it would be difficult to refute a negative assessment with regard to subjective criteria. And consumers will not only have difficulty understanding a ratings system, they may not equally endorse the varied commands of the HRC program. Instead, we have chosen—at least initially—to have a much simpler and limited coverage that is targeted at eradicating the core wrong—intentional disparate treatment on the basis of sexual orientation. To this end, we propose that the mark should be licensed only to companies that privately promise not to violate the ENDA commands of nondiscrimination. The license agreement expressly states that its goal is "to privately commit [the Licensee] to nondiscrimination as defined in the Employment Non-Discrimination Act."

By crafting the substantive license simply to prohibit the core concept of discrimination—treating people differently because of their sexual orientation—and by expressly privatizing the effects of the proposed federal legislation, the mark can appeal to and piggyback on the substantial preexisting support for ENDA. In a 2003 Gallup poll, 88 percent of respondents said that "homosexuals should . . . have equal rights in terms of job opportunities."[22] Dozens of corporations (including behemoths AT&T, Coors, and Quaker Oats) have already officially endorsed the passage of ENDA and so might be willing to embrace privately what they have claimed should be the law of the land.

In the spirit of incrementalism that informs much of this book, we would propose that the mark evolve over time. While the initial mark only commits companies to the nondiscrimination mandates of ENDA, subsequent editions of the mark might encompass more far-reaching goals. For example, once ENDA is enacted, the mark as written would be wholly redundant with the mandated federal right. At that point in time, it might be appropriate to require that licensees provide domestic partnership benefits (at least to same-sex partners in states that deny the right to marry civilly). Alternatively, it might be appropriate to add gender identity to the covered groups to extend protection to transgendered workers. But we should be careful not to impose an ever escalating set of duties on employers. Corporations will be chary of using a mark if they expect it to become increasingly burdensome (because there will be costs in adverse publicity if in the future they discontinue the mark's use).

Finally, it might be appropriate to require users of the mark to certify that affiliated corporations—particularly major suppliers—have also agreed to be bound by the nondiscrimination mandate of the mark. Other labeling schemes have dealt more rigorously with the problem of suppliers. For example, the "leaping bunny" mark of the Coalition for Consumer Information on Cosmetics (CCIC) certifies that neither the manufacturer *nor the suppliers of ingredients* for marked cosmetics and household products perform tests on animals.[23]

In order to insure a critical level of participation, we have crafted the Fair Employment license only to apply to the licensee's own employment practices. Again, this mimics the coverage of ENDA itself—as corporations are not responsible for discriminatory practices of their suppliers. Of course, one danger is that an essentially empty "gay friendly" shell could be devised to bear the label, while the entire manufacturing process is conducted by companies that discriminate against gay, lesbian, and bisexual employees. But we find it unlikely that corporate forms will be manipulated because of the possibility of disparate treatment liability, and we are reluctant to require an adopting company to enforce nondiscrimination up the supply chain (at least in the first version of the mark).

Efficient Enforcement

The most obvious group of enforcers are the people who are supposed to get the greatest benefit: gay, lesbian, and bisexual people who work for companies adopting the mark. The certification license expressly empowers this group by naming the corporation's employees and applicants as third-party beneficiaries and clothing them with the same rights they would have under ENDA:

> The Licensee and Licensor intend that these third-party beneficiaries will have the right to sue the Licensee for any breach of this agreement and have a legal right to the same remedies (including damages and injunctive relief) to which they would be entitled if ENDA was in effect.

Thus, the Fair Employment license mimics not just the substance but also the procedures of the proposed ENDA statute. These third-party beneficiaries would be entitled to sue for compensation (back pay or benefits) or injunctive relief (reinstatement or promotion) that would be available under the statute. Gay and lesbian employees will have the strongest incentives to police the licensee's conduct, and the cheapest access to information regarding violations. Therefore, using the licensing agreement to create rights of action in the employees—who are, after all, the intended beneficiaries of the whole arrangement—would be sensible.

By creating rights of action in gay, lesbian, and bisexual employees, the mark might worry some employers who fear an additional source of litigation. But many employers are already subject to that risk because they operate in states or cities that forbid sexual orientation discrimination. For these companies, the mark offers some payoff for a policy they already follow. For employers that have not yet adopted nondiscrimination policies because they fear litigation, the mark could alter their calculation by creating new marketing benefits to offset expected litigation costs.

In order for current or potential employees to assist in enforcement efforts, they must be educated about the mark and the rights it guarantees. Some licensees would use the mark not only to promote products with consumers but also to recruit potential employees who are gay, lesbian, or bisexual. Employers will have independent incentives to inform employees and applicants that they are Fair Employment Mark licensees. Other companies will consider the mark much more a marketing than a recruiting tool. These companies may adopt the mark with hopes it will increase sales, but play down the mark and its meaning with employees. Gay rights advocacy groups could collaborate with the owner of the mark in a program to educate workers about their rights. Employers may not be motivated to distribute this information to employees on their own. But gay workers are likely to learn very quickly when their employer has chosen to start marking its product.

Certification marks usually involve the licensor as an active monitor in certifying the compliance of the mark user. The mark users pay fees to the licensor to cover these monitoring expenses. But we have opted for a much more decentralized structure that obviates the need for licensor monitoring and the payment of licensing fees. The licensor merely certifies that the licensee has promised not to discriminate. This certification does not require licensor effort because the very act of validly using the mark constitutes the promise of nondiscrimination itself. The employees of the licensee are then left (just as under ENDA) to do the hard work of enforcing the underlying promise.

Far more complex enforcement schemes than the Fair Employment Mark have succeeded with regard to other certification marks. For example, consider the Orthodox Union emblem (a letter *U* inside a larger circle) certifying that a product is kosher.[24] The Orthodox Union certification service employs a staff of "over 1,000 rabbinic coordinators, kashruth supervisors, food chemists and support personnel." It certifies "250,000 brand names, hotels, restaurants, services and 2,505 companies in 54 countries around the globe."[25] Substantial paperwork and close attention to detail are required of companies using the OU emblem.[26] In contrast, the Fair Employment Mark is a model of procedural licensing simplicity.

There is, however, an important respect in which the licensing agreement does not replicate the ENDA enforcement regime. Under ENDA, both the Justice Department and the Equal Employment Opportunity Commission would be empowered to sue employers who discriminate. The licensing agreement names as third-party beneficiaries "all persons and entities who would be entitled to sue if ENDA was in effect." This is an attempt to grant government actors enforcement power. While this provision is sufficient consent upon the part of the corporate licensee for such enforcement, at the moment the government actors are not empowered by statute to bring an ENDA-like enforcement action. However, in the spirit of incrementalism, the license could become an invitation to Congress to pass ENDA-like enforcement protection—at least with respect to those corporations who consent. Such an "opt-in" approach might garner the support of legislators who have been reluctant to impose ENDA's requirements on unwilling companies.

An alternative way of supplementing private employee enforcement would be to specify that particular gay rights organizations would have standing as third-party beneficiaries to enforce the agreement. Such organizations have standing to enforce other civil rights laws.[27] And extending such enforcement powers might be particularly appropriate in a world where government enforcement was not forthcoming. Indeed, if an organization such as Human Rights Campaign or its division Worknet would act as the licensor itself, it would have direct standing as a certifier to ensure that its licensees were complying with the promises of the license. Even if HRC did not act as licensor, it might be listed as a third-party beneficiary of the agreement, again creating the right to enforce the standards of fairness in employment contained in the agreement.

The power of advocacy groups is also related to the question of auditing. To facilitate enforcement by agencies and organizations, the licensing agreement could require the licensee company to permit "testing"—what some might call "deceptive audits"—by which people who do not really intend to take jobs or remain in jobs pose as applicants or employees in order to test the company's compliance with the licensing agreement. In the housing context, testing is done regularly. Similarly here, testers could apply for a posted job opening and present themselves as openly bisexual, gay, or lesbian. They could ask about discrimination policies, domestic partner benefits, or LGBT employee groups. They might even take the jobs temporarily, without a bona fide intention of working for the company, just to see whether the policies are actually followed once employees enter the company.

Corporate consent to potential auditing is important because it can reduce the risk that the auditor will be sued by the corporation. In one case, a company subject to similar testing sued and obtained a large jury verdict against the testing entity. In *Food Lion v. ABC,* Food Lion brought a tort action when ABC broadcast videotape of unwholesome food-handling practices. The videotape had been obtained by ABC reporters who gained employment in Food Lion supermarkets by misrepresentation. The plaintiff alleged fraud, employee disloyalty, and unfair trade practices. The jury returned a verdict for the plaintiff, awarding $1,402 in compensatory damages and over $5 million in punitive damages, which the trial judge reduced to $315,000 through remittitur. On appeal, the court rejected Food Lion's fraud claim, because the reporters were at-will employees for an indefinite period, and Food Lion could show no reliance on their misrepresentations in training them and paying their wages. With respect to the claims of employee disloyalty, however, the court held that the reporters intended to act against the interests of the plaintiff and were liable in tort. The reporters' disloyalty also caused the reporters to exceed the consent Food Lion granted them to enter plaintiff's premises; the reporters therefore committed trespass. The court rejected Food Lion's claim that misrepresentations on the job applications alone could vitiate Food Lion's consent.

To avoid anything resembling the Food Lion case, the entity licensing the Fair Employment Mark might include in the licensing agreement a clause making clear that use of the mark is conditioned upon consent to random testing. This could create incentives for licensees to comply with the mark's requirements, and in the event testing did occur, preempt any claims of fraud or trespass they might bring.

While there are strong arguments for empowering advocacy groups like HRC to both audit and bring suit against licensees, we have chosen, in the spirit of incrementalism, to maintain a narrow set of potential plaintiffs and enforcement tools for the initial version of the license. Real progress can be made just by endowing the direct victims of discrimination with a power to sue. And to our minds, the costs of scaring away potential licensees could outweigh these concrete benefits if the licensing scheme becomes too ambitious or complex.[28]

Balancing Subtlety and Signaling

Consumers who care about gay rights—and here, again, we can include many heterosexual people—can learn about the mark and its meaning through a variety of sources. Gay rights organizations could launch a campaign to promote the mark and inform their members and contributors about it. These organizations could take out advertising space in publications likely to reach a broad group of progressive readers—gay and straight—and use the ads to introduce readers to the mark and its meaning.

It would be foolhardy, however, to ignore the risks inherent in a mark that represents fairness on the basis of sexual orientation. The very hostility toward gay, lesbian, and bisexual people that makes the mark a good idea could also work against it. Enemies can read product labels as well as allies can, and some companies may refuse to use the mark out of fear of boycotts.

The kosher symbol provides one possible response to this point. The Orthodox Union emblem appears on a broad array of products (those associated with traditional Jewish dishes as well as more mainstream products), but it is so innocuous that many anti-Semites miss the signal, even though they might wish to punish companies that affirmatively market products to Jewish consumers. The Fair Employment Mark proposed here would be similarly opaque. For consumers "in the know," the mark could create incentives to buy particular products. But there is nothing about the appearance of the mark to tie it to gay rights or gay people generally. Other, more explicitly "gay" symbols—a pink triangle, a rainbow flag, or the Greek letter lambda—would certainly be more transparent. Even consumers who'd never heard of the mark would know that the company using the symbol is positioning itself in sympathy with the gay community. But this more explicit positioning would also run the risk of alienating consumers who are hostile to gay rights (who will react to an explicitly "gay" symbol but not to a neutral one).

A second response to fears about backlash would involve a thorough and critical assessment of boycotts and the loss they could cause. In very concentrated industries, where a few companies have captured the market, each company has a lot to lose if it alienates a significant portion of the market. In such markets, a boycott could cause real economic loss if antigay consumers far outnumber progay consumers. In such circumstances, it will always be in at least one company's self-interest to reject the mark—being known as the one company that is not "gay friendly" could help that company capture the antigay consumers' business (just as the Fair Employment Mark would help companies capture the business of progay consumers).

Most industries in the United States are sufficiently deconcentrated that boycotts would not pose a significant danger. Indeed, in deconcentrated markets the potential upside in business gained through use of the mark could far outweigh the downside risk of business lost to boycott. To see how this works, let's imagine a stylized market consisting of ten hammer makers. Suppose that hammers are so uniform that consumers are completely indifferent about the source of hammers they buy; consumers purchase randomly, so each manufacturer gets 10 percent of the market. Suppose further that if we were to poll consumers, we would find that 5 percent support equal employment for gay men and lesbians so strongly that they will go out of their way to buy hammers from the company that treats gay employees fairly.[29] But imagine that four times as many consumers—20 percent—actively dislike or disapprove of gays (enough that they'll avoid purchasing from companies that treat gay employees fairly). The remaining 75 percent of the consumers don't care one way or the other.

Now consider what happens to the first company adopting the Fair Employment Mark. Even if that company loses all of its business from the antigay consumers, that difference is more than made up by the progay consumers who are induced to buy hammers bearing the mark. The first mover increases from a market share of 10 percent (before using the mark) to a 12.5 percent market share after adopting the Fair Employment Mark. This increase results despite the fact that the company loses its share of the anti-gay customers' business (one-tenth of 20 percent = 2 percent). The company is still getting its random tenth of the consumers who don't care (one-tenth of 75 percent = 7.5 percent), plus *all* of the consumers who support gay rights (5 percent).

Indeed, in this example, a second firm will have an incentive to use the mark as well. The two "marked" firms will now split the progay consumers, so each gets 10 percent of the market (7.5 percent [one-tenth of consumers who don't care] plus 2.5 percent [half the progay consumers]).[30] This example suggests that the Fair Employment Mark could create some very strong first-mover advantages, if only to capture the loyalty of gay-supportive consumers, who might remain brand loyal even after other brands start sporting the signal. The first mover also has a better chance of selling the product to antigay consumers before they catch on to the meaning of the mark. But there is also a very strong incentive for another company to become the "second mover."

If we more realistically assume that distribution of premark market share is not random, we can see that small producers might have stronger incentives to adopt the mark. Assume a ten-company industry in which five companies had 15 percent market shares and five companies had 5 percent market shares. If one of the smaller-share companies were to adopt the mark, it could stand to move from a 5 percent share to a 7.75 percent share (all of the progay consumers [5 percent] plus one-twentieth of the neutral consumers [3.75 percent] minus one-twentieth of the antigay consumers [1 percent]). This is a sizable jump, one that would raise the company's sales by more than 50 percent.

Just as small states have the strongest economic incentives to respond to a vacation pledge, small business will have the strongest incentives to send a gay-friendly signal. In both contexts, the unconcentrated structure of our federal political system and of our economic markets makes the buycott "carrot" much bigger than the boycott "stick." Buycotts are powerful at starting the ball rolling—they create incentives for first movers—but these examples also show that the economic incentives quickly dissipate for subsequent movers. The buycotts need to be viewed as first steps that demonstrate the possibility of nondiscrimination both in government and in markets.

Conclusion

The preceding example shows that the potential benefits of using the Fair Employment Mark could outweigh the potential costs, at least for a few companies. With more specific information about consumer attitudes toward homosexuality in various markets, companies could better predict the mark's likely effect on sales.

M. V. Lee Badgett has examined the three distinct roles that gay, lesbian and bisexual people can play in an economic system: consumers, investors, and producers.[31] Many companies have recognized the LGBT community as an important group of consumers, and have developed advertising to target this market. The concerns of gay people and their allies as investors are reflected in rating systems that grade companies for their gay friendliness.[32] As producers, LGBT people get some recognition in nondiscrimination policies, statutes, and local ordinances, fair employee benefit programs, and other incentives offered by companies that wish to recruit talented people, regardless of sexual orientation. Tools like the HRC Equality Index can help potential employees to identify the companies that respect LGBT people as producers. The Fair Employment Mark complements these existing strategies, as it conveys information about companies' employment practices to a wider audience in a decentralized way. In a sense, the mark completes the circle by allowing gay and nongay consumers to tie their purchasing decisions to the fair treatment of LGBT employees.

A key characteristic of the mark is that it could facilitate heterosexual support for gay rights in ways that need not be public. This could create opportunities to work for gay rights for a new group of "stealth" supporters—people who, for any number of reasons, are not able or willing to act publicly but who wish at the very least to spend their money responsibly. As heterosexual consumers begin to feel aligned with the cause through their purchasing decisions, other, more public forms of support might start to feel comfortable as well. Perhaps most importantly, from simple, everyday consumer choices, an internal sense of connection to, and identification with, LGBT people could grow. As emphasized in chapter 9, remaining open to these internal changes could be a key component of gay rights advocacy for many heterosexual supporters.

Part II

Disabling Privilege

In part I we explored strategies that would permit allies to exercise privilege—to identify themselves as heterosexuals, in some cases, and to exploit the voice, access, and purchasing power they possess to promote equality for gay, lesbian, and bisexual people.

The next two chapters take a very different approach to privilege, discussing strategies that render sexual orientation less powerful by obscuring it. We introduce the concept of ambiguation in chapter 5, showing how it can been used to change the meaning of words and social categories. Through ambiguation, allies can sometimes support gay rights by leaving their own sexual orientation unclear. This lack of clarity disables privilege because it makes rewarding heterosexuality or punishing homosexuality more difficult.

In chapter 6, we apply the ambiguation principle to the integration of sexual minorities in the U.S. military. We propose inclusive commands, which would permit openly gay and willing nongay people to serve together. The inclusive command is an application of ambiguation because nongay recruits who join the units would forgo the opportunity to join units that exclude openly gay people. By joining an integrated unit, nongay service members would express their willingness to be associated with, even mistaken for, gay people.

Ambiguation

When you say, "I am a heterosexual person who supports gay rights," you offer a kind of support that is important to the gay rights movement. We explored in part I just how straight allies can use their position as heterosexuals to advance gay rights. But this chapter considers the possibility that the first phrase in this sentence, "I am heterosexual," should not be uttered, at least in some contexts.[1] When someone says, "I support gay rights," the audience may assume the speaker to be gay. This raises the question: When is it legitimate or even necessary to "correct" this assumption? When should allies make listeners wonder if they are gay?[2]

When someone speaks about race, gender, age, or disability, observers can usually tell whether the person is part of the group in question—that is, if the speaker speaks not only about the group but also for him- or herself.[3] A white woman talking about racial justice needn't qualify her remarks by revealing her race or gender; each member of the audience will have a set of assumptions about the speaker's sex or race, and some might be inclined to give greater or lesser weight to the speaker's views based upon these characteristics.

Sexual orientation is different. People's behavior can send signals about sexual orientation, but it's not marked on the body, as race and gender are. When someone speaks about sexual orientation, words rather than appearance will reveal his or her status, if it is to be revealed at all. As we choose these words and actions, we can adopt strategies that might not be possible in other civil rights contexts.

In 1995, Lawrence Lessig published an article, "The Regulation of Social

Meaning," in which he discussed some of the rhetorical devices that can change a society's shared understanding of the meaning conveyed by a given word or action. One of these is *ambiguation*, which gives "a particular act, the meaning of which is to be regulated, a second meaning as well, one that acts to undermine the negative effects of the first."[4] Ambiguation has long been deployed by gay, lesbian, and bisexual people when they permit the default presumption of heterosexuality to stand—their "true" sexual orientation is obscured as a way of controlling the meaning others might assign to it—or, perhaps more accurately, the meaning and value others might assign to *them* if their sexual orientation were known.

But the blurring operates in two directions. By permitting (or, more accurately, requiring) gay, lesbian, and bisexual people to pass as heterosexual, the closet also "ambiguates" what it means to be heterosexual. The meaning of heterosexuality, in a society in which the closet operates, is flavored with the possibility of closeted homosexuality. It's possible that anyone you meet could be gay. Nowhere is this more apparent than in the military, where the "don't ask, don't tell" policy preserves the appearance of a heterosexual fighting force even as everyone knows that gay, lesbian, and bisexual people are serving.[5] The closet ambiguates the category we call "heterosexual people" even as it preserves stereotypes of homosexuality.

Coming out, in contrast, can ambiguate the meaning of homosexuality. Granted, coming out now ties the individual to homosexuality in ways that might (in the minds of the audience) be "clarifying"; it allows people to apply their own meanings of *homosexuality* to an individual who has come out. But coming out can be ambiguating, too, because the people who come out are bound to defy the preconceptions of their audience—by being individuals, not categories. When you commensurate knowing someone as a "friend," "sister," "competent, responsible coworker," or "reliable neighbor" with also knowing that she is lesbian, you are almost inevitably forced to loosen any preexisting meanings on what it means "to be gay." The process of coming out can thus ambiguate—in the core sense of producing multiple and more varied meanings.

If gay people's "coming out" is ambiguating, so too might be heterosexual people's "going in." In this chapter, we explore how allies can use ambiguation. This "going in" for heterosexual people could include a variety of moves: permitting confusion about whether or not they are gay; forgoing opportunities to identify opposite-sex partners as spouses; making affirmative statements that align them with gay, lesbian, and bisexual people, and *not* qualifying those statements with disclosure of their own heterosexuality.

To see how this might work, consider the case of Denmark, King Christian, and the Star of David.[6] Legend has it[7] that when the Nazis invaded Denmark and demanded that Danish Jews wear the yellow Star of David on their clothing, King Christian X (loved and honored by his subjects) decided to protect Jews by hiding them. Instead of secreting them away in cellars, attics, and barns—as was done by many courageous gentiles throughout Europe—King Christian decided to "hide" Danish Jews by making them indistinguishable from other Danes. He set the example by wearing a Star of David on his own clothing. His subjects soon began to follow suit. The legend is that soon all Danes were wearing the star, confounding Nazi attempts to set the Jews apart from their countrymen.[8] As Lawrence Lessig explains,

> The Nazis required Jews to wear yellow stars. Wearing a star had then a particular meaning, in part constructed by disambiguating who were Jews and who were not, thereby facilitating the expression of racial hatred. Danes who opposed the racism of the Nazis then began to wear stars themselves. Their action then ambiguated the meaning of wearing a star. Now wearing a star meant either that the person was a Jew or that the person was a Dane supporting the Jews. Their action also tied the Danes to the Jews: now Danes were seen as supportive of the Jews.[9]

Can we find contemporary analogs to the Star of David, symbols of homosexuality that could be appropriated by nongay people in liberating directions?

Consider another example: Sikhs after the terrorist attacks of September 11. In the wake of the attacks, many people in the United States began to feel and express anti-Muslim sentiment. Attacks on people who were perceived to be Muslim (women in veils, men in turbans) occurred in various places. Sikhs, who wear turbans but are not Muslim, were often perceived as Muslim, though their culture and religion are distinct. An intense debate arose among Sikhs about "how to go about distinguishing themselves from Muslims while not implying that attacks on Muslims are justified."[10] Some argued that any effort to disambiguate Sikhs and Muslims would be morally wrong.

> "It would be antithetical to our faith to have materials saying, 'We are not Muslims,'" said Inderpreet Singh, a Sikh in Boston. "It's understandable that people now are worried about being mistaken for Muslims, but we have to be very careful not to do that."[11]

A cover illustration on the *New Yorker* magazine depicts disambiguation with a sort of bleak humor in the weeks immediately following September 11. A Sikh cabdriver cowers in his taxi with a frightened but hopeful look on his face; from the roof of his cab he is flying at least ten U.S. flags, and along the side of the cab he has attached a sign reading "God Bless America."

But ambiguation can be uncomfortable. Heterosexuals who are mistaken for gay—but who don't want to be—want to remedy the situation. Consider the case of the University of Hawaii football team, which has used the name Rainbow Warriors for several years, because the school is located in the Manoa Valley and enjoys rainbows on an almost daily basis. The university's athletic logo incorporated a rainbow to capture this unique feature of the school's physical environment. But in 2000, the University of Hawaii decided to disassociate itself from the rainbow symbol. The school renamed the team "the Warriors" and removed the rainbow from its logo.

Some gay activists complained that the school's decision sent "a very bad message." Other observers were less troubled. In their view, the rainbow has been appropriated by the gay community as a symbol of pride. To use it for other purposes, they argued, diluted gay expression—a good use in their view. Perhaps saving the symbol for the exclusive use of gay activism is a good way to preserve the power of gay politics. Still, it is unfortunate that the university's decision was motivated not by a desire to honor gay expression, but by an effort to separate itself from gay-identified symbols. Retaining the use of the rainbow—even as the rainbow became increasingly known as a symbol of gay pride—would have sent a powerful message to the broader world, not only about the university's exquisite geography but also about its atmosphere of tolerance and diversity.[12]

The case of the rainbow bumper stickers in Traverse City, Michigan, demonstrates the potential power of ambiguation and the lengths to which people will go to resist it. To counter a growing trend of intolerance in this city of fifteen thousand, culminating in acts of vandalism and violence against African-American, Jewish, and gay citizens, city leaders wanted to send a message that Traverse City should be an open city embracing diversity. They designed a bumper sticker to be placed on city vehicles and distributed to the public. The sticker featured human figures of various colors resembling interlocking puzzle pieces against a rainbow background. Above these figures were emblazoned the words: "We Are Traverse City." Although the color scheme was slightly different from the gay pride flag,[13] the resemblance was close enough to alarm some social conservatives. They accused Traverse City of promoting homosexuality and supporting "the homosexual agenda." Gary Glenn, president of the American Family Association of Michigan, located in Midland, made his concerns known on Christian radio stations across the country, energizing conservative activists throughout the United States to complain to Traverse City leaders about the sticker.

City leaders, now on the defensive, disclaimed any intention to tie the city with symbols of gay pride. One city commissioner, perhaps disingenuously, disclaimed any intention to invoke gay symbols. "I'm a child of the '60's," she said. "There were damn rainbows everywhere. It wasn't a gay thing. It was love, peace, happiness, inclusive, an Age of Aquarius thing."[14] Others argued that the rainbow symbolized empowerment of all minorities, including gay people and people of color. Mayor Larry Hardy backpedaled most violently, claiming that he had "no idea it had anything to do with the gay community."[15] Indeed, he said, "I personally think I was kind of conned. . . . I was stupid not to know what the symbol stood for."[16]

The substantive outcome of the controversy is not what makes it most interesting. It is unfortunate that the city appeared to capitulate to the voices of conservative activists, but there may have been legitimate concerns about using the sticker on public vehicles. Perhaps the city attorney was correct that the bumper sticker was not neutral, and when affixed to city vehicles, it created a public forum broadcasting only one view. Perhaps he was right to worry that the bumper sticker would set a dangerous precedent, permitting groups with contrary views to claim space on city vehicles as well.[17]

But the outcome is not as interesting as the violent disclaimer of identification with gay people and gay rights. City officials might have withdrawn the stickers citing constitutional concerns while nonetheless embracing the gay community. They might have said something like, "We are distressed that this show of support for our LGBT citizens is so alarming to some people. We do not want to create a public forum on our vehicles or give those who espouse antigay viewpoints a claim to public space for the airing of their views, so we will remove the stickers. Nonetheless, we stand behind the message these stickers convey and we encourage private citizens to display the stickers on their own property." Instead, the city officials claimed not to recognize the meaning of one of the central symbols of gay rights advocacy, further distancing themselves from the gay rights movement and the LGBT citizens of the city.

Gay rights groups have taken advantage of opportunities to use ambiguation. On National Coming Out Day, many people wear buttons or stickers expressing gay-affirmative messages. These messages range from declarations of one's own orientation ("Out" or "This is what a bisexual looks like"), to assertions of positions on public policy ("Gay rights are civil rights"), to the nonverbal, and more ambiguous, pink triangle in a black circle. When, even for a day, people identifying with a broad range of sexual orientations all wear the pink triangle, they literally replicate the Danes' legendary appropriation of the Star of David.[18] For that one day, at least, sexual orientation is ambiguated, because it is not clear: does a person wear a triangle to come out (on that day of all days of coming out) or to express support for and solidarity with LGBT people as *they* come out? And does it matter *why* we wear the triangle that day?

Similarly, some LGBT student groups on college campuses and gay-straight alliances in high schools have sponsored "wear blue jeans if you're gay" days. Because denim jeans are practically a uniform for most Americans between the ages of twelve and twenty-four, many people would wear jeans on such a day as a matter of course. The declaration that people should wear jeans if they are gay, however, changes the default understanding of what it means to be wearing jeans. On these days, people who want to avoid potential identification with homosexuality must go out of their way to do so. And those who fail to take such measures are, perhaps involuntarily, ambiguated. They might be wearing jeans to come out; they might be wearing jeans because that's what everyone wears in the ordinary course of things.

Muddying the signals creates interesting opportunities for heterosexual people to show their alliance with and support for gay people. Traverse City's bumper stickers provide another example. To prevent the stickers from going to waste, the group Hate-Free TC acquired and distributed five thousand to private citizens who support diversity in Traverse City.[19] One could see the display of the bumper stickers as another instance of voluntary ambiguation. By displaying the bumper stickers, heterosexual people not only express their support for diversity in their city, but also display a symbol that they know at least some people take to be a gay pride symbol.

Allies, we argue, can deliberately use the power of ambiguation. We know a woman in Madison, Wisconsin, we'll call Sarah, whose home was vandalized. The vandals broke a window and burned the gay pride rainbow flag Sarah had flown from her front porch. When Sarah talked with her neighbors about the attack on her home, one of her neighbors, who is heterosexual, suggested that all of the houses on the street should put up rainbow flags to show solidarity with and support for Sarah, who is a lesbian. A secondary benefit perhaps received less attention. If every house on the street flew the gay pride flag, they could create an ambiguating effect. The flags would say to the vandals, in effect: "Do you want to persecute gay people? Well, you'll have to come after all of us, too. But how will you be sure that it's a gay or lesbian person you are harming?" Of course, harming a gay rights supporter might be as satisfying to this criminal as harming a person who is actually gay or lesbian. But like the non-Jewish Danes who wore the Star of David, a street full of gay pride flags ambiguates in ways that could help Sarah, physically and emotionally.

Our next example emerges from pop culture, but it so vividly illustrates an instance of liberating ambiguation that it deserves mention here. A scene in the film *In and Out* shows the graduation ceremony at a high school in a small town in Indiana. Howard Brackett, played by Kevin Klein, is an English teacher and track coach who has recently discovered his own homosexuality. After Howard openly acknowledged that he is gay, the principal of the school fired him. When a former student of Howard's interrupts the ceremony to demand an explanation for Howard's firing, the principal nervously explains that it is a "matter of influence." The principal acknowledges that he fired Howard to prevent him from persuading his students to become gay or lesbian. The former student turns to the graduating seniors and demands, "You've all had Mr. Brackett; is that the way it works?" One could read the question as an inquiry into the students' sexual orientation. If Brackett has, indeed, been exerting his "influence" on students, many or all of them should, in theory, be gay. To reaffirm their heterosexuality will be to prove that Brackett either has not been exerting influence or that his efforts have been futile. The seniors remain silent for several moments, and it appears that the graduation will get back on track.

Suddenly, a student named Jack stands and says, "'Scuse me . . . I'm gay!" He explains all the ways in which Mr. Brackett worked with him in English class and on the track team, crediting the teaching with helping him get into college, and concludes: "It must have rubbed off. I'm gay."

Before the audience has a chance to absorb this information, the young woman sitting next to Jack stands and shouts, "Oh my God! I had Mr. Brackett all year and I'm gay!" And then, in a determined tone: "If there's something wrong with Mr. Brackett or with Jack, then there's something wrong with me." The young woman on the other side of Jack stands and declares that she is gay. The two young women then turn expectantly to an aggressively heterosexual young man in their crowd. He reluctantly succumbs to the pressure and states: "All right! I'm gay! I'm a homo! I like guys! I mean, I still do it with chicks every chance I get and I'm totally good at it . . . but I hate it and I'm gay!"

Additional students stand to declare their own homosexuality; the principal falls back to a second argument about the community's values, and how they won't stand for the continued employment of an openly gay teacher in the school. A man in the audience stands to declare, "I'm a member of the community and I don't mind that Howard's gay." The principal dismisses this speaker by pointing out that he is Howard's brother. The man then says, "You know what that means . . . I must be gay!" A second man stands to say, "I'm a parent. I've lived in this town all my life. I'm Howard's father . . . and I'm gay!" Howard's mother then declares, "I'm Howard's mother and I'm very proud of him . . . and I'm a lesbian!"

A fashionable woman near the rear of the auditorium, who runs the bridal shop in town, declares, "I'm gay!" The town barber (who insists on being called a "hair stylist") says, "I'm gay!" (He adds, removing his toupee, "And I'm bald!"). The elderly mail carrier in town says, "I'm a federal employee . . . and I'm gay!" The entire fire department of the town, filling a row of the auditorium, simultaneously stands to shout, as one, "Gay!"

By the time the scene concludes, all of the people in the auditorium have declared that they are gay or lesbian. The group seems to say: "We are *all* gay. We are *all* lesbian. We are *all* queer." And then they silently demand of the principal: "What are you going to do about it?"[20]

Several things about this scene interest us. First, the former student who comes to defend Howard challenges the graduating seniors to respond to the principal's fears about influence. The most obvious way to do this is to deny that they are gay (the influence, if it exists, has been unsuccessful in converting them to homosexuality). Jack disrupts this by apparently using the occasion to come out. The young woman next to him—who is apparently heterosexual—further disrupts the planned defense by aligning herself with Howard and her friend Jack: "If there's something wrong with Mr. Brackett or with Jack, then there's something wrong with me!" The planned defense would have required some gay, lesbian, or bisexual students to closet themselves, denying their own sexuality to follow the party line that a gay teacher does not "influence" his students. Instead, by the end of the scene, many heterosexual people have embraced and affirmed homosexuality as a way of supporting Howard Brackett.

A second aspect of this scene that interests us is the extent to which any one speaker ambiguates his or her own sexual orientation. Jack, for example, may be coming out when he says, "I'm gay." His friend, on the other hand, seems to be declaring her homosexuality as way more clearly to stand in solidarity with Jack and Howard. Is she understood by her audience actually to be coming out? Do they understand the statement, uttered with mock alarm, "Oh my God! I'm gay!" to be merely a rhetorical device and not a statement of fact? Or is there some mixture of messages here—the very essence of ambiguation—bringing to the surface the underlying truth that any individual standing in that room really could be gay, lesbian, or bisexual? The words themselves ("I am gay!") must create some sense of vulnerability, because even as he says them, Jack's aggressively heterosexual male friend feels compelled to make clear he still desires women. Surely for some percentage of the people in the room, the declaration of homosexuality serves not only to support Howard Brackett but also to describe their own sexual orientation. The statement is ambiguating because for any one individual it may or may not be "true." By the time the scene concludes, all of the members of the audience have said that they are gay, which leaves us where we started: someone is closeted. But because the default is that we are all gay, it is the heterosexuals who are closeted, not the gay people.

Or are they? If everyone understands the statement "I am gay" to be supportive of Howard rather than an accurate description of the speaker's sexual orientation, then the default has not really changed. The people in the room are understood to be a group of heterosexuals who, for the sake of politics, are saying they are gay. Lost in a sea of pseudogays, the people who truly identify as gay, lesbian, and bisexual may feel the need to come out again, or in a new way.

If the statement "I am gay" is understood simply as a statement of support for Howard, this raises the question: why not just say, "I support Howard"? What is added by the appropriation or acceptance of gay identity in the statement of support?

To demonstrate just how confusing things can become, consider Michael, a real person whose sexuality became the stuff of conversations, all because of one simple action he took. In 1996, the Association of American Law Schools began to publish in its annual directory a list of law professors who self-identified as "Gay, Lesbian and Bisexual Community Law Teachers." [21] Michael, then a junior professor at a Midwestern law school, appeared on the list a few years later. Some who knew him expressed surprise; they assumed he was heterosexual. There ensued some conversation about Michael's appearance on the list. Some people, taking the list at face value, slipped into idle gossip: "I thought he had a girlfriend." Others speculated about the *meaning* of his appearance on the list: "Maybe Michael isn't gay or bisexual, but has placed himself on the list in an act of solidarity." Still others wondered whether Michael had joined the list in an effort to subvert sexual orientation categories, distinctions he might view as artificial or oppressive. Most of these conversations were silly. Some of the conversations about Michael's appearance on the list were substantive and constructive, however, because they caused people to focus on the purpose of the list, the basis for appearing on it, and the criteria for legitimate membership in the group it purported to represent.

We may never know Michael's motivations for joining this list.[22] If Michael is indeed gay or bisexual, the story may be much simpler than all the gossip and analysis would suggest. Suppose for a moment, though, that Michael identifies, for the most part, as heterosexual. Suppose that he joined the list not to declare anything new about his own sexual orientation but rather to change the social meaning of the AALS list of "Gay, Lesbian and Bisexual Community Law Teachers." Suppose he joined the list as an act of solidarity, that is, to declare himself a member of the *community* that includes (but is not limited to) gay, lesbian, and bisexual law professors. Such a move would not only ambiguate the list, it would be a voluntarily self-ambiguating move. Later we'll discuss the pros and cons of Michael's action, assuming these suppositions are true. For now, let us mark this as a real-world attempt at the sort of ambiguation suggested in the movie *In and Out.*

Another example of voluntary ambiguation comes from the realm of law. In her review of Richard Posner's book *Sex and Reason*, law professor Robin West critiqued some of Posner's underlying premises about the nature of sex. West addressed "the central metaphor [Posner] uses to describe both our quest for sexual pleasure and the moral attitude we should bring to it: that sex is like 'eating ice cream.'"[23] She particularly objected to his assertion that one's sexual desires are knowable in the same way that preferences for a particular sort of ice cream are knowable. To explain her objection, she invoked the well-known research conducted by Alfred Kinsey, which introduced a scale (often referred to as the Kinsey Scale) purporting to characterize a person's sexual attraction or identity. At either end of the scale are those who are "exclusively" heterosexual (0) or homosexual (6). In the 1–5 range lie those with varying proportions of sexual attraction to members of their own sex versus the opposite sex.[24] To demonstrate that Posner's assertions about the nature of sexual orientation were off base,

West explained that she would have no idea where she herself would fall on the Kinsey scale:

> To put this point autobiographically, I know with utter confidence what flavors of ice cream I prefer, but I am no clearer now than I was twenty years ago in what direction my sexual orientation lies, or what my "preference" is, or even whether or not I "have" one. I have no idea whether I'm a "Kinsey one" or a "Kinsey three" or a "Kinsey six."[25]

West's statement about her placement on the Kinsey scale—her disavowal of any knowledge about that placement—had the effect of ambiguating her own sexual orientation in a very public way. She disclaimed clear identity as heterosexual, lesbian, or bisexual.[26]

Moving outside the law, think about Richard Gere and his refusal to clarify his sexual orientation. Many celebrities are the subject of rumor and speculation, especially when it comes to matters of sexuality. Gere is a Hollywood actor whose sexual orientation is often discussed in the media. Writer Michael Gross explains, "Straight men like the indestructible rumor that Gere is gay, because it reduces his threat. He is in fact aggressively heterosexual, but that hasn't stopped men from hoping."[27] In response, Gere usually refuses even to acknowledge or discuss the rumor that he is gay, "except to say that denying it would denigrate homosexuals."[28] By refusing to deny rumors of his homosexuality, Gere declines the invitation to place himself outside of a group of people he wants to validate and uphold. He implicitly permits the public to assume that he is gay, since his position is that being gay would be a good, legitimate identity for him to have.[29] Here again, an apparently heterosexual person voluntarily creates ambiguity about his own sexual orientation, in part to reinforce the goodness of, and to align himself with, gay identity.[30]

The Pros and Cons of Ambiguation— and Some Questions That Might Prevent Misuse

Even as we propose ambiguation as a way of creating new space for the expression of heterosexual support for gay rights, we recognize risks inherent in this strategy. It is important to be sensitive to the fact that ambiguation will not be appropriate always and everywhere. At times, it might run counter to the goals of LGBT groups and individuals.

Am I Trivializing Sexual Orientation?

Ambiguation can be viewed negatively if it appears to be "playing" with homosexuality in trivializing ways. Consider the resentment Roseanne Barr engendered when she toyed with techniques of ambiguation. Barr, an actress and comedian who identifies as heterosexual, was reported to have hinted at her own lesbianism, but only in a temporary way, and with such a wink and a nudge that the liberating purpose of her words may have been undermined. Here's what she said, as reported by *Girlfriends*, a magazine targeted to lesbians and bisexual women.

> In a recent sound bite for the *New York Post*'s Page Six, comic genius Roseanne Barr teased, "What would you think if I came out as a lesbian?" Having gotten the interviewer's attention, the TV diva admitted she wasn't about to, "but wouldn't it be cool to say so, even just for a week?"[31]

The reporter for *Girlfriends* didn't think so. She wrote, "Sometimes our favorite straight celebs confuse perception with reality. Like when it comes to lesbian chic. . . . As if talking about talking the talk were anything like walking the walk."

Why did Barr's statement, no doubt intended as gay-affirmative, fail as ambiguation? First, Barr exerted energy to clarify even as she ambiguated her sexuality. By making clear that she "wasn't about to," she created no ambiguity at all about her own understanding of her sexual orientation. Indeed, she may have exploited the stigmatized status of lesbians by using the tantalizing hint of coming out merely to "get the interviewer's attention," thus perpetuating the marginalization of lesbians. Further, by suggesting that she could achieve her goals by coming out as a lesbian "even just for a week," she trivialized the process of coming out for the millions of women who do so as a lifetime commitment. In all these ways, she treated the notion of an apparently heterosexual woman coming out as a lesbian as a sort of temporary frolic.

Do I Predict That My Audience Will Think Less of Me
If They Perceive Me to Be Gay, Lesbian, or Bisexual?

Ambiguating may be most constructive if the audience is likely to hold a negative view of homosexuality.[32] When heterosexual allies allow such an audience to place them in a disfavored category, they not only gain an opportunity to challenge some of the assumptions leading to that disfavor, they also gain a chance to empathize a bit with gay, lesbian, and bisexual people. Douglas Morrison, a manager in Levi Strauss's human resources department, attended a 2002 Workplace Summit sponsored by Out and Equal Workplace Advocates, an organization devoted to LGBT employment issues. Douglas, who describes himself as a "straight white Christian male," visited Walt Disney World's Pleasure Island one evening with a group from the conference. He noticed "stares, glares, gawking" and "turning away" from strangers he encountered that evening, and then noticed that he and other members of the group were still wearing their Out and Equal conference ID badges. Though he found the negative judgments "frustrating and demoralizing," he was more impressed by the "sickening realization that many LGBT people deal with this day in and day out." "Talk about walking a mile in someone else's shoes," he wrote; "[t]his profound epiphany will not be forgotten."[33] Even if Douglas's (perhaps inadvertent) ambiguation failed to teach his judgmental audience much, he apparently learned a great deal. These lessons would have been less clear to him if he'd encountered a friendlier audience.

Michael, the Midwestern law professor who appeared on the AALS list of gay lesbian and bisexual community law professors, was subject to criticism on the assumption that he is a heterosexually identified man who joined the list in order to ambiguate its meaning. Why did this attempt at ambiguation fail to convey the gay-affirmative message Michael may have intended to send?

Actually, it is not clear that Michael's act of ambiguation *did* fail its intended purpose. At the very least, he caused people to talk about the meaning of that list of professors, the purposes of creating it, and the aspects of identity that qualified people to join it. Suppose that Michael's action engendered some resentment or mistrust; perhaps this proves only that his action was truly brave, because it subjected him to criticism even from the people with whom he sought to stand in solidarity. He did not join the list in a pandering way.

In the case of the AALS list, however, context makes a tremendous difference. Here is a description of the AALS list that many of its members would probably adopt: it is a list that gay, lesbian, and bisexual professors can join if they wish to be "out" to a wider community within the AALS and even beyond. The list is purely voluntary, at the option of the individual professor. It is a tool for networking within the community of gay, lesbian, and bisexual professors, to assist them in finding fellow travelers with similar experiences. It can be a recruiting tool, useful for schools interested in enhancing the diversity of their faculties by hiring professors who are openly gay, lesbian, or bisexual.

Nowhere in this description, you'll note, did we say anything about the list serving as a tool for the exclusion or stigmatizing of gay, lesbian, and bisexual law professors. This use of the list is precluded by the AALS's own policy of nondiscrimination on the basis of sexual orientation, which is strongly held and strongly enforced.[34]

Here's a quick principle for ambiguation: will the suggestion that I might be gay bring me up or down in the view of my audience, or will it have no effect? We suggest that heterosexual people should ambiguate only when ambiguating will lower the audience's estimation of them. If the audience for the ambiguating act is gay-friendly or gay-neutral enough that it would make no difference to them, then ambiguation may be misappropriation of gay identity.

The AALS list is not a Star of David. It carries no negative connotations—for the AALS that created it or for the now hundreds of people who appear on the list. Standing in solidarity with an oppressed group of people who are under attack is one thing; joining the group when it is being affirmed is another thing entirely. The AALS list was not created as a way to stigmatize, so joining the list was not likely to bring Michael into a disfavored status. Indeed, the list was created for positive, gay-affirmative purposes that may be subverted if the meaning of the list is ambiguated.

Should Sexual Orientation Be Irrelevant to the Discussion or Transaction at Issue?

Ambiguation does carry larger social risks if its pushed too far. If too many nongay people engage in it, the process can "recloset" gay, lesbian, and bisexual people. It may be difficult for gay people to come out if nongay people steal their signals. In a sea of people all claiming to be gay or bisexual, those who have truly lived the experience may be hidden. In some cases, this is good—where it disrupts discrimination against gay men, lesbians, and bisexuals. But in other contexts, if coming out becomes more difficult for gay people, it is also more difficult for them to accomplish the ambiguation Lawrence Lessig describes, where the meaning of homosexuality in mainstream culture undergoes change as diverse people acknowledge their own homosexuality.

To address this risk of recloseting, heterosexual people might ask themselves, "Do I think that sexual orientation should be irrelevant to the conversation or transaction that would provide the context for my ambiguating speech or act?" Ambiguation creates noise or distortion in the signal of sexual orientation. If signals about sexual orientation are being used in a way that disempowers or oppresses gay, lesbian, or bisexual people, then interfering with those signals might be the moral thing to do. If, on the other hand, people's "true" sexual orientation—that is, sexual orientation as lived and experienced—is appropriately part of the conversation or transaction, then "noise" created by ambiguation will disrupt a constructive, desirable process.

We've already seen an example of each situation. When Sarah's house in Madison, Wisconsin, was vandalized and her gay pride flag burned, safety and security in that neighborhood appeared to be conditioned on sexual orientation, something that ought to be irrelevant in determining how safe people are. If every home on Sarah's street had flown the gay pride flag, her heterosexual neighbors would have obscured the sexual orientation of any individual homeowner on that street. This might have helped to take sexual orientation out of the calculus of whose home would be safe, rendering sexual orientation irrelevant. In the case of the AALS, on the other hand, the list of gay, lesbian, and bisexual community law professors may have been intended for purposes that appropriately turn on sexual orientation. To facilitate networking among and recruitment of gay professors, a list of openly gay, lesbian, and bisexual professors makes sexual orientation relevant in ways that are liberating and gay-affirming. To the extent Michael's appearance on the list inserts noise into the signal, it might actually run counter to the goals of the list.[35]

Once again, analogizing sexual orientation to race or ethnicity helps to illustrate the distinction we're drawing here. What is gained by preventing people from opting into racial identities that are not theirs? In many settings, the social consensus may be that race should be irrelevant to the discussion or transaction. But when an organization or institution has undertaken affirmative action to benefit an historically marginalized category of people, majority members may subvert the program if they ambiguate or opt into the marginalized category. A controversial example of this may be found in the willingness shown by some Hispanics of European ancestry to opt into programs designed to benefit Hispanics of Latin American ancestry.[36]

Answering the question about relevance might help heterosexual allies decide when it is important to be "out" about their heterosexuality. Professor Carbado has cautioned against the appropriation of gay identity by people who lack the lived experience of gay men and lesbians. He warns that heterosexual people weighing in on issues of gay rights can "create the (mis)impression of gay authenticity" if they are not clear about their own position in the debate.[37] If sexual orientation is relevant in ways that would empower gay, lesbian, and bisexual people—including giving their experiences and ideas greater credibility or weight in the discussion—ambiguation by heterosexual people should be avoided.

Can I Entertain Some Internal Ambiguity about My Own Sexual Orientation?

In some contexts, the interior motivation of a person who ambiguates can make a difference. Consider a rather reductive description of two "types" of ambiguating heterosexual people.

Type A has no internal doubt about his or her own heterosexuality. Certain of it, this person ambiguates with a wink and a nudge, in a playful way just to muddy the waters. This is Roseanne Barr.

Type B entertains some internal doubt about his or her own heterosexuality. This person "comes out" to himself or herself at least to the extent that he or she leaves open the possibility of love, attachment, or attraction to persons of the same sex. This person ambiguates internally as well as externally, and acknowledges his or her location in that vast, bisexual middle of the Kinsey scale. For such a person—even one who, for all external purposes, identifies as "straight"—the signal of the identity category is democratized ever so slightly. Some affiliation is more genuinely created between "gay" and "straight" within that expanded identity category. This internal ambiguation does less to rob gayness of its signaling quality, because the person claiming membership in the identity category has actually reworked his or her own self-conception and sense of sexuality. This seems to be what Robin West was doing in her statement of self-ambiguation. Thus, it appears that ambiguation may be more effective when it reflects an internal indeterminacy about sexual orientation.

Obviously, these are extremely difficult questions for many people to ask themselves. Most of us, straight and gay, have absorbed negative messages about homosexuality. Our own homophobia, much as we struggle against it, can prevent us from acknowledging any internal ambiguity about sexual orientation. If the process of ambiguating and the rationales for it help us to examine and perhaps resolve some of this homophobia, it is constructive.

One key point about ambiguation is that it should be authentic and true. In an area such as sexual orientation where so much harm has been done by the closet—all the deception and lies it requires—we should avoid remedies that also call for deception or statements that are not true, even if they have noble goals.

Would Lambda Approve?

Instead of asking the substantive questions (concerning trivialization, self-sacrifice, irrelevance, and truth), it may be appropriate to ask a procedural question: would the LGBT community support the attempt at ambiguation? Deferring to the preferences of others is itself a metastrategy that has difficulties and limitations (which we will explicitly take up in chapter 9). One must decide who is the appropriate representative of the community. But the larger point is that the decision whether or not to ambiguate is not one that needs to be made alone—as it were, in the closet. You can ask others.

Or you can at least ask yourself what you think others would want. In some ways, our substantive questions reflect concerns that community members have often raised. The LGBT community is less likely to support trivializing or self-aggrandizing attempts at ambiguation and more likely to support ambiguation that reflects genuine ambiguity or is deployed where sexual orientation or lived experience should not be relevant to the question at hand.

Ambiguation in Action

Finally, if it's OK, then how exactly would an ally go about ambiguating? The following list provides a few suggestions of the things one could do or say to create an ambiguating effect. Note that each of these suggestions falls short of actual misrepresentation. Each of these suggestions can raise questions about sexual orientation, however, and to the extent the speaker allows those questions to go unanswered, others might rethink their assumptions about when and why sexual orientation is relevant.

1. Heterosexuals who are married, instead of referring to *husbands* or *wives*, could talk about *spouses*, a gender-neutral term. Better yet, *partner* is the term more commonly used by committed same-sex couples. In addition, using the term *partner* renounces some of the heterosexual privilege inherent in marriage (in jurisdictions where same-sex couples do not have identical access to this status).

2. When describing their spouses, heterosexual parents could avoid references to their child's *mother* or *father*. The term *parent* leaves open and unspecified the gender of that parent.

3. Heterosexuals could fly gay pride flags from their homes, or put them in sticker form on their cars.

4. Heterosexuals could wear pink triangle buttons or other gay-affirmative symbols. These need not be explicit statements of sexual orientation. Simply wearing a T-shirt that says, "I support gay marriage" can send a powerful message in part because it is unclear whether the wearer is herself gay. Less verbal and therefore more ambiguous messages (such as the simple pride flag or pink triangle) also convey support for gay rights and leave open the wearer's own sexual orientation.

5. When discussing gay people and their perspectives, heterosexuals might experiment with phrasing that aligns them with gay and lesbian people without clearly identifying their own sexual orientation. For example, they might say something like, "Those of us who are gay might take umbrage at the claim that child rearing does not occur in families headed by same-sex couples." This sentence is ambiguous, because it is not clear whether the phrase *who are gay* modifies *those* (conveying "those who are gay among us") or *us* (conveying "we who are gay"). Particularly if the audience for this sentence contained people with antigay sentiments, a sentence that potentially aligns the speaker with gay people may be an equality-enhancing move. Similarly, in conversations that include gay men, lesbians, or bisexuals,[38] heterosexuals might introduce some remarks with phrases that include the words "we," "us," and "our." So, for example, they might say, "From our perspective, legal recognition for same-sex couples *is* a profamily policy change," or, "We believe that LGBT youth need more support and protection in high school from administrators, teachers, and peers."

6. When a person says something to suggest that he or she has misperceived the sexual orientation of a heterosexual supporter of gay rights, that supporter should think carefully before jumping to correct. If correcting the misperception will raise the person's estimation of the supporter, it might be better to remain in the disfavored category. If, on the other hand, homosexuality registers as a positive or neutral characteristic with the person, a heterosexual supporter might disclose her own sexual orientation, so as not to claim status or experience she lacks. Similarly, if sexual orientation is relevant to the discussion or transaction in which the misperception of orientation has occurred, so that permitting the misunderstand-

ing to persist would misappropriate gay identity or authenticity, then "coming out" as a heterosexual might be a good idea. For example, (from a woman), "Well, actually, I am married to a man" or "Actually, I am heterosexual."

The key element in all of these examples is a willingness to occupy a large, uncharted space in which sexual orientation is unassigned, where multiple realities or possibilities are entertained, and where heterosexual people reflect long and hard before they expend any energy to distinguish themselves from gay, lesbian, and bisexual people.

Maybe most radically, the chapter asks us to interrogate our own behavior. Why, for example, do most heterosexual men in the United States choose not to kiss a man in greeting when they routinely kiss women? At the level of the individual, some men probably are reluctant to violate any existing social norm (such as tie wearing). But for some men—even allies—part of the reason surely has to do with a reluctance to be thought of as gay. This chapter, then, calls for men to do something at once trivial and at the same time almost unimaginably difficult—to kiss all our friends.[39]

The next chapter will describe in some detail a strategy of ambiguation for integrating sexual minorities into the military that turns crucially on the willingness of some heterosexual people to be aligned with gay people, even at times to be misperceived as gay. Finding—or creating—critical masses of heterosexual people willing to take these "risks" could be one of the central challenges of gay rights advocacy in the twenty-first century.

The Inclusive Command
Voluntary Integration of the U.S. Military

> What we do and what we think is fascinatingly dependent, much of the
> time, on what we believe that other people do and think.
>
> *Cass Sunstein*

Many opponents of gays in the military will accept the proposition that gay
and lesbian soldiers, most of them closeted, have served their country
bravely and well.[1] General Colin Powell has referred to gay service members
as "proud, brave, loyal, good Americans"[2] who have "served well in the past
and are continuing to serve well."[3] General Norman Schwarzkopf agrees:
"homosexuals have served in the past and have done a great job."[4]

What these opponents find harder to accept is the proposition that heterosexual people can effectively serve their country if openly gay people are in the
military with them. The fear is that if openly gay and lesbian people are allowed to serve, they will make other soldiers uncomfortable, cause a breakdown in morale and discipline, and destroy the "unit cohesion" that is essential for effective soldiering. To show that these fears have perpetuated an
exclusion policy that is overbroad, this chapter proposes the creation of inclusive commands in the U.S. military. Gay and nongay soldiers would volunteer
for inclusive commands by indicating that they are willing to serve with gay
and lesbian soldiers. Soldiers who were not willing to serve with openly gay
people could assign themselves to alternative, exclusive commands. Placement
in an inclusive command would therefore be entirely voluntary.

This chapter also is an application of chapter 5's theory of ambiguation. The very act of saying that you are willing to serve with gay soldiers may make some people wonder whether you yourself are gay. This would challenge some heterosexual soldiers to "come out" as supporters of gay rights and in so doing raise questions about their own sexuality. The fact that soldiers are forced to answer the question "yea" or "nay" also marks a turn in the book toward more uncomfortable choices. Some soldiers might prefer not to have to answer this type of question. But when faced with the question, we will ultimately argue, many soldiers today will opt for the inclusive command.

And as in earlier chapters, we explicitly seek incremental progress. To that end, we propose two distinct, intermediate stages on the path toward nondiscrimination. In stage 1, our system would not require any changes in the current "don't ask, don't tell" (DADT) policy, and soldiers in both types of commands would remain closeted. All soldiers would be asked two questions.

> Question No. 1: Your answer to this first question will be kept confidential (and your answer will have no effect on your future assignments or treatment).
> *Would you be willing to serve in a command with openly gay service personnel?*

> Question No. 2: Your answer to this second question will not be kept confidential. If you answer "no," you will be assigned to an "inclusive" command. If you answer "yes," you will be assigned to an "exclusive" command.
> *Would you prefer to serve in a command without any gay personnel?*

The first question elicits information about whether service members are comfortable serving with "openly" gay colleagues. Since the answers to this question will be kept confidential, it is likely to provide feedback on the level of discomfort that is the premise for the "unit cohesion" concern.

In stage 2 of this evolving plan of integration, the statutes and regulations comprising the DADT policy would require amendment to permit but not require gay and lesbian members of inclusive commands to come out. All soldiers would be asked a single question.

> Your answer to this question will not be kept confidential. If you answer "yes," you will be assigned to an "inclusive" command. If you answer "no," you will be assigned to an "exclusive" command.
> *Would you be willing to serve in a command with openly gay service personnel?*

In the second regime, DADT would still be in effect for the exclusive command—so that soldiers who wanted to avoid serving with openly gay soldiers could do so. But in the second stage, the inclusive command would become a space in which openly gay and lesbian soldiers could serve their country and willing heterosexual soldiers could serve with them. Even stage 2 would be an intermediate, evolutionary step in the progression from exclusion, through DADT, to the ultimate goal: mandatory, wholesale integration of sexual minorities into the armed services.

The inclusive command would help to unpack and challenge the changing justifications for disqualifying gay people from military service. In early periods, the rationales were always centered on the gay soldiers themselves: they were said to be security risks, mentally unstable, cowardly, and lacking in discipline.[5] Over time, however, these rationales started to erode. This change was inevitable as highly decorated, clearly effective soldiers came out or were exposed as gay or lesbian.[6] The many promotions and glowing reviews these soldiers received during their service showed that they had discipline and courage.[7] The almost universal opinion within the psychiatric community that homosexuality is not a mental illness[8] made it untenable for the military to argue that gay people were inherently less stable than any other group. The illogic of the ban started to become clear as gay rights advocates pointed out that emotional problems and security breaches were more likely to occur if soldiers were forced to hide their sexual orientation; lifting the ban would mitigate rather than aggravate these risks.

Nonetheless, when President Bill Clinton proposed to lift the ban in early 1993, Congress balked. Ultimately, the compromise DADT policy emerged—a policy that, in theory, forbids military officials from asking whether soldiers are gay or lesbian, but also forbids gay and lesbian soldiers from being open about their orientation.[9] While this policy may have many flaws,[10] the congressional debates leading to its implementation achieved something valuable: they showed that some rationales for the ban on gays in the military were off the table. Security risks, cowardice, and mental illness of gay people have, for the most part, lost respectability in this debate.

The argument shifted. The new mantra became "unit cohesion." Indeed, when gay and lesbian service members have challenged the DADT policy, the government has defended it not by raising any of the old justifications for excluding homosexuals, but by resting upon "unit cohesion," protecting "the privacy of heterosexuals," and reducing "sexual tension."[11]

If we examine "unit cohesion" more closely, however, we see that the point of concern has actually shifted; the anticipated source of rule violations, breakdown in discipline, and insubordination has changed. The problem, it turns out, is not so much the gay soldier himself, but the reaction he is likely to elicit in others: their fear of the "gay gaze," their feelings of invaded privacy, their hostility. Put more pointedly, the fear is not so much that openly gay soldiers will violate military rules or underperform, but rather that one soldier's open homosexuality will cause another soldier to fall short in executing his duties.[12]

Military officials faced a similar dynamic when they proposed racial integration of the armed forces. Military commanders believed that white and black soldiers could not live and work together; morale, discipline, and unit cohesion would suffer. Notwithstanding these fears, officials determined that wholesale integration was necessary. Many contend that this integration has been a success, proving that prejudice and fear can be overcome when soldiers subject themselves to the discipline demanded by military life.[13] While some critics have argued that the military should follow the same path in integrating the armed forces with respect to sexual orientation, congressional repeal of DADT in the short term is unlikely. Therefore, this chapter proposes a more incremental approach, one that does not launch a direct, normative attack on DADT, but instead attempts to demonstrate that the policy rests upon fears that are baseless—even in a military setting. Stage 1 calls for changes that could be implemented by executive order, without congressional action.

If, as Judge Eugene Nickerson has asserted, "the only conceivable way that the presence of known homosexuals could undermine the cohesion of the unit is 'by the negative reactions of service members who disapprove of homosexuality,' "[14] military officials should consider instituting policies that seek out and nurture heterosexual soldiers who are tolerant of homosexuality. Our proposal does just this by allowing the perpetrators and victims of discrimination to voluntarily separate themselves into two distinct groups.

As a purely descriptive matter, our screening mechanism is likely to have two channeling functions that would be mutually reinforcing. First, gay soldiers would likely opt for the inclusive command. While gay and lesbian soldiers could also opt for an exclusive command,[15] the screening mechanism would probably reduce their incentives to do so.[16] After all, fellow soldiers in the exclusive command are there because they've expressed a preference not to serve with gay people.

Second, intolerant heterosexual soldiers are likely to opt for the exclusive command. Intolerant soldiers—taking into account the channeling effect on gay soldiers—can reduce their expected contact with gay soldiers by opting for the exclusive command. And intolerant soldiers are also likely to be less willing to ambiguate their own sexuality by expressing even minimal support for gay rights.

The remaining individuals—those that don't fall into either of these two categories—might be classified as tolerant heterosexuals. They are neither gay (who we expect, overall, will choose the inclusive command), nor identifiably intolerant toward gays (who we expect will choose the exclusive command). As we discuss in depth later, the choice of these individuals is more complex, and may depend in part on the magnitude of the two channeling effects. Tolerant soldiers will be less likely to choose the exclusive command if it is a small, stigmatized group. But they will also be less likely to join the inclusive command if it is small enough to potentially mark them as gay.

The Benefits of Self-Segregation

This tendency of self-segregation will produce three distinct types of benefits: *amelioration* (of current discrimination), *demonstration* (that the unit cohesion rationale does not require the exclusion or closeting of gay and lesbian soldiers), and *realignment* of political allies and enemies (creating a common cause for progay legislators on the left and prodefense legislators on the right) (see table 1).

At first blush, the inclusive command might appear to aggravate rather than ameliorate discrimination. One of the clear consequences of the proposal is to create "safe" spaces, but those spaces protect both those who support *and those who oppose* the inclusion of gay men and lesbians in the military. The exclusive command, by insulating some soldiers from openly gay and lesbian soldiers, might be seen as legitimizing the desire for such insulation. Granted, to the extent the inclusive command rests upon a system of "separate but equal" classifications, it will strike many readers as distasteful, and even quite harmful. Certainly, compared to a world in which gay and lesbian citizens are freely admitted into the service without restrictions peculiar to their sexual orientation, the inclusive command is not attractive. But if we take as our starting point the world we actually occupy, where the DADT policy constrains gay people's speech and conduct, heterosexual people are never given the opportunity to show that they are capable of working effectively with openly gay soldiers, and gay people are regularly discharged from the service because of their sexual orientation, the inclu-

TABLE 1. EVOLVING EFFECTS OF THE INCLUSIVE COMMAND

Type of Effect	Stage 1	Stage 2
Amelioration	More supportive environment	Speech and conduct discrimination eliminated
	Reduced chance of harassment, abuse, outing, or witch hunts	Safe haven for gays in exclusive unit if outed or come out
Demonstration	Testing number of soldiers willing to serve with gay people	Testing whether heterosexual and openly gay solders can work together effectively
	Testing relative performance of inclusive and exclusive commands	Testing whether openly gay soldiers are more likely to violate military code
Realignment	Attract supporters of individual choice	
	Attract supporters of unit cohesion	
	Attract supporters of strong defense; boost recruitment	

sive command gains important ground, if only as a set of temporary strategies. At the very least, the inclusive command increases the options available to gay and heterosexual soldiers, and thus improves their situations.

The inclusive command would *ameliorate* the discriminatory character of the DADT policy in the day-to-day lives of gay soldiers. In stage 1, the inclusive command would ease the lives of gay and lesbian soldiers by allowing them to work in units filled with fellow soldiers who have suggested that they are not prejudiced with respect to sexual orientation. The "buddy system" already in place in the United States military would complement the inclusive command strategy well, for even now heterosexual service members become accidental allies when their "buddies" come out to them. One openly gay former infantry man we know recounted the support and even protection he received from his buddy, who was straight. The inclusive command simply increases the chance that such mutually supportive pairings would form, maximizing everyone's performance. In the inclusive unit, this reduction in prejudice would presumably lead to a drop in homophobic jokes and comments, harassment on the basis of sexual orientation, and other antigay behavior.[17] These benefits would be felt immediately, because it would not be necessary for gay and lesbian service members to be out of the closet in order to appreciate a more supportive environment. Simply knowing that their fellow service members are tolerant of homosexuality could ease the strain of DADT. Heterosexual service members in the stage 1 inclusive commands, as well, would feel some amelioration of the harassment and discrimination they can suffer if they express support for gay rights under the current regime. Even in stage 1, while DADT still applies, the inclusive command would ameliorate discrimination by creating a space in which gay and nongay service members could safely and openly express their support for gay rights.

In stage 2, the inclusive command would ameliorate discrimination even more dramatically. Because the DADT policy would no longer apply to inclusive commands at this stage, gay and lesbian soldiers would be permitted to be open about their orientation. The stage 2 inclusive command would alleviate the stress of secrecy that so many gay and lesbian soldiers must bear. It would give gay and lesbian soldiers the same rights of free speech enjoyed by heterosexual soldiers.[18] Gay and lesbian service members who opt for the exclusive units could also benefit. Although DADT would continue to apply in exclusive commands, the consequences of that policy could be changed in time of transition. Closeted soldiers in the exclusive command whose sexual orientation became public (through their own decision to reveal it or because of others' investigations) could avoid discharge by transferring to an inclusive command.

The inclusive command would also have evolving *demonstration* effects. In stage 1, the inclusive command would demonstrate, if nothing else, the extent to which new recruits support gay rights. The first question directly solicits recruits' preferences about serving with gay soldiers. Because this question is confidential and unrelated to the respondent's assignment or career path, it provides powerful information into whether DADT is necessary as a recruitment device.

Moreover, the second question facilitates a limited test of the unit cohesion hypothesis itself. The self-segregating of people based upon attitudes toward homosexuality would allow military commanders to measure and compare the performance of these two distinct groups of people. Under some versions of the "unit cohesion" theory, one might expect soldiers in the exclusive command to work more effectively (because they were less likely to have to interact with gay colleagues). But this prediction can be tested. We might find that the service members who selected the inclusive unit work more effectively with people who are different from them in multiple ways than do those who express unwillingness to serve with homosexuals. Or it is possible that *both* groups would perform better when segregated than they do when mixed together under the current system. These are empirical questions that are impossible to answer before we have any data. But even while DADT still applies in stage 1, the inclusive command creates a structure for gathering data and comparing the performance of people with distinctly different attitudes toward homosexuality.

In the second stage, when gay and lesbian members of the inclusive command are permitted to be open about their orientation, a broader test of the unit cohesion theory is possible. It would then be possible to test whether heterosexual soldiers are rendered less effective by the "gay gaze"—that is, when they work alongside openly gay colleagues.[19]

Gay and lesbian soldiers have already demonstrated that the early rationales for exclusion—emotional instability, security risks, and ineffectiveness—are without merit. But these men and women could only show that *closeted* gays could serve effectively. Never have we created an environment in which *openly* gay people could prove their abilities.[20] The inclusive command takes us that additional step. And it takes us there not by creating a segregated unit just for gays[21] (as the United States has at times maintained for African-American and Japanese-American soldiers), for this would prove only that gays could serve in units reserved for gays. An exclusively gay command would fail to address the unit cohesion problem head on. Only a regime that places gay and nongay soldiers together—bunk to bunk, shoulder to shoulder, showerhead to showerhead—can prove that openly gay people can serve and (perhaps more importantly) that *heterosexual people can serve with them.*

The final effect of the inclusive command would be realignment of political interests. As this book goes to press, George W. Bush is preparing for a second term. The "don't ask, don't tell" policy is likely to remain in place. During this period, the inclusive command would offer at least incremental progress toward integration.

Such incrementalism could help even a prointegrationist president, if such a person were to suceed Bush. Bill Clinton's attempt to integrate in the early days of his first term backfired when Congress resisted. The controversy resulted in the elevation of the "don't tell" rule from a Department of Defense regulation (more easily changed through presidential action) to a federal statute (now requiring congressional action to eliminate). Congress could similarly resist integration by refusing to repeal the "don't tell" statute. Even under a progressive, prointegration president, therefore, the inclusive command could provide a useful compromise, especially if a majority of Congress remains opposed to integration.

By allowing gay people to serve without forcing uncomfortable heterosexual people to serve with them, the inclusive command structure could create a common cause for gay rights advocates on the left and various groups of conservative legislators on the right. This effect would be particularly pronounced in stage 1, when DADT remains in place for both types of commands. Indeed, during stage 1, the inclusive command proposal appears to be superior to the current DADT system, as every relevant participant's position improves. By channeling gay and lesbian soldiers toward the inclusive command, the sorting mechanism used in stage 1 would give homophobic service members a greater sense of insulation from homosexuality in the exclusive command. Finally, stage 1 should also dominate DADT in the minds of the military commanders who are morally neutral on homosexuality but fear, in a purely instrumental way, the effect integration will have on unit cohesion. Allowing people to sort themselves according to their attitudes toward homosexuality could actually boost unit cohesion in both the inclusive and the exclusive commands. Indeed, it seems the only people who would not be made better off by the move to inclusive commands would be people who do not like gay people and derive enjoyment from harassing and harming them. It would be surprising to hear any legislator argue publicly that the interests of such people must be included in the calculus.

Initially, one might suspect that liberals would be against an inclusive command because it doesn't go far enough in eliminating DADT, while implicitly condoning and legitimizing antigay sentiment by making it the basis for a new exclusive command. But when it is framed as part of a broader goal (the move from stage 1, to stage 2, to full integration), liberals should accept the program, if only as necessary data-gathering to support their position.[22]

A less positive way to describe the realignment effect is that an inclusive command might create a wedge in traditional antigay coalitions, giving legislators who are generally unsympathetic to gay rights a reason to defect from their usual political alignment. For example, a conservative lawmaker might tell her constituents that the inclusive command will more fairly distribute the burdens and dangers of military service, requiring gay and lesbian as well as heterosexual citizens to show their patriotism.[23] Particularly when the military has great need for soldiers (such as when the country is waging an unpopular war, or a strong peacetime economy makes it more difficult to find talented recruits), conservative legislators might see greater appeal in a policy that finds a way to include gay citizens in the military. The fact that the exclusive command offers some soldiers a way to decrease their probability of serving with gays only adds to the appeal for such legislators. At the very least, the inclusive command could give conservative legislators who support a strong national defense a way to trade off the benefits of a potentially larger, stronger military against the "moral values" that would otherwise lead them to oppose any expansion in gay rights.

Historical Parallels

The foregoing arguments for incremental progress are likely to be offensive to readers impatient for a simple regime of nondiscrimination. We share this impatience. But it is useful to remember that racial integration of our schools and of the military did not occur in one fell swoop. Instead, various intermediate forms of (admittedly discriminatory) inclusion were important precursors to the ultimate mandate of integration. This section reminds of us of these histories to make more plausible the idea that intermediate steps of the kind suggested in our proposal might be a necessary evil.

The history of racial integration of public education might, in stylized fashion, be broken into four core stages: exclusion, segregated inclusion, voluntary integration, and mandatory integration (see table 2). In the exclusion stage, African-American children in the United States were at first denied the right to education. The country then moved to a system of segregated inclusion, the "separate but equal" regime found constitutional in *Plessy v. Ferguson*.[24] African-American children were permitted to go to school, but only to schools designated specifically for them. White children continued to attend schools that were exclusively white.

The U.S. Supreme Court's nominal holding in *Brown v. Board of Education*[25] was to reject *Plessy*'s segregated education system. But *Brown* of course did not lead to immediate integration. Notwithstanding the court's mandate, *Brown* was followed by either continued segregation or by various

TABLE 2. STYLIZED STAGES OF INTEGRATION

Core Stage	Race in Education	Race in Military	Sexual Orientation in Military
Exclusion	African-American children denied right to education	African-Americans denied the right to serve	Homosexual exclusion policy
Segregated Inclusion	"Separate but equal" schools	Segregated units	Never used
Voluntary Integration	"Freedom of choice" Whites have option of busing to black schools White suburbs have option of accepting black students from urban areas	Never used	Proposed inclusive commands
Mandatory Integration	Nominal holding of *Brown v. Board of Education*	Integration order by Truman	Long-range goal

attempts to desegregate through voluntary action. These sporadic efforts at voluntary integration in public education may provide the most powerful historical parallel for the inclusive command proposed here.[26]

In the shadow of *Brown*, some localities adopted so-called freedom of choice plans that gave white and black families the option of participating in the integration of the schools. Because it was understood that white students would not opt to attend predominantly black schools and black students would be intimidated and pressured not to attend predominantly white schools, the "freedom of choice" plans were used by southern school districts as a tool of resistance to court-imposed integration orders.[27] Although the U.S. Supreme Court eventually struck down such plans when other methods, such as rezoning, could more quickly achieve the ends of desegregation, the Court suggested that the concept could—at least in theory—be used to integrate schools fairly.[28]

Some school boards instituted integration plans that were asymmetrically voluntary; they were optional for whites but required for blacks. Under some plans, for example, white children were permitted but not required to be bused to attend schools in predominantly black neighborhoods; many children from those neighborhoods were required to ride the bus to predominantly white schools.[29] Just as some states gave white families the choice to integrate, others gave white school districts analogous choices.

Volunteerism is still alive and well today as a dominant tool of desegregation. Several desegregation plans ask whether suburban school districts would volunteer to accept students who would be bused out from predominantly black urban districts.[30] A strategy employing elements of volunteerism can be found in ever-popular magnet schools. Majority and minority families have the option of registering for such schools, and school districts attempt to lure a racially mixed group of students to these schools by offering special programs and resources there. Instead of mandated busing, the preference is for voluntary integration.

The history of racial (and gender)[31] integration of the military is also partially analogous. We did not move directly from a regime of exclusion to one of mandatory integration. As in the educational context, African-Americans were officially excluded from service at various points in our nation's history.[32]

The objections to racial integration of the armed forces bear striking similarity to the antigay rhetoric that currently supports the ban on gays in the military.[33] For example, in the Civil War, some Union generals "feared that the presence of black soldiers in the army would create disharmony and drive away white volunteers."[34] In 1940, Admiral W. R. Sexton wrote to the secretary of the navy that if "colored men" served in the navy, "team work, harmony, and ship efficiency [would be] seriously handicapped" because of the attitudes of white sailors.[35] As late as 1971, Lieutenant General Edward Almond wrote that racial integration "weakens" the "efficiency" of the armed forces.[36] As in the case of homosexuality, unit cohesion served as a general objection to the integration of the services by race.

From nominal exclusion we moved (as in education) to a regime of segregated inclusion. After the Emancipation Proclamation, black men were officially allowed to enlist in the Union army during the Civil War as part of the "United States Colored Troops."[37] Four black units fought in the Indian wars of 1870–90, and black soldiers also fought in Cuba, where they rode with Teddy Roosevelt as part of the Rough Riders.[38] Racial segregation within the armed forces continued during World War I and at the start of World War II.[39]

But unlike education, the military moved directly from segregated inclusion to mandatory integration. When the United States suffered a shortage of combat personnel during World War II, platoons of black soldiers were ordered to serve in previously all-white companies, but this was not by choice of the black or white soldiers. This experimental combination was instead a move to mandatory integration, made complete with President Truman's executive order of 1948 officially outlawing segregation in the U.S. military.[40] By the time the United States fought in Korea, black and white soldiers fought side by side without incident.[41]

Stepping back, we see that racial integration of the military was incremental, but it bypassed the voluntary integration stage that has been much more present in the evolution of educational integration. So the natural question arises whether voluntary integration is needed with regard to sexual orientation in the military. If this stage could be bypassed with regard to race (and sex), maybe it could be bypassed with regard to sexual orientation as well.

Our answer is that the voluntary integration stage with regard to race might have been less needed because the military went through a stage of segregated inclusion that had sufficiently demonstrated the competence and valor of African-American soldiers. But if this is so, shouldn't we instead be embracing segregated integration (instead of voluntary integration) as the intermediate step to full integration?

The problem here is that segregated integration of gays and lesbians (even if we wanted it) is really not feasible. The idea of segregated inclusion for gays and lesbians would mean "gay only" units that would parallel the "black only" or "women only" units of the past. As a practical matter, the military does not have the option of using a segregated inclusion strategy, because gay men and lesbians have the option of remaining in the closet and thereby "passing" as heterosexual.[42] This passing strategy is generally not available to women and people of color. The closeting option means that any attempt to (exclude or) segregate on the basis of sexual orientation in an absolute sense is bound to fail.[43]

The difficulty of passing in the context of race and the relative ease of doing so with sexual orientation means that segregated inclusion could progress toward mandatory integration more effectively in the context of race than in sexual orientation. While black soldiers had to be "openly" black and simultaneously to demonstrate their abilities as soldiers, gay and lesbian soldiers have never had this opportunity. As soon as a soldier's orientation is known by her superiors, her resulting separation from the military prevents her from serving while openly gay. As Kenji Yoshino explains,

[T]he military has been careful to rely on stereotypes that gays cannot disprove through infiltration. Because these stereotypes rely on what "open" or visible homosexuals will do to a unit, an invisible homosexual cannot, by definition, disprove the stereotype until she comes out of the closet. At that point, of course, she is generally removed from the military and the stereotype remains largely uncontested.[44]

So while racial integration could move directly from segregated inclusion to mandatory integration, the integration of sexual minorities may have to proceed with a different intermediate step to counter the effects of the closet. Voluntary integration suggests itself as candidate in part because of the important role it has played and continues to play in the integration of public education.

Our inclusive command proposal suggests that the military use voluntary integration as a substitute for segregated inclusion as the core intermediate step, a step the military was able to skip in the context of race. The voluntary integration stage, as the name suggests, permits every participant to choose, fully informed and free of coercion, whether to join or avoid the integrated group.

The history of racial and sexual integration suggests that potential demonstration effects of any system that creates segregated groups are not just hypothetical. For example, the army has conducted experiments to determine what ratio of women in a unit might lower the performance of units in combat and noncombat contexts. The army found that women had no adverse affect on performance up to the level of 35 percent women, the highest ratio tested.[45] This same spirit of experimentation could be applied to test the relative performance of the inclusive and exclusive commands in both stage 1 and stage 2.

Keeping with a major theme of this book, the volunteerism of the inclusive command mobilizes the power of heterosexual allies—forcing them to decide whether they prefer to stand with the intolerant or the tolerant. Some heterosexuals might prefer not to make this choice, but when confronted with the decision, many—like the jurors in *Twelve Angry Men*—will step away from the table of bigotry.

The inclusive command strategy admittedly treats integration of the forces as an incremental process. It permits some service members to keep themselves apart (or, under the don't ask, don't tell policy, to persuade themselves that they are staying apart) from people they dislike. Such a system of separation would not offer a satisfying end point for any attempt to integrate gay and lesbian soldiers. But one of the central qualities of the inclusive command strategy is that it is dynamic rather than static—a means to an end rather than a goal in itself. Creating separate spaces (based upon the level of openness about homosexuality and people's preferences for that) can contribute to the overarching goal of ultimate, undifferentiated integration of the armed forces by sexual minorities.

Granted, inclusive commands might begin as much smaller entities than exclusive commands. As homosexuality gains acceptance in our society, however, the number of people opting for inclusive commands should increase. Over time, exclusive commands might shrink, eventually becoming a sort of vestigial organ, so dispensable that the costs of maintaining separate facilities outweigh the military benefits. At that point, soldiers with the real "problem"—an inability or unwillingness to serve with fellow soldiers who are openly gay—would be subject to exclusion. In this dynamic version of integration strategy, the stigma eventually falls on soldiers who are prejudiced rather than those who are gay. This in turn might create incentives for soldiers to rid themselves of their prejudices, or at least put those prejudices aside when it is time to serve their country.

Implementing the Inclusive Command

The foregoing analysis lays out the theoretical arguments for adopting the self-segregation of the inclusive command. But we did not delve into the details of implementation and a host of nitty-gritty inquiries: Can the military effectively function with both inclusive and exclusive commands? Will anyone actually opt for the inclusive command? It is to these practical questions that we now turn. In essence, we hope to have already convinced you that the idea has appeal. Here we try to answer the question: will it actually work?

What Questions Should Be Asked?

There are many different ways to frame the basic questions in stages 1 and 2. And, as in other contexts, the framing can have important impacts on the way that people would respond. In stage 1, we have suggested that the self-sorting question be phrased in the following way:

Would you prefer to serve in a command without any gay personnel?

But we might have framed the question in the affirmative instead: "Would you be willing to serve in a command with gay personnel?" Or "Would you volunteer to serve in a command with gay personnel?" These different phrases might tease out different levels of support. Some soldiers who wouldn't "volunteer" to serve with gays might nevertheless "be willing" to serve if asked. Many soldiers simply might not care whether their colleagues are gay or not. We have chosen to frame the question in the negative—as a way of partitioning those who have an affirmative desire to avoid gay colleagues from those who are merely neutral. We predict that soldiers who don't care or don't have a problem with gays will answer this question "no," and be channeled into the inclusive command.

One might argue that the phrasing will have little effect on the answers, because the soldiers will quickly see through the question and focus on what turns on it—whether they will be assigned to the inclusive or exclusive command. By this argument, the question itself becomes irrelevant, and you might as easily base assignments on the question, "Is the moon made of cheese?" But from the perspective of an individual soldier, what turns on her answer is importantly determined by how *other* soldiers answer the question. A soldier's perception of how many other soldiers are neutral about gay personnel versus how many affirmatively desire to serve alongside gays is likely quite different. Framing the question differently is likely to produce different focal points. We have chosen a frame that attempts to channel the truly intolerant toward the exclusive command, while channeling the tolerant and the indifferent toward the inclusive.

One interesting issue regards the timing of the question. On the one hand, it might make sense to pose the self-sorting question to recruits as soon as they enter the armed forces, channeling them into training programs that separate inclusive from exclusive command members. On the other hand, commanders might wait to pose the sorting question until recruits have completed basic training. The central messages of training are unity and tolerance. As they emerge from training, recruits have absorbed the military's message that "we are one" in battle. Tolerance for difference is a central value of training as well, as personal characteristics such as race, gender, or ethnicity fade in importance relative to survival and mutual support. Training also introduces recruits to the military's antiharassment policies. Once recruits have gone through training with unsorted soldiers, they have experienced service alongside people who might be gay, and they know this. With the bonding experience of training already in hand, it is possible that recruits would answer the sorting question differently than they would at the outset of service, recognizing that the sexual orientation of fellow soldiers might not matter to them as much as they would have expected prior to training. Individuals who still want to avoid serving with gay and lesbian soldiers—despite the messages of unity and tolerance imparted during training—would then be given the option of joining the exclusive command.

We have also considered whether the question should expressly respond to potential "tipping" anxiety of heterosexual soldiers. Some soldiers might be willing to serve in an inclusive command, but only if the proportion of the unit that is gay remained below a certain level. Even if heterosexual soldiers responded in the abstract that they were willing to serve with openly gay people, in actual practice they might feel differently. Each soldier might have a "tipping point" beyond which his enthusiasm for an inclusive command would wane.

For example, while some heterosexual soldiers would be happy to serve in a command where 10 percent of the soldiers were openly gay, they might be less comfortable in a command where 75 percent of the soldiers were gay. This could be true for a number of reasons. In the 75 percent command, heterosexual soldiers might fear that the ambiguity of the inclusive command would be reduced, and that observers would assume that any given individual within the unit is gay. Other heterosexual soldiers might worry that the atmosphere of the command would change if the percentage of the unit that was gay exceeded a certain point. Between 10 and 75 percent, however, the tipping point is unclear. At what point would the proportion of gay soldiers in the unit become so large that no heterosexual soldiers would wish to remain in the unit, thus rendering it a "gay command" rather than an "inclusive" one? Heterosexual people who genuinely support gay rights might still avoid gay bars or certain sections of Fire Island.

This tipping anxiety is of course related to the last chapter's discussion of ambiguation. Some heterosexuals might be comfortable with letting their audience entertain the possibility that there is a 5 percent chance that they are gay, but would become very uncomfortable if the audience thought there was a 50 percent chance that they were gay. This tipping anxiety was vividly displayed on a plane trip we took to Boston. By chance, the flight included several dozen members of the New York City Gay Men's Chorus. The heterosexual men on the flight were in the minority and some seemed to go to unusual conversational lengths to disambiguate themselves.

Collective action problems of this type could make it difficult to form a truly inclusive command from the very outset; heterosexual soldiers might be unwilling to opt for this command unless they felt assured that a significant number of other heterosexual soldiers would do the same. Just as we might ask the maximum percentage of the command that could be gay within an integrated unit before tipping would occur, so too we could ask the minimum percentage that would have to be heterosexual in order to get it off the ground.

In stage 1, the tipping problem might be suppressed because soldiers would be much less aware of the percentage of the command that is gay. The tipping problem in stage 1 might also relate to the size of the inclusive command. Especially early in the experiment, there may be fear among heterosexual soldiers that low total participation in the inclusive command will result in the assumption that only gay soldiers opted in. For example, an "inclusive" command that is 5 percent of the armed forces would be more susceptible to the suspicion that all its members are gay than would one that makes up 30 percent. Thus, in stage 1, total participation in the inclusive command will act as a proxy for what percentage of each command is gay, since that factor is unknown. Heterosexual service members may be hesitant to join an inclusive command unless the total participation in such commands comprises a substantial percentage of the armed forces. This would combat the presumption that all the members are gay because there would just be too many. Most service members likely assume that approximately 10 percent (the highest, but also most popular estimate) of the population is gay. Thus, if twice that percentage were to join the inclusive command, fears may be assuaged. This doesn't contradict the idea that every soldier has a specific theoretical tipping point. However, even if a particular soldier's theoretical tipping point were exceeded by the actual number of gay people in the command, he would not know this and thus would not engage in the "straight flight" that would cause the tipping to occur. On the other hand, the very fact that a soldier has a tipping point and cannot know when it has been exceeded might cause him to avoid the inclusive command altogether. Thus, the inability to measure the percentage of the command that is gay does not necessarily help the inclusive command to recruit heterosexual soldiers. What starts as a tipping problem becomes a recruitment problem—we don't have to worry about heterosexual soldiers tipping out of the command if they won't join it to begin with.

Some recruits might prefer to qualify their willingness to serve in the inclusive command by indicating that if the percentage of gay people exceeded a certain level (10 percent, 35 percent, 50 percent, for example), they would prefer the exclusive command. To these people, the military could

offer conditional membership in the inclusive command; they could specify their tipping point and would be free to transfer to the exclusive command if the number of gay people in the inclusive command exceeded their
disclosed tipping point. However, a cascade effect might occur in such a system: when individuals at the 10 percent point are allowed to transfer, the
command may as a result reach 35 percent gay, allowing more service members to transfer.

Moreover, this approach would be difficult to implement, because the
stage 1 screening mechanisms proposed thus far do not ask (and under
DADT cannot ask) about soldiers' sexual orientations, only their preferences with respect to the sexual orientations of their peers. Without a separate question that seeks to discover soldiers' sexual orientations, military officials could not know who was gay, making it impossible to tell when the
maximum gay percentage had been reached.

For information-gathering purposes, then, the armed forces could ad-
minister an anonymous survey, asking each recruit to state his or her sexual
orientation. Two problems immediately arise with such a survey: accuracy
and legality. The results from any such survey might be wildly inaccurate.
Promises of anonymity are often insufficient to induce truthful answers to
questions about homosexuality. And directly asking the question would violate the "don't ask" portion of DADT.

But the military might get a more accurate count of gay and lesbian soldiers if it used a "randomized response" approach, in which respondents are
instructed to privately flip a coin. If it is heads, they answer the question,
"Are you gay" truthfully; if it is tails, they answer the question "yes" no matter what the truth is. A "yes," in other words, does not require respondents
to reveal anything about themselves, because only the individual soldier
knows the result of the coin flip. But if 53 percent of one thousand respondents should answer yes, the military would have a good idea that 6 percent
of the group was gay.[46] This randomization preserves anonymity by giving
the "yes" responders plausible deniability, but allows researchers to estimate
the proportion of gays in the aggregate.[47]

If this coin-flipping survey revealed that the number of gay people in the
inclusive command had exceeded the tipping points of some members,
then the military even in stage 1 could respond to "tipping" anxiety. The
armed forces could offer transfers to soldiers who had expressed a discomfort with serving with too many gays. In this way, the military would manage tipping by keeping track of aggregate numbers; and it would not be
necessary to know the orientation of any given soldier.[48]

Ultimately, we reject the idea of soliciting detailed discriminatory preferences from the troops—in part, because it might reify and reinforce the very preferences we are trying to obliterate. The military should take seriously the risk that "straight flight" will turn the inclusive command into a de facto segregated gay command. But the solution to the tipping problem is found in effective training, not in catering to homophobia. Prior to assignment, every recruit could receive information that would describe the inclusive command in detail. In this training program, recruits would learn that DADT's prohibition on asking about service members' sexual orientation prevents military officials from knowing ex ante the proportion of any command—inclusive *or exclusive*—that is actually gay or lesbian. Recruits who opt for an inclusive command in stage 1 would accept the assignment on the premise that DADT would prevent gay and lesbian members of the command from identifying themselves. In stage 2, recruits would join the inclusive command knowing that they would be free to seek transfer to an exclusive command if the inclusive command at some point exceeded their own personal tipping points. If this training program also included accurate, up-to-date information about homosexuality, it is possible that many heterosexual soldiers would internally adjust their tipping point upward.

What Should Turn on the Answers?

Arguably, the assignment given to a soldier who says he is willing to serve with gay people should have no special label at all; it should just be "the armed forces." This complete integration is the ultimate goal of the strategy of inclusive and exclusive commands. As a first step, however, giving labels to the two different commands can help create the appropriate focal point for self-segregation of the tolerant and intolerant. Naming the two commands is problematic, however. It could prove difficult to find word pairs that avoid any connotation of hierarchy or stigma.

But we should pause to consider whether the military should stigmatize those soldiers who opt for the exclusive command. Identifying and stigmatizing bigots is a worthy goal for reasons besides the recognition of gay rights. Research on anti-Semitism shows that people who express prejudice on the basis of one characteristic (such as religion) are likely to express prejudice on the basis of other characteristics as well (such as race or national origin).[49] In an organization that relies upon soldiers' ability to work together and defend each other, prejudice can be costly. A soldier who is willing to express prejudice on the basis of sexual orientation may also be harboring prejudice on the basis of race or religion, not so willingly expressed (because such prejudices are less socially acceptable than homophobia). Soldiers who opt for the exclusive command might be inadvertently signaling an inability to work not only with openly gay people, but with people of diverse races, religions, or ethnic backgrounds as well. Soldiers who join an inclusive command, on the other hand—particularly heterosexual soldiers who do so—might in general be more tolerant of and receptive to differences within the ranks. This receptivity could foster greater unity in an already diverse military force.

There is, however, a serious risk attendant to any stigmatization of the exclusive command. Social attitudes, like sexual orientation, can be masked. If soldiers join an inclusive command not because they are comfortable serving with gay people, but because they wish to avoid the negative aspects of the alternative command, then some soldiers with antigay prejudice (people we might call "closeted bigots") could end up in an inclusive command. These closeted bigots could be bad for unit cohesion in the inclusive command. In stage 1, although DADT would prevent them from identifying gay or lesbian soldiers with certainty, they could nonetheless decrease morale by making derogatory remarks about gay men and lesbians. In stage 2, in addition to harassing the soldiers who came out, the closeted bigots might seek to pit heterosexual soldiers against openly gay soldiers within an inclusive command. If the inclusive command is to have its desired demonstration effect, then soldiers who are likely to display or foment antigay prejudice should be discouraged from joining it. Stigmatizing the exclusive command could drive some soldiers to an inclusive command who are not really "qualified" to join it. In this sense, the inclusive command has its own exclusive qualities, because it bars people who express antigay sentiment.

If we wish to avoid stigmatizing either of the commands, we should devise names that are parallel and politically neutral. But this could prove difficult. If the command admitting openly gay people is "inclusive," is the other command "exclusive"? The word *exclusive* sometimes connotes a kind of elitism or superiority. But other word pairs—*tolerant/intolerant; may ask, may tell/don't ask, don't tell,* and so on—are also value laden. Labeling the divisions by number does not solve the problem, because the lower number will inevitably communicate priority or hierarchy. To avoid these problems, we could choose labels that are not descriptive in any real sense, such as animals (Cougar Command/Tiger Command) or colors (Green Unit/Red Unit).

And for parallel reasons, the substantive assignments and career opportunities of soldiers who opt for the exclusive command should not be impaired. The military should resist the urge to statistically discriminate against these intolerant soldiers, again because such discrimination is likely to cause them to suppress their true feelings. A reverse tipping problem in which all soldiers opted for the inclusive command in stage 1 would not be an advance on the current system. Of course, at some level it will be difficult to avoid the politicization of choice. Just as judicial nominees are judged on their decisions to join restrictive clubs, candidates for the joint chiefs of staff one day would likely be judged on whether they preferred to associate with the intolerant. The point here is that the military should to the extent practicable reduce and disconnect the careerist and social consequences of opting for one command or the other. Over time, any word that we give to the exclusive command is likely to become tainted by repeated connection to its unworthy substance. But the mechanism should at least begin by putting the commands on an equal and neutral footing.

Whatever the name attached to the inclusive command, it should be integrated rather than exclusively gay. Creating a "gay ghetto" within the military could more severely stigmatize the soldiers who join this unit, singling out the people are not the sole or even the primary cause of the problems surrounding sexuality and the military. Given the hostility many feel toward homosexuality, a command that was exclusively gay could be vulnerable to hostile reactions from soldiers outside the unit, reactions that could range from a general lack of support to "fragging," in which service members fire on their own people with malicious motive.[50] The presence of heterosexual soldiers within an inclusive command would help to dilute this effect, insulating gay and lesbian soldiers from the negative reactions they would likely engender in some fellow soldiers outside the unit.

In her defense of the ban on gays in the military, Melissa Wells-Petry argues that grouping or segregating soldiers by certain behaviors can be detrimental to their relationships with fellow soldiers.

> This phenomenon already is observed in military culture when soldiers are grouped—in social, not official, terms—by behavior, or potential behavior, that is considered substandard for soldiering. The groups of soldiers frequently become a focal point for reinforcing the military identity of the larger group. . . .

Desirable or not, this social phenomenon is a reaffirmation of the larger group's identity as "*real*" soldiers. Nevertheless, this social phenomenon clearly can go too far and result in divisiveness. Controlling this natural social phenomenon would be more difficult if soldiers were grouped by non-military behavior as a matter of official policy.[51]

The inclusive command system would group soldiers by their expressed willingness to serve with openly gay colleagues. This willingness would not be, in Wells-Petry's words, "non-military" or "substandard" behavior, but rather would be crucially tied to work as members of the armed services.

At this point it is important to remember the role commanding officers play in implementing strategies like the inclusive command. One might even enlist the support of "norm entrepreneurs" such as Norman Schwarzkopf, Wesley Clark, or Colin Powell. They might make clear that if *they* were called upon to answer the key question, simply on their own behalf, they would indicate a willingness to serve with gay and lesbian service members. Indeed, given their praise of gay and lesbian former service members, Schwarzkopf and Powell could likely express this personal view without contradicting their congressional testimony on unit cohesion. If norm entrepreneurs were able to endorse the inclusive command as a good thing, such statements might play a role analogous to the U.S. Supreme Court's pronouncement in *Brown*, creating an environment conducive to voluntary integration efforts.

But even if the problems of tipping and stigma proved so intractable that the inclusive command became in actuality a gay command, we needn't conclude that the experiment has failed. Instead, we might see the gay command as an interim step (stage 1a, perhaps) toward an integrated inclusive command (probably renamed, to disrupt the signal that "inclusive" equals "gay"), which in turn would be an interim step toward full integration. The process of integrating gay and lesbian soldiers would be broken into smaller increments, but the cause of gay rights would nonetheless move forward.

Administrative Burdens

The inclusive command system this chapter proposes would admittedly impose on military administrators additional layers of cost and procedure that could prove onerous. First, we must acknowledge the additional costs if the military attempted to implement an inclusive command system by creating two duplicative sets of resources—one for each type of command. The costs of keeping the inclusive and exclusive commands separate but indeed equal could be prohibitive.

The greater the administrative burden created by a dual-command system, the more difficult it becomes for the military to meet other demands on commanders' time and energy. The very process of determining the appropriate command for a new soldier, for example, would consume precious resources. If soldiers retained the option of moving from exclusive to inclusive commands (or vice versa), this too could impose additional administrative costs. While soldiers are trained to be flexible, able to adapt to new conditions and requirements, it is also a hallmark of military training to emphasize esprit de corps. Undue movement of personnel from one command to another could jeopardize unit cohesion in ways that a few openly gay soldiers staying in one place never would.

Military officials might also object that the division of soldiers into inclusive and exclusive units would be artificial and potentially temporary. If the soldiers were called to combat, it would be difficult, if not impossible, to maintain the separation of the two units. They might fight in coordinated or even combined fashion. Experiences of gay and lesbian soldiers who have served suggest, however, that the more exigent the circumstances under which soldiers are working, the less important anyone's sexual orientation seems to be.[52] It is perhaps not a coincidence that in wartimes, the military has been willing to overlook members' homosexuality in order to maximize personnel.[53] As the United States has coordinated peacekeeping efforts with other members of the United Nations and NATO, moreover, American troops have worked closely with soldiers from countries that permit openly gay people to serve.[54]

In the wake of the ruling by the European Court of Human Rights requiring Great Britain to include openly gay people in its military forces,[55] such interaction can only increase. Britain has been the United States' greatest supporter in the war on terrorism declared in response to the terrorist attacks of September 11; the United Kingdom has also deployed thousands of troops in Iraq. Not only do gay soldiers serve this and other countries' interest in staffing at times of crisis, they may disturb the average heterosexual soldier less at such times than in peacetime. Geoffrey Bateman and Sameera Dalvi studied openly gay, non-American service members who have served with Americans in multinational military units or operations. They concluded that U.S. personnel are able to interact and work successfully with acknowledged gay personnel from foreign militaries. Institutionally, they found, neither NATO nor the United Nations has addressed the coordination of divergent policies concerning sexual orientation in an official manner. This appears to be the case "largely because these organizations are preoccupied with more pressing concerns, and because homosexual personnel are not seen as sources of tension, even for U.S. personnel."[56] As studies like Bateman and Dalvi's multiply, military leaders will gain further assurance that inclusive and exclusive commands could be coordinated and even combined in times of crisis without sacrificing military effectiveness.

Although "unit cohesion" is the central rationale now for excluding openly gay and lesbian citizens from the military, commanders and commentators have from time to time cited other administrative rationales for the ban, such as health care costs and security risks. Just as voluntary, incremental integration can solve the "unit cohesion" problem, so too the inclusive command could demonstrate that these additional administrative rationales are unfounded. Some military warnings of increased administrative burdens are empirical claims unsupported by relevant data. The inclusive command system creates an opportunity to gather relevant data. Only in this way can we determine the strength of these empirical claims masquerading as normative statements.

But Will Anyone Join?

Although behavior under changed norms can be difficult to predict, it is not unrealistic to think that a substantial number of heterosexual soldiers would opt for the inclusive command. The very premise of this book is that many nongay people are looking for ways to stand up for the rights of gay, lesbian, and bisexual people. For supportive heterosexual people inclined to serve in the military, the inclusive command would provide yet another way to work for the equality of gay people.

Randy Shilts writes about Greg Teran, a heterosexual man who attended MIT with the help of an air force ROTC scholarship. Teran was troubled by the military's antigay policy. When assigned to do a full briefing on "any military-related issue" for an ROTC class, he "delivered a report to the fifteen other Air Force cadets and his unit commander arguing that the regulations banning gays should be rescinded."[57] Teran eventually began to work for change, attending a national conference of organizers whose goal was the elimination of ROTC chapters from college campuses unless the Defense Department lifted the ban on gays.[58] Teran once told a flight commander that his goal for military service was to "serve in an Air Force that did not discriminate on race, sex, or sexual orientation."

In his book *Honor Bound*, Joseph Steffan writes that when he was expelled from the Naval Academy because of his homosexuality, his heterosexual friends were loyal supporters.[59] Greg Teran and Steffan's friends give us reason to believe that some heterosexuals already in the armed forces would choose an inclusive command if it were an option.[60] Moreover, it is possible that the existence of an inclusive command might draw people to the military who would otherwise forgo service.[61]

Recent surveys suggest that public acceptance of LGBT people in the U.S. military has grown since DADT was first implemented. A study found that between 1994 and 1999, the percentage of U.S. Navy officers who "feel uncomfortable in the presence of homosexuals" decreased from 57.8 percent to 36.4 percent.[62] A CNN/Gallup poll conducted in December 2003 found that 79 percent of all Americans believed that gay and lesbian service members should be able to serve openly in the military. Among respondents between the ages of nineteen and thirty, the percentage was even higher: an astounding 91 percent supported the right of openly gay people to serve.[63] This last statistic is particularly important, since it reveals the views of the age group most likely to be serving in the U.S. military. If these trends continue, there may be reason to expect that a critical mass of service members would express a willingness to serve in an inclusive command. Better yet, these polls may suggest that the time for full integration is now—without the interim step of the inclusive command.

Conclusion

This chapter proposes a new, incremental way to integrate sexual minorities into the U.S. military: inclusive commands. Built on a system of voluntary self-assignment, the inclusive command and its counterpart, the exclusive command, would permit soldiers to sort themselves by their attitudes toward homosexuality.

But is integration of the military really a worthy goal for gay rights advocates, allies, and policymakers? Certainly, many theorists have raised legitimate concerns about the ways the military reinforces patriarchy and constructs masculinity to the disadvantage of women and people of color.[64] One might point out that exclusion from the military, especially combat, keeps openly gay people out of harm's way.

But focusing exclusively on the costs and dangers of military service ignores the fact that inclusion in the military is a right and duty of citizenship. It also confers undeniable advantages. Military service has symbolic value: it simultaneously demonstrates and creates patriotism and full citizenship. Military service also carries with it material benefits: job training, education, health and retirement benefits, and political clout. It is not happenstance that military service is an important correlate with success when candidates run for public office.

"Don't ask, don't tell" is an inadequate means of giving gay men and lesbians access to these benefits. To move the debate further and break down antigay assumptions, we must create an environment where the assumptions can be tested and proven to be unfounded.

The inclusive command would be one such environment. With the support of commanders who are behind the integrationist goals of the unit, soldiers could demonstrate that unit cohesion need not suffer in the presence of openly gay soldiers, that sexual tensions can be managed, and that privacy can be respected. In the process, much of the harm currently imposed by the DADT policy could be ameliorated.

The importance of this support from higher-ranking officers cannot be overemphasized. As the RAND report concluded when it summarized its recommendations: "Any sense of experimentation or uncertainty invites those opposed to change to continue to resist it and to seek to 'prove' that the change will not work."[65] Although this chapter has referred repeatedly to the demonstration effects of the inclusive command and the opportunities for gathering data that it offers, commanders would have to make clear to all service members that the new regime is not an "experiment," but rather a process that they support toward a final goal of full integration. Through the inclusive command, the armed forces could come one step closer to the ideal Judge Nickerson has described: "A Service called on to fight for the principles of equality and free speech embodied in the United States Constitution should embrace those principles in its own ranks."[66]

Part III

Renouncing Privilege

Chapter 6 began to move toward some uncomfortable choices. Some soldiers would prefer not to choose between the inclusive and exclusive commands described in that chapter; even if they generally support equal rights for LGBT people, they prefer to ignore the fact that the military discriminates. In the chapters that follow, we're going to push further with the theme of uncomfortable choices—choices that give people opportunities (sometimes unwelcome) to renounce the benefits of their heterosexual privilege.

Consider, for example, the story of Barry, who for several years had volunteered as a leader for his son's Boy Scout troop. On a troop trip to a rock-climbing gym, Barry overheard a father, not connected with the troop, say, "That's too bad. They're wearing Boy Scout shirts, and the Boy Scouts discriminate against gay people."

Barry's first reaction was annoyance. He thought, "What an obnoxious thing to say! Who's he to criticize?" Barry didn't think of himself as embracing prejudice or antigay attitudes. But based on his Scout uniform, this other father could accuse him of discrimination. This gave Barry pause. He had read media accounts of the Supreme Court case against the Scouts by the gay Scout master, and he knew the Scouts had kicked the guy out because he was gay. He hadn't agreed with the Scouts' policy, but he didn't think it would have much bearing on the activities of his troop. But now he questioned what sort of message he was sending by continuing to lead the troop. Could he continue to wear the BSA insignia with pride?

To Barry's credit, he was able to get past his defensive reactions and engage in some genuine introspection. The confrontational approach of that nearby father might not have found so receptive an audience in most cases. We hesitate to promote in-your-face strategies because they are often counterproductive: they ask too much of the ally, and they can alienate their audience—people who are, after all, potential allies. At the end of the day, we do not call upon all allies to publicly confront anyone in a Scout uniform. But at the same time, we find it difficult to chastise those who do speak up. Sometimes, renouncing privilege means bearing the consequences when you identify injustice.

In chapter 7, we offer a legislative strategy that would have helped Barry realize and acknowledge—to himself and others—that he was in fact supporting a discriminatory organization. Allies should consider just when they ought to speak from inside an organization and when they should publicly renounce and quit a discriminatory organization, the subject of chapter 8.

The Informed Association Statute and the Boy Scouts of America

[W]hen a "message" is kept secret, many individuals will invest in an organization they would not have joined had they known of the "message." How many pro-gay individuals are now deeply troubled that they ever sent their boys to the Scouts, or gave the Scouts their money or their time as volunteers?

Kenji Yoshino

In *Dale v. Boy Scouts of America*,[1] the U.S. Supreme Court reinforced the principle that no matter how large or apparently public an organization might be, the decision to join it is imbued with meaning; a person signals something by associating with an organization. Thus, the Boy Scouts of America and its members had rights of "expressive association" that would be violated if they were forced to extend membership to someone who failed to meet the BSA's admission standards. The trouble, of course, was that one of those standards came into direct conflict with New Jersey's public accommodation statute, which prohibits institutions and organizations of a sufficiently public nature from discriminating on the basis of enumerated characteristics—including sexual orientation. Based on this statute, James Dale, an openly gay man, sought to retain his position as scoutmaster. In ruling for the BSA, the Court effectively held that the constitutional right of expressive association trumps the statutory right to be free of discrimination.

The effects of *Dale* extended far beyond James Dale and the administrative offices of the BSA. The ruling affected millions of people who were or are now involved in scouting. Some of these people, no doubt, breathed a sigh of relief. But others felt a keen disappointment—and even embarrassment—that the organization to which they had devoted much of their time and energy had committed itself to an exclusionary policy with which they disagreed.

The *Dale* case was framed as a battle between an organization's First Amendment rights of expressive association and a state's interests in eradicating discrimination.[2] But those individuals who were embarrassed by the BSA's stance on homosexuality found themselves at odds with the Scouts because they may not have known that the BSA discriminates against homosexuals. And if they did know, perhaps they didn't really expect the BSA to follow through. And so a third interest deserves greater attention: the interest of individuals in knowing *what* they express by associating with a particular organization. The right of expressive association has meaning only when the decision—to join or not to join—is informed and deliberate. Only then can a person actually signal something by joining. If an organization's failure to disclose discriminatory policies allows it to recruit people who would refuse membership if fully informed, a kind of associational fraud can occur. The state as well as potential members and donors have an interest in preventing this sort of fraud. People should know exactly what they're signing up for.

One of the core questions in the Boy Scout case is how easily a private organization should be able to show that its members knew about and approved its discriminatory policies. The answer to this question profoundly affects people who would prefer to know about such policies up front and avoid discriminatory organizations. The decision *not* to associate with an organization is also expressive, and that right of expression also deserves protection.

When the decision not to associate is collective and coordinated, it becomes a boycott. Through boycott, people can critique and discipline organizations.[3] But boycotts are difficult to pull off, because individual decision-makers must coordinate their activities. This chapter proposes a legislative initiative—the Informed Association Statute—that would make it easier for people to *avoid* organizations holding policies they disagree with. Because the statute would increase the amount of information about an organization available to potential members, it would also facilitate more meaningful decisions to join organizations when people agree with their policies.

At the core of our proposed statute would be a requirement that organizations, like the Boys Scouts, obtain written acknowledgments from their members.

> I, the undersigned, acknowledge that I am choosing to associate with an organization that retains the right to discriminate on the basis of sexual orientation.

This requirement would help secure the state's interest in preventing people from mistakenly associating with discriminatory organizations. The statute is an example of a strategy that asks allies to "renounce privilege": when faced with the choice, many people—even people who don't consider themselves to be activists—will be unwilling to sign the written acknowledgment.

A statute requiring disclosure of, and explicit consent to, an association's discriminatory policies would in no way force gay and lesbian people on unwilling organizations. But it would force some heterosexual people to come to terms with their own acts of discrimination. They would lose the plausible deniability that currently allows them, in some cases, to enjoy the benefits of organizations they would feel compelled to quit if discriminatory policies were revealed. Ignorance would no longer be an excuse. The informed association statute, therefore, would force decisions on heterosexual people: fish or cut bait.[4]

For some people, the statute would thus create an uncomfortable space—but one from which support for gay rights could emerge. Social change often depends upon people being put to hard choices. While President John F. Kennedy may have preferred to sidestep the civil rights battles of his day, the moral claims of activists such as Dr. Martin Luther King Jr. forced JFK's hand.[5] Forty years later, history credits JFK with providing much of the momentum that propelled the Civil Rights Act of 1964 through Congress. At times there may be a productive role for more extreme agitators—such as Malcolm X or Act Up—that provide a kind of good cop/bad cop synergy in the struggle for civil rights. The people addressed by this chapter are not only legislators and political leaders, but perhaps more importantly they are the great center of the heterosexual majority. Their choices—even ones that are difficult or uncomfortable at first—could make all the difference for the cause of gay rights in this country.

The chapter ends with a personal turn. Besides supporting law reform, heterosexual allies can lobby for the idea of informed association in their own private organizations. For example, if your religious congregation does not have the power to stop discrimination in the celebration of marriage rites, it might consider asking its members to acknowledge that they are associating with a discriminatory organization. On a more individual level, it may be illuminating for allies at least to think about signing actual acknowledgments whenever we choose to associate with discriminatory organizations or events.

Dale v. Boy Scouts of America in the U.S. Supreme Court

In the now familiar case giving rise to this proposal, the Boy Scouts of America terminated James Dale as a Boy Scout leader because he was gay, and Dale challenged his expulsion. When the case reached the U.S. Supreme Court, Justice Rehnquist told the story in this way.

> The Boy Scouts is a private, not-for-profit organization engaged in instilling its system of values in young people. The Boy Scouts asserts that homosexual conduct is inconsistent with the values it seeks to instill. Respondent is James Dale, a former Eagle Scout whose adult membership in the Boy Scouts was revoked when the Boy Scouts learned that he is an avowed homosexual and gay rights activist. The New Jersey Supreme Court held that New Jersey's public accommodations law requires that the Boy Scouts admit Dale. This case presents the question whether applying New Jersey's public accommodations law in this way violates the Boy Scouts' First Amendment right of expressive association. We hold that it does.[6]

Justice Rehnquist's summary tells a simple story, one in which the conclusion (requiring the BSA to admit Dale will violate the BSA's right of expressive association) seems to flow almost inexorably from the very identity of the characters (an organization "engaged in instilling its system of values in young people" on the one hand, an "avowed homosexual and gay rights activist" on the other).

Dale sued the Boy Scouts in New Jersey Superior Court, alleging that the organization had violated New Jersey's common law and public accommodations statute[7] by excluding him from membership based solely on his sexual orientation.[8] The case wended its way to the New Jersey Supreme Court (after a victory for the BSA in the trial court[9] and a reversal in Dale's favor at the intermediate appellate level). The New Jersey Supreme Court held that due to its size and public nature, the Boy Scouts was a place of public accommodation and was therefore subject to the public accommodations statute. The court further held that the Boy Scouts violated the statute by excluding Dale based on his sexual orientation.[10]

The New Jersey Supreme Court rejected the BSA's claim that subjecting it to the public accommodations law would violate its federal constitutional right "to associate for the purpose of engaging in protected speech."[11] The court acknowledged that "Boy Scouts expresses a belief in moral values and uses its activities to encourage the moral development of its members."[12] The court could not accept the notion that "a shared goal of Boy Scout members is to associate in order to preserve the view that homosexuality is immoral."[13] Because the court believed that Dale's membership "would not 'affect in any significant way [the Boy Scouts'] existing members' ability to carry out their various purposes,'" it ruled that being forced to include Dale would not violate the Boy Scouts' right of expressive association.[14]

The U.S. Supreme Court reversed the New Jersey court's decision. A deferential review of the Scout Oath and Law persuaded the majority that homosexuality is counter to the values BSA seeks to instill in its members. The BSA asserted that homosexual conduct is inconsistent with the Scout Oath and Law, particularly the Scout Oath to remain "morally straight" and the Scout Law requiring scouts to be "Clean." The Court acknowledged that the Oath and Law do not mention homosexuality expressly, and that the terms "morally straight" and "clean" are "by no means self-defining."[15] Notwithstanding the ambiguity of phrases such as "morally straight," the Court deferred to the organization's interpretation of its own doctrine and accepted the BSA's assertion that it views homosexuality as immoral.[16] More importantly for this analysis, the Court accepted the BSA's assertion that it had clearly and consistently expressed this view of homosexuality in the past.

According to the majority opinion in *Dale*, admitting Dale would force the BSA to acknowledge homosexuality's "straightness" and "cleanliness" and prevent it from expressing its professed opinion. As Justice Rehnquist explained, "The fact that the organization does not trumpet its views from the housetops, or that it tolerates dissent within its ranks, does not mean that its views receive no First Amendment protection."[17]

In the wake of *Dale*,[18] a nationwide movement has developed to remove various forms of community support for the BSA, principally meeting space and money. This movement has involved people who are gay and straight, has not been orchestrated in any central way, and has involved people in a diversity of roles (BSA members, parents of members, and people who are not involved directly with the BSA).

Many communities and organizations have withdrawn sponsorship of the BSA. Under such sponsorship, space for meetings is a valuable resource that churches and schools provide the Boy Scouts free of charge (even when other groups might pay a fee for the space). In the wake of *Dale*, organizations have started to pull this "in kind" support. In Taunton, Massachusetts, for example, the Union Congregational Church ended a two-year relationship with the BSA[19] during which the church had subsidized the Scouts and provided them with meeting space. Pastor Beverly Duncan explained that gay and nongay members of the church expressed concern about the ruling in *Dale*. Although the church had experienced no problems with the local scout troop, it could not ignore the "stark contrast" between the national organization's stance on homosexuality and the church's beliefs.[20] One Oak Park, Illinois, church turned the tables on the BSA to force the organization's hand: The Cornerstone United Methodist Church's application for a charter to sponsor a Cub Scout pack was denied by the BSA because the church stated an intention to run an "open and inclusive program."[21]

School districts, too, have sought to restrict BSA access to meeting space. Nine months after the Supreme Court ruled in *Dale*, directors of the New York State School Boards Association passed a resolution urging boards to deny building access to any group that engages in discrimination. In the October newsletter, Vice President Harris Dinkoff wrote, "We cannot tell ourselves and our children that it is OK to exclude and be biased against one group of people and then say we are not biased against anyone else. By accepting bias in any form, we condone what we profess to condemn."[22]

On December 1, 2000, Chancellor Harold O. Levy announced that New York City schools could no longer sponsor Boy Scout troops.[23] The BSA could no longer use public schools as sites for recruiting new members, and the organization was barred from bidding on school contracts. Troops could continue to hold meetings in public schools, but only on the same basis as all other organizations that have access to public schools as meeting places.[24]

The Broward County, Florida, school board took more extreme measures. It voted unanimously on November 14, 2000, to ban the BSA entirely from its schools pursuant to the board's nondiscrimination policy, which forbids use of school facilities by "any group or organization which discriminates on the basis of [a series of characteristics including] sexual orientation."[25] Before the vote, individual board members expressed their desire to send a message not only to the BSA but to the community generally that discrimination "would not be tolerated."[26] When the BSA challenged this action in federal court, the court scrutinized the various aspects of the board's decision independently. The court held that "the District was within its rights" when it terminated sponsorship of the Scouts; the court permitted the school board to cancel "a five-year agreement that gave the Scouts free use of the school buildings and established an annual 'School Night for Scouting' at which the school assisted the BSA in recruiting new members." But when the school board further excluded the BSA "from using the limited public forum of school property on the same basis as other private groups," the court held, the board violated the First Amendment.[27] Although the school board could speak for itself and fashion a message disapproving "intolerance toward homosexuality," it was not free to punish the BSA for its contrary message.[28]

The U.S. Congress stepped into this fray in June 2001, when the Senate approved the "Helms Amendment," which would withhold federal funds from public school districts that deny "equal access" to meeting space for the Boy Scouts and any other youth groups that "prohibit the acceptance of homosexuality."[29] The House of Representatives passed a similar amendment in May 2001. Congressional opponents of these measures pointed out that the Helms Amendment amounts to little more than gratuitous antigay rhetoric, because the U.S. Constitution and existing civil rights laws *already* prevent schools from denying the Boy Scouts (and other groups that discriminate) access to meeting space on the same basis as other groups.

Gay civil rights groups and their allies in Congress worked with a House-Senate conference committee to remove the language they deemed most harmful.[30] The final legislation makes clear that nothing in the statute "shall be construed to require any school, agency, or a school served by an agency to sponsor any group officially affiliated with the Boy Scouts of America."[31] The final version of the Boy Scouts of America Equal Access Act thus appears to extend no further than preexisting case law; it requires schools to permit the BSA to use facilities on the same terms provided to other outside organizations. Schools remain free to cancel sponsorships. But the legislation did allow legislators to expressly state their own preferences—just as the Informed Association Statute would for individual members.

The second institutional reaction to *Dale* has been an effort to remove the BSA from lists of local United Way funding recipients. In Broward County, Florida, for example, the United Way announced that, beginning in 2002, the BSA would be ineligible for program grants due to the organization's discriminatory policy.[32] This sort of funding boycott can be powerful, because people opposed to Boy Scout policies can express their disapproval and impose costs on the organization, even if they are not potential members or parents of potential members. This strategy requires groups to take action, and inertia is difficult to overcome. According to the United Way of

America, the national organization permits local groups to set their own funding policies, but only fifty-three local groups—out of fourteen hundred total—have changed their policies regarding Scout funding.[33]

The political stakes can sometimes be high. In Tempe, Arizona, Mayor Neil Giuliano attempted to disqualify the BSA from city employee donations to United Way, which triggered a recall effort against him.[34] In the face of substantial opposition, Giuliano said that city employees should determine their own contributions to the United Way.[35] Although Giuliano abandoned his effort, the controversy seems to have suppressed donations to the United Way by city employees.[36]

Corporate donors to the Boy Scouts mirror actions by local United Way chapters and their donors. Novell, a computer software firm headquartered in Provo, Utah, announced that it would no longer match employee contributions to the BSA. The company announced this new rule as an effort to comply with its overarching policy not to make charitable contributions to discriminatory organizations.[37] Only five days after the announcement, however, Novell modified its stance, agreeing to match employee contributions to the local United Way chapter.[38] In December 2000, Wells Fargo Bank instructed the United Way not to allocate any of its four-hundred-thousand-dollar annual corporate gift to the Boy Scouts.[39]

Some regional councils and local chapters of the BSA are defecting from the national position on homosexuality, attempting to substitute their own policies of inclusion and nondiscrimination.[40] In Rhode Island, where the statewide public accommodations law covers discrimination on the basis of sexual orientation, a Cub Scout pack and a Boy Scout troop in Providence informed the BSA that they would ignore the national policy.[41] Daniel Gasparo, chief executive officer of the New York council of the BSA, asserted that the local New York Scout organizations do not discriminate based on sexual orientation.[42] Such statements of inclusion and nondiscrimination may be subject to monitoring and discipline by the national body of the BSA. But this is a result the Providence pack and troop are prepared to face; they refuse to enforce the antigay policy even if the national organization retaliates by terminating their charters.[43]

Individuals have taken action here too. Steven Spielberg resigned from the BSA advisory board in the wake of *Dale*.[44] Thousands of people—including Eagle Scouts—have signed a national petition urging the BSA to end its discrimination. You can join this effort. Indeed, we suggest that you pause for a moment, visit the web site of Scouting for All, and sign their online petition right now: http://www.scoutingforall.org/onlinepetition.html. Receiving disapproval—especially from former Scouts—undermines the organization's claims about the importance of the antigay policy to the scouting experience.[45] Indeed, even without active coordination, individual decision-makers seem to be steering clear of the Boy Scouts. According to *Newsweek* magazine, internal BSA documents show that Cub and Boy Scout membership dropped 4.5 percent in 2000—7.8 percent in the Northeast region of the United States—while membership rates in the same period increased for youth organizations that do not discriminate on the basis of sexual orientation (such as the Boys and Girls Clubs and the Girl Scouts).[46]

The BSA's response to all of this agitation has been to dig in its heels and resist the inclusion of gay men even more vehemently. On February 6, 2002, the BSA issued a press release announcing that "the national officers further agree that homosexual conduct is inconsistent with the traditional values espoused in the Scout Oath and Law and that an avowed homosexual cannot serve as a role model for the values of the Oath and Law."[47] In support of the ultimate resolution, the BSA cited the following finding.

> WHEREAS, the national officers reaffirm that, as a national organization whose very reason for existence is to instill and reinforce values in youth, the BSA's values cannot be subject to local option choices, but must be the same in every unit.

This resolution sends a strong signal to the local chapters in New York and Rhode Island: inclusive policies will not be tolerated.

James Dale's challenge to his exclusion from the Boy Scouts forced the BSA to publicly disclose its official policy of discrimination on the basis of sexual orientation. Indeed, some organizations have cited the Boy Scout policy's newfound notoriety as the factor forcing them to pull their support for the BSA. As one Broward County school board member explained:

> The Scouts wanted to make a statement and that they did by pushing this point to the Supreme Court. By so doing, they put us on notice of something that we were unaware of previously. Had it not gone to court, had it not gotten the publicity that it did, we may never have known about it and may not be having this discussion. . . . If we have no knowledge . . . we can't take action.[48]

The Boy Scouts' policy has thus become a matter of public record, and individuals and corporations can now act on complete information. But what about the organizations whose exclusionary policies remain more obscure? If anything, one would expect that they've learned to avoid such publicity, and they find themselves able to hide their policies.

The U.S. Supreme Court in *Dale* made it pretty easy for an organization to invoke a "message" important enough to displace a state's antidiscrimination statute. Even rather ambiguous statements publicized after litigation has arisen will apparently suffice. This raises the troubling possibility, as Professor Kenji Yoshino has argued, that an organization can simply opt out of an antidiscrimination statute anytime it wants. Moreover, because courts are now instructed to adopt a deferential approach—taking organizations at their word regarding their own discriminatory aims, goals, or philosophies—the possibility of after-the-fact invocation of discriminatory "messages" is particularly troubling.

While the Court's decision in the *Dale* case does acknowledge the state's interests to squelch discrimination, it does not find that those interests can justify trampling a private organization's First Amendment rights to associate with whomever it wants to. Specifically, the Court held that "the First Amendment prohibits the State from imposing such a requirement through the application of its public accommodations law."[49] So, clearly, the state can't use its public accommodation law to force private organizations to be inclusive. But the Court's holding does not preclude the state from trying other ways to further nondiscrimination, and the state clearly has other options.

In our Informed Association Statute, silence is a covenant not to discriminate. That is, if you join an organization and it doesn't mention anything about discrimination, then members would be safe in assuming that the organization would not discriminate against anyone. In fact, this is what most people today assume when they join most organizations, and what most Boy Scouts assumed before the *Dale* case. To discriminate, organizations would have to affirmatively "opt out" of this covenant by adequately informing their membership of just how and against whom they planned to discriminate.

Since this is a proposal for a new law, and because we're lawyers, we want to briefly address the constitutionality of such a statute. Certainly nothing in the *Dale* Court's holding would suggest that an organization would be constitutionally barred from affirmatively opting to be bound by a nondiscrimination duty. As long as the law is a default rule, the organization under either an opt-in or an opt-out regime would have the freedom to choose whether or not to be bound by a duty not to discriminate. And if an opt-in statute would be constitutional, there is nothing in the Court's opinion (or logic) to suggest that an opt-out statute would be per se unconstitutional.

Indeed, the state in this context, as in others, must as a matter of logical necessity give meaning to silence.[50] Either organizational silence means that the organization retains the right to discriminate, or organizational silence means that the organization does not retain the right to discriminate. Defining the legal meaning of organizational silence is necessary not only as a means of defining the implicit contract between an organization and its members, but also as a way of reducing fraud. Organizations that dupe individuals into joining "under false pretenses"—even implicit pretenses—are guilty of fraud in the inducement of a contract. The state is well within its rights to discourage such reliance-inducing deceit.

Clearly, the opt-out procedure would have to avoid "materially interfer[ing] with the ideas that the organization sought to express."[51] We do not require that the organization register its policy on discrimination publicly with the state or reveal its membership list. We only require that it inform its potential members and that it receive from them an acknowledgment that they are choosing to associate with "an organization that retains the right to discriminate."[52] Nothing in the acknowledgment would require that all members agree with the discriminatory policy (or potential policy),[53] only that they are choosing to associate with an organization that retains the right to adopt such a policy.[54]

For people who prefer to join organizations that discriminate on the basis of sexual orientation, the statute also has some benefits. The *lack* of opt-out disclosure and acknowledgment would signal to potential members that the organization submits itself to the general nondiscrimination rule, alerting people who would be distressed to learn after-the-fact that the organization they have joined *refuses* to discriminate on the basis of sexual orientation.

Unlike a public disclosure filed with the secretary of state,[55] the private acknowledgment approach would give organizations greater control over whether and how they express their views to the general public.[56] Under our proposal, the state would not have access to the organization's statement of its core values, nor would it speculate about the likelihood of damage to those core values if the organization were prevented from discriminating. Our statute would give an organization substantive carte blanche to claim that discrimination is or might be necessary in order to preserve the organization's First Amendment rights of expressive association. Kenji Yoshino's concern, that "the Court . . . simply took the Scouts at its word, according 'deference to an association's assertions regarding the nature of its expression,'" would go unaddressed.[57]

But our statute would reduce one of the negative consequences of such deference identified by Yoshino, that keeping an organization's "message" secret can lead individuals to "invest in an organization they would not have joined had they known of the 'message.'"[58] The statute would accomplish something important: people thinking about joining an organization would receive information at the time when it is most useful. "Point of purchase" disclosure often will have a higher salience and impact on a negotiation than information that comes long before or long after the moment of decision. In some ways, our proposal in this chapter is similar to chapter 4's Fair Employment Mark. In that chapter, we tried to give potential consumers point-of-purchase information about particular sellers that did not discriminate. Here, we try to give potential members point-of-purchase information about particular organizations that have retained the right to discriminate.

If you fear that an informed association law will suppress people's rights of association, keep in mind that favoring undisclosed policies (as the Court in *Dale* did) can also burden individuals' associational rights. Individuals may be reluctant to associate with organizations unless they can credibly ascertain that the organizations have not adopted abhorrent policies. Requiring organizations to disclose to their members when they opt out of generally applicable civil rights law may thus spur more association. Members need not fear waking up to learn that they have been supporting a discriminatory organization for years.

The signed acknowledgment of the disclosure is particularly important. As in other contract contexts, written acknowledgments provide evidence that disclosure was both made and received. In the normal contract setting (for example, a bank or car dealership), we expect most people to go forward and sign a form acknowledging disclosure. With organizations that retain the right to discriminate, in contrast, we expect that some people would not be willing to sign a statement that they are choosing to associate with an organization that discriminates against gays and lesbians. Just as Steven Spielberg was not able to continue associating with the Boy Scouts, we believe that many people who currently associate with such groups would be unwilling to put pen to paper.

When applied to an organization like the Boy Scouts, an informed association statute would raise some difficult, interesting questions. How meaningful, after all, is the disclosure of a potentially discriminatory policy when most of an organization's members are children? Few if any eight-year-old boys joining the Cub Scouts could understand a statement by the BSA that it excludes gay men from membership, or that it does so in order to uphold rules requiring Scouts to be "clean" and "morally straight."

The probable response to this problem is that the acknowledgment (like other consent forms) would need to be signed by the boys' parents rather than the boys themselves. The parents would decide whether or not to associate with a potentially discriminatory organization. Parents and children might disagree, but parents often overrule their children's wishes "for their own good." Like soda pop and Pokémon, the Boy Scouts might be chosen by some children but vetoed by their parents. For other children, the Boy Scouts might be more like spinach or a good night's sleep: something the kids would avoid but the parents insist upon. Indeed, expressive parental decision-making can cut both ways: supporters of gay rights might pull their boys from scouting despite the boys' ardent wishes to join.

Personalizing the Informed Association Approach

At this point, many readers may wonder whether this chapter has any personal relevance: "This informed association statute is fine in theory, but what does it tell me about the ways *I* can promote gay rights?" We've already mentioned a web site where you can petition the Boy Scouts to end its official policy of discrimination. And in the notes to this chapter, we've included a model informed association statute for which you could lobby in your home state.

We think that informed association acknowledgments can be powerful at the personal level as well. Many discriminatory organizations would not qualify as "public accommodations" and would fall outside the reach of our statute, but we think they should still own up to their views and behavior. If they're going to exclude people, then they ought to let their members know, "This is what we stand for." To these groups, you could still experimentally apply the notion of informed association. To see how this might be, take a personal inventory. Do you currently associate with organizations that have explicitly discriminatory policies? If you are a member of a house of worship, chances are you do. For example, we are members of an Episcopalian parish. Though we are working with others in the church to open the marriage rite to same-sex couples, we are pained by the church's current refusal to sanction such blessings officially. In this sense, we not only associate with a discriminatory organization, we force our children to attend as well (no doubt violating our own parenting "do's and don'ts" in chapter 2). As residents of the United States, we all are forced to associate with state and federal governments that discriminate, most notably in marriage and the military. We may not be able to disassociate fully from discriminatory institutions, but we must nonetheless take responsibility for the choices we do make.

Consider, for example, the choice we faced a few years back. A student of Jennifer's who was a military officer in training invited us to a formal spring dance at the local military base. Normally, we would have accepted. But it occurred to us that this dance was one where gay and lesbian service members would not be allowed to dance with their preferred partners (indeed, it seemed unlikely that they would even invite their preferred partners). For these gay and lesbian service members, something as innocent as a dance might be "telling" under DADT and could trigger an investigation leading to discharge.

We chose not to go. This was not costless—Jennifer genuinely liked and enjoyed this student, and would like to have accepted the invitation. It wasn't easy to explain our basis for declining the invitation without sounding sanctimonious; at this, we may very well have failed. But the experience sensitized us to the fact that we volunteer to participate in discriminatory institutions more frequently than we might think. Even if you don't go to church regularly, chances are you have attended marriage ceremonies that were formally unavailable to same-sex couples.

As you complete your personal inventory, think about the institutions that you support from time to time. Also consider whether your organizations engage in informal or de facto discrimination. Is your country club or condo or employer more likely to reject a qualified applicant who is gay or lesbian? If your written inventory is still empty, you should probably think again. It is very hard to walk through life at the beginning of the twenty-first century without associating from time to time with some organization that engages in formal or informal forms of sexual orientation discrimination.

Now that you've compiled your inventory (however long it might be), for each item on the list, prepare the same sort of acknowledgment that we proposed for members of the Boy Scouts. Now, sign it. It's not easy, is it? Even though your acknowledgment is not going to be kept on file by anyone else, we bet you'll have difficulty putting pen to paper and fessing up that you are voluntarily choosing to associate with a discriminatory organization. We know how you feel: our church discriminates, and we voluntarily worship there. And though we can draft that last sentence on a word processor, we have been unwilling to actually sign the very acknowledgment that we propose in this chapter. For us there is a palpable shame in both signing and being unwilling to sign. Shame can be disabling, even paralyzing.

But shame can also be productive if it spurs us to action—if it motivates us to change the conditions that embarrass us. In this way, the acknowledgment of informed association represents a new tool for change.

Consider again our church. It is a warm community that is explicitly welcoming, where gay and lesbian parishioners are valued, embraced, and woven into the fabric of the place. What would it mean for our church to take informed association seriously? Well, at a minimum, it might mean that the church has a responsibility to inform potential members that it discriminates against same-sex couples. How would it word such a disclosure? Try to imagine an announcement in the church bulletin that simultaneously welcomed new members and warned them that the parish discriminates against gays and lesbians when it comes to marriage. Unthinkable. Emphasizing the ways in which the institution falls short could effectively prevent it from ever reaching its ideal. Instead, the announcement might emphasize that the parish welcomes all people regardless of sexual orientation, that it is actively working toward inclusion and equality within the church, but that it is regrettably forbidden by the diocese from marrying same-sex couples. A parish may not have the power to stop discriminating, but it can and should make clear to potential members what they're in for and what the parish's hopes and goals are.

Furthermore, in trying to imagine how such a disclosure would be worded, it becomes clear that when an organization discloses a discriminatory policy, it is likely to feel a need to explain why it is maintaining the policy. Indeed, this thought experiment leads to the possibility that an organization might even *apologize* for its discrimination. You might respond that if the organization's members felt that guilty about the discrimination, they would simply end it. But organizations are often multilayered. Most members of our parish, for example, support gay rights *and* also feel bound by diocesan law. Apology is one way that people express their shame and regret, distance themselves from wrongful conduct, and send signals that they embrace norms inconsistent with that conduct.[59] Seen in this light, the amazing thing is that liberal parishes have not apologized for the wrong of their continuing discrimination.

The larger point here is that informed association is a neutral principle that might attract support from people who are not yet ready to rescind a formal policy of discrimination or break from a larger institution that imposes the policy. If you associate with an institution that discriminates against gay men and lesbians, you might work to make sure that it does so transparently. Potential members can then choose whether or not to join with full information. And, equally importantly, the organization itself would have to be clear where it stands and what, if anything, it hopes to do.

Informed association could thus be another step on the path toward equality. It generates movement because just the thought experiment of formulating appropriate disclosure leads toward the simple but radical steps of apology and compensation. A conversation about informed association may quickly evolve into a conversation about ending the discrimination itself.

Eschewing Silence

To bring his majority opinion in *Dale* to a close, Justice Rehnquist quoted Supreme Court justice Louis D. Brandeis (1856–1941) and underscored the importance of "discovery and spread of political truth" as First Amendment values. "Believing in the power of reason as applied through public discussion, [the Founders of this nation] *eschewed silence* coerced by law—the argument of force in its worst form."[60] The statute proposed in this chapter would promote the "spread of political truth." It would permit organizations and their members to "think as [they] will," but it would also require them to "speak as [they] think" rather than concealing their discriminatory policies.[61] Such an approach would protect the associational rights of people who want to join organizations that discriminate as well as those who wish to avoid such organizations. If, as the Supreme Court suggests, the First Amendment effectively grants the Boy Scouts a license to discriminate, the Informed Association statute would at least force the Boy Scouts to post that license prominently for its members to see.[62] Members and potential members would then be free to do as they saw fit.

And once an organization has disclosed the necessary information, it needn't go out of its way to make antigay statements or continually reaffirm its intention to discriminate on the basis of sexual orientation. Potential members can look to the safe-harbor disclosure as the definitive statement of the organization's policies on the topic and decide whether or not to associate based on that statement. This prevents an organization from having it both ways: claiming an intent to discriminate as defense against subsequent liability under the state accommodation statute, but simultaneously embracing nondiscrimination norms as a recruitment device.[63] It also might dampen public antigay rhetoric, because organizations that have complied with the safe-harbor provision would not be pressured to continually declare their antigay policies.

When informed that they belong to a discriminatory organization, some straight people would no doubt heave a sigh of relief or utter words of strong approval. Others might mount a challenge to the discriminatory policy only to find that the majority of the organization's members support it. Indeed, in response to an attack on the policy, the organization might take reinforcing action, for example by converting an otherwise informal norm into a codified rule.[64] The "push back" effect could polarize the membership of the organization, actually worsening the position of its closeted gay or lesbian members by bringing antigay sentiment to the surface. The subsequent exit of people opposing antigay policies could make dialogue and reform more difficult.

On the other hand, supporters of gay rights can't even begin to attempt reform if they don't know that an organization is discriminatory in the first place. If members of an organization learn of an antigay policy only after the fact, as many members and supporters of the Boy Scouts did, working for change from within the organization is difficult. By the time the antigay policy comes to light, the organization may have committed itself in ways that make compromise difficult. If people know about antigay policies before a case or controversy arises, they can work to repudiate the policies through inclusive, even incremental, discussions within the organization. Therefore, the Informed Association Statute should be viewed as a mechanism that enables not only exit from discriminatory organizations but also dialogue and reform within the organizations.

Inevitably, some battles for reform would be lost. But no organization should be permitted to invoke First Amendment rights to facilitate the extraction of time, energy, and financial support from members who, if fully informed of the organization's discriminatory policies, would choose to devote those resources elsewhere.

Renounce or Share?

This chapter asks a seemingly simple question: Can it ever be ethical to take a benefit that is invidiously denied others? To a question couched this way, the appropriate answer seems to be "no." Few of us would advise a friend (or a child) to accept a scholarship that was only open to whites. If you are white, would you drink from a whites-only water fountain? Of course not. But at the same time, many of us take benefits that are unfairly denied others. Bill Clinton took a Rhodes Scholarship that was only offered to men. In 1982 Ian accepted a Yale scholarship that was only available to males from Jackson County, Missouri. And many, many heterosexuals voluntarily accept the benefits of marriage that are invidiously denied to their gay friends and family. We have done so ourselves. This chapter is an attempt to reconcile this conflict.

Chapter 7 focused on informed association as a precursor to action. As with Alcoholics Anonymous and other twelve-step programs, first you must acknowledge that you have a problem: "I am choosing to associate with an institution that discriminates." But the discussion in that chapter suggested a variety of ways that people might respond to this knowledge. Some might cut their ties (refuse figuratively or literally to sign the acknowledgment); others might work for change within the institution (calling for apologies, compensation, and nondiscrimination). This is the classic dichotomy between strategies of "exit" and "voice."[1]

In this chapter, we explore factors that might lead straight allies to choose one strategy over the other. In chapter 9, we'll suggest *how* you should use your voice, which rests on the core idea of qualified deference to the victims of discrimination. But this chapter will focus on *how much* of your voice is owed. We suggest a way of thinking about how much of your time and money should be devoted to the cause of change. Our take-home message is that beneficiaries of discrimination (people who do not exit but retain the benefits of continued association) owe a qualified duty of what we'll call *pro rata sharing*.

The voice versus exit conundrum that we tackle here arises in virtually every context of discrimination. Is it moral

To join the Boy Scouts when they refuse to appoint gay scout masters

To join the military when they refuse to allow openly gay soldiers

To attend a church that refuses to ordain gay priests

To take a job from an employer that refuses to give equal employment benefits

To adopt a child from a state that bars same-sex parents from adopting, or

To join a club that refuse to admit gay members?[2]

We'll first outline our theory of pro rata sharing, and then we'll apply this rather abstract theory to the concrete question of whether it is moral for heterosexuals to marry in a world that denies equal recognition to same-sex couples. An alternative version of the question is whether heterosexuals should feel free to marry, but surrender some of the benefits—by devoting some of their time and money to the cause of change. We conclude that reasonable people may differ on the better course. And indeed, the movement for equality may best be served by people adopting a mixture of "voice" and "exit" strategies. But one thing is crystal clear. Silent acceptance of discriminatory benefits is not a morally acceptable alternative.

Responding to Inequity: Two Ethical Approaches

Over millennia, moral philosophers have developed frameworks to guide decision making in situations like this one. Although important themes distinguish one approach from another, one can crudely divide these ethical standards into two categories, based upon the extent to which they highlight the importance of the consequences. Deontological theories of ethics focus on the moral rightness of action as an end in itself.[3] This approach would tend to counsel toward exit.[4] Accepting the benefits invidiously denied others is aesthetically abhorrent, regardless of whether declining the benefit makes a difference in real-world conditions. We wouldn't drink at a whites-only fountain even if no one else was around to see.

163

In contrast, consequentialist rationales, as the label implies, attend to the consequences that flow from action. This is sometimes categorized as *teleological* (or end-driven). Teleological views could also encompass—but need not be limited to—utilitarianism, where the desired end is creating a better state of the world or achieving human happiness. Here, cost-benefit analysis of the effects of a decision would be the central concern.[5]

In particular settings, either voice or exit could make sense under consequentialism. Individual or group boycotts might put pressure on organizations to end a policy of discrimination. But giving voice to your concerns might also be effective. Explaining to others in the organization why the discrimination is wrong and why it has hurtful consequences can powerfully persuade. Which strategy will prove more effective is a horse race.

The consequentialist would account for the impact of a particular action on both the likelihood of causing an end of discrimination and on social welfare with and without change. Particular action—voice versus exit—would be preferred the greater the predicted chance of effecting change, the greater the benefits that would flow from that change, and the greater the costs if no change occurs. Some consequentialists rail against exit strategies, arguing that they have no impact on the probability of change and only force a needless sacrifice on the people who exit. But thoroughgoing consequentialism should also take into account the potential distaste that people experience in associating with discriminatory organizations, the happiness of excluded people who see others standing in solidarity, and the possible sense of loss of nonexiters when they see their friends exit.

Thoroughgoing consequentialism is often a difficult task because it is hard to weigh these cross-cutting effects and assess the impact of action on change. From one perspective, individual action in large groups is rarely likely to effect change. But individual voices can persuade others, and individual exiting can lead to cascade effects of exodus (the so-called tipping point). To assess the effect of voice, you must also realistically evaluate how much time you are likely to give to the cause of change. Discrimination against gays may be invidious, but spending all of your time working on change is unrealistic. While such devotion might be very effective, most of us are only going to spend a small part of our lives on this issue (more of our lives than we used to, if this book has its hoped-for effect). A consequentialist should compare the impact of exit versus the impact of *realistic* voice.

Pro Rata Sharing

Silence is immoral, but devoting your entire life to a cause is impractical. So how much voice is enough? Here we can help. We propose that people who choose not to exit and instead accept the benefits of associating with a discriminatory organization should be guided by a principle of *partial* or *pro rata* sharing.

We think that if you take a benefit that is invidiously denied others, you are duty-bound to give up part of the benefit. Your first impulse might edge toward full disgorgement—indeed a person poised on exit might be disinclined to retain any of the benefits of discrimination. But pro rata sharing, if adopted by all beneficiaries, would (at least conceptually) extinguish the monetary discrepancies wrought by discrimination. If all the beneficiaries surrender this prorated amount, their benefit net of the amount surrendered would equal the moneys available to the victims of discrimination.

Here's a simple monetary (and therefore quantifiable) example. If a person takes a one-hundred-thousand-dollar college scholarship that is invidiously denied to 20 percent of qualified beneficiaries, we believe that at a minimum the person should give up 20 percent of the scholarship. In this example, there are four beneficiaries for every victim. If the four beneficiaries each surrender twenty thousand dollars, then both the beneficiaries and the victim end up with a nondiscriminatory allocation of eighty thousand dollars.

Pro rata sharing is also an attractive moral precept because it makes the moral duty literally proportional to the magnitude of the harm. It would be bizarre to require people to give up all the benefits of a scholarship, regardless of whether 1 percent or 90 percent of the qualified beneficiaries were unfairly excluded; under our scheme, there's some proportionality.[6] Pro rata sharing represents a kind of individualized insurance against social discrimination.

Of course, in the real world, many beneficiaries will not give up any part of their benefit. One reaction to this kind of shirking might be to share up to the point where your net benefit is the same as the worst-off victim. In many contexts, this will lead to surrendering virtually all of one's benefits. But there is an argument for sticking with the initial pro rata formula. Pro rata sharing makes up for your individual contribution to inequity. If other individuals fail to make up for their own contribution to inequity, that might be seen as their problem, not yours. This is especially so if the pro rata sharing idea is viewed merely as a minimum requirement. Even people who exit (shunning the benefits of association) may still feel called to give their time and money to the cause of equality. But for present purposes, we view these additional efforts as above and beyond.

It may seem odd that while we began by talking about "voice" and "working for change," our examples are focused on money and redistributing benefits to the victims of discrimination. But this slippage is not as great as it first appears. Your time and your money can both help bring about change. Sometimes writing a check to Lambda or Love Makes a Family can be just as efficacious as speaking up and literally exercising your voice.[7] Campaign finance law teaches us that there is a close connection between money and speech.[8]

The sharing principle gives you a way to start thinking about how much you owe in total. It becomes a subsidiary question whether you pay off this moral duty via expenditures of your time, contributions to advocacy organizations, or compensation to victims. Indeed, the next chapter will advise that we be guided by (actually or hypothetically) asking victims how they think the surrendered sums would best serve. If you have a duty to share one thousand dollars and your leisure time is worth fifty dollars an hour, let a representative of the victims' group decide whether they would prefer twenty hours of your time or a one-thousand-dollar contribution (or some combination thereof).

This principle naturally follows the call in chapter 7 for a personal inventory. There we asked you to set down the ways that you benefit from associating with discriminatory organizations. Now we are asking you to monetize those benefits—to assign dollar values even to intangible advantages. Admittedly, this is not always easy to do. Many of the freedoms and protections we take for granted are, when we stop to think about them, priceless. But consider: how much would you have been willing to pay to retain the right to marry the person you love? How do you value the ability to hold hands or kiss on the street without threat of being beaten (or kicked out of the military)? If 3 percent of the people who are otherwise qualified for these benefits are invidiously denied them,[9] you should think about giving 3 percent of this value in some form of advocacy or compensation.

The principle of pro rata sharing is far from self-actuating. One needs to answer a host of questions—identifying the arenas where one is a beneficiary, determining how much one is benefiting, learning the percentage of otherwise qualified beneficiaries who are being invidiously excluded, and finally choosing the form that sharing should take. But even if it is impossible to apply precisely, the idea of pro rata sharing is attractive. It calls for intermediate sacrifice on the part of the beneficiaries of discrimination—instead of the all-or-nothing demands of the unrealistic or the uninterested.

Now we can turn to the question, "Is it moral to marry in a world that prohibits gays and lesbians from marrying?" Until recently, this question was almost never asked. While people saw the problem of accepting other types of discriminatory benefits, few people who married before 1990 wondered whether it might be immoral to marry when gays and lesbians could not. Indeed, Ian remembers putting this precise question into an anonymous question box at an "Engaged Encounter" seminar he endured in 1993 as a prerequisite to marrying Jennifer in the Roman Catholic Church. When the question was later read to the group of engaged couples, it was met by prolonged silence. Finally, a septuagenarian Jesuit priest responded, "The church doesn't prohibit gays and lesbians from marrying." (He meant lesbians can marry men, and gay men can marry women.) He and others at this Silicon Valley event could not conceive of this as a moral question.

Fortunately, things have changed. In April 2004, Randy Cohen, "The Ethicist" for the *New York Times Magazine,* fielded the same basic question:

> My partner and I have discussed marriage . . . (we are heterosexual). We believe that gays and lesbians should have the same rights as heterosexuals. Why should we be privileged with the rights and protections of marriage when others are being denied? Is it ethical for us to walk down the aisle?[10]

Cohen's response was reasonable, but far too one-sided. He unequivocally rejected the exit strategy.

> I share your opinion of the marriage laws but not your conclusion that you must defer your wedding until utopia arrives. Many who sincerely denounce the inequities of our society inevitably profit from them. If you're a man who works at a job where the lack of flex time or on-site day care disadvantages women who do the bulk of child care, you benefit from sexism. If you're a middle-class white person who attended a decent high school and then applied to college, you had a huge advantage over a poor kid or an African-American from an inferior high school. It is impossible to lead an immaculate life in an imperfect world. The task is not merely to insulate yourself from being a beneficiary of injustice—even if that were possible—but to combat injustice.
>
> Were there an organized boycott of marriage as a way to reform the law, you should observe it. But without that, I see no point in your becoming refuseniks. Doing so would not influence the marriage laws. You would do better to lobby

your state and federal representatives and contribute money to freedom-tomarry.org or similar organizations. You should seek ways to bring about change, not just to make self-comforting gestures.

Cohen's response is certainly pragmatic, and suggests helpful steps supporters can take while the world persists in its "imperfect" stage. But is this enough? The flaw in Cohen's response is that it ignores nonconsequential approaches. Wouldn't the Ethicist refuse to drink at a whites-only drinking fountain? Or would he also reject this act of denial as merely a "self-comforting gesture?"

The salience of the deontological concern can be heard explicitly in a growing number of what Eric Baard in the *Village Voice* has termed "hetero holdouts"—different-sexed partners who refuse to marry in a world where same-sex marriages are forbidden.[11] For example, Andrea Ayvazian, the dean of religious life at Mount Holyoke College, has chosen with her partner, Michael Klare, not to marry because they "don't want to be part of an institution that's actively discriminatory."[12] Similarly, Mame McCutchin, a female technology professional in a relationship with male artist/webbie Kyril Mossin, draws more contemporary parallels to explain why they are not marrying: "I wouldn't join a country club that excluded blacks or Jews."[13]

Some people might reject the country club analogy because there are many clubs but only one institution of marriage. But increasingly this is not the case. People desiring a religious ceremony could join the Unitarian Universalist marriage club, which, unlike the Roman Catholic club, does not discriminate. On the civil side, heterosexual allies can now join the Massachusetts marriage club, which unlike Connecticut or Utah clubs, does not discriminate (not, at least, in summer 2004).

In a country where most states have unequal marriage laws, Massachusetts's reform creates new choices—for both the victims and the beneficiaries of discrimination. Now that it is possible to marry in a jurisdiction that does not discriminate on the basis of sexual orientation, the question isn't whether it is moral to marry at all, but rather whether it is moral for heterosexuals to marry in a discriminating state.

Cast your mind back a few decades. Suppose you were living in Virginia when the state still prohibited interracial marriage. Even if you wanted to marry someone of the same race, wouldn't you consider traveling to a neighboring state that did not discriminate? Now every heterosexual couple that wants to marry must face the same question. In fact, heterosexuals (unlike same-sex couples) can marry in a nondiscriminating jurisdiction without risking nonrecognition back in their home state.

Indulge us as we revert to an old law professor trick: let us start with the smallest question. Wouldn't you at least be willing to cross the street to avoid marrying in a discriminatory jurisdiction? This hypothetical may not be so unworldly. It is not unfathomable that some states will adopt "home rule" on the question of same-sex marriage. Just as with other contentious social issues in the past (divorce, gambling, drinking), a state may see fit to give individual counties the authority to decide whether to be "wet" or "dry."[14] In a state that has a checkerboard pattern, heterosexuals may literally have a choice of crossing the street to avoid discriminatory jurisdictions.

Or even without crossing the street, it may become possible for heterosexuals to take the benefits of marriage without participating in discrimination. Imagine a state that had civil unions as an alternative to marriage for both same-sex and different-sex couples and conferred on these unions the same rights and responsibilities given to marriages.[15] What possible excuse could a heterosexual couple give for *not* entering a civil union rather than a civil marriage?[16] Would the word *marriage* be so important that the ally would bypass the nondiscriminatory equivalent? The case for boycotting civil marriage would grow even stronger.[17]

The unwillingness to participate in discrimination as a categorical imperative has also had increasing salience for celebrants. The person who performs weddings—the priest, the rabbi, or the city official—might also "refuse to marry." And some have. About a dozen clergy from Connecticut and Massachusetts in 2003 refused to sign marriage licenses for heterosexual couples until unions between same-sex couples are legally recognized.[18] As explained by Reverend Fred Small of the First Church Unitarian in Littleton, Massachusetts, "We continue to marry people, joyfully, in a religious ceremony, but heterosexual couples must have someone else sign the license."[19] Here the motive is not to insulate oneself from the tainted benefits of discrimination, but to avoid facilitating the discrimination itself. There are always two ways to end disparate treatment; in a world where same-sex couples can't marry, refusing to legally marry everyone does the trick.

The nonmarriage movement is not limited to lefty UU ministers. In March 2004, Benton County, Oregon, stopped issuing licenses to everyone. The county had earlier planned to start issuing marriage licenses to same-sex couples (another way to end discrimination), but reversed its earlier decision and decided instead to refuse to issue marriage licenses to anyone—heterosexual or homosexual—until state courts decide the issue.[20]

But Will It Ultimately Lead to Equal Marriage Rights?

None of these deontological impulses, on their face, respond to the Ethicist's concerns. Cohen's exclusive focus on consequentialism parallels the thinking of Representative Barney Frank: "Too often people on the left want what they call 'direct action' because it's more satisfying to them in some way. . . . It's well-intentioned but not helpful. When two very good heterosexual people refuse to get married, I don't see how that puts pressure on politicians."[21]

Yet even from a consequential perspective, a stronger case can be made for the strategy of individually boycotting marriage. Even if it doesn't put pressure on politicians to change the law, the act of refusing to marry might have positive effects. It dramatically signals your solidarity with gay men and lesbians—showing your friends and acquaintances that you are willing to absorb some of the same costs and inconveniences that same-sex couples must bear outside legal marriage.

As chapter 5 discussed, heterosexual people at times can promote gay rights by ambiguating—by resisting the urge always and everywhere to distinguish themselves from gay men and lesbians. Refusing to marry is in a small way ambiguating because it rejects a marker of heterosexuality. When people who identify as heterosexual are willing to be "mistaken" as gay or lesbian, and have created this possibility by giving up some of the privileges and institutions that serve to distinguish gay from straight, the cause of gay rights is in some ways promoted.[22]

Conceptually, the refusal of heterosexuals to marry also could, contrary to Frank's assertion, put pressure on politicians to legalize same-sex marriage. Refusing to marry might put "an economic dent in the wedding industry" reducing expenditures not just on marriage licenses, but on wedding receptions, bridal dresses, photographers, and honeymoon excursions.[23] A movement of heterosexual holdouts could incentivize the wedding industry to more actively embrace equality as a mechanism to revitalize sales.

This is especially true if *heterosexuals who marry* respond to a state's legalization of same-sex marriages. Mitt Romney said he did not want Massachusetts to become the Las Vegas of "gay marriages." But legalizing same-sex marriages could also make Massachusetts the Las Vegas of straight ally marriages—as "hetero holdouts" travel to the commonwealth to avoid marrying in a discriminatory jurisdiction.

Heterosexuals' refusal to marry may even create a noneconomic motive for legislators who think that marriage is an essential social institution. Legislators who genuinely want to promote marriage because of the stability they believe it brings to family and social life should be troubled by heterosexual couples' refusal to participate in marriage. If the group of refuseniks became too large, even legislators who initially opposed same-sex marriage as undermining heterosexual marriage might grudgingly support legalization as a way to bring heterosexuals back to the institution. Thus, while Representative Frank and others view a marriage boycott as pointless, a mass refusal like the civil rights boycotts of the past might in fact highlight the political and nonpolitical factors supporting equality.

At the moment, however, it seems inconceivable that a mass boycott movement will arise. As argued above in chapter 3, there are sound structural reasons why buycotts are likely to be more effective than boycotts. We agree that refusing to marry is not strongly supported as a method to bring about law reform.

But what seems implausible today may not seem so implausible tomorrow. Few people in 2003 would have predicted the dizzying pace of positive decentralized change that has already taken place on the marriage front—from San Francisco to New Paltz, from Massachusetts to Oregon. Most heterosexuals weren't even spotting the ethical concerns five years ago. Now there is a blossoming—dare we say—movement of refusals. Individual actions, especially early on, can sometimes create ripple effects and cascades. We shouldn't be overconfident in predicting the impact of these individual acts or how far this nascent movement will evolve.

It is true that some heterosexuals may have ignored the deontological impulse—the abhorrence of taking a benefit that is unfairly denied others—because they don't consider discrimination against gays and lesbians to be as serious a concern as discrimination based on race or sex. Other heterosexuals feel that they don't have to make this sacrifice because the gay rights movement hasn't asked them to. Remember, even the reassuring Ethicist column advised, "Were there an organized boycott of marriage as a way to reform the law, you should observe it."

But as it turns out, there already are gay activists who are calling on heterosexuals to boycott marriage. In 2000 after California's Proposition 22 against gay marriage was adopted, Eric Rofes, a professor of education at Humboldt State University, expressly called upon justice-minded heterosexual couples to boycott marriage until the institution is democratized. His manifesto pulls no punches.

> During a period when same-sex couples cannot marry, the taking of such vows by mixed-sex couples will increasingly be named for what it is: an act of willful participation in an institution that is neither democratic nor open to all. In the year 2000, heterosexuals getting married parallels Christians joining a club that excludes Jews, men working as partners in a law firm that has no female partners, or whites supporting the flying of the Confederate flag over public buildings intended to serve people of all races. No matter how one wishes to frame them, such choices are inherently ethical choices: participation in rituals and institutions that exclude sectors of society puts you on the side of discrimination and oppression. [It may be time] for true heterosexual allies to say NO to marriage until all people have equal access.[24]

Consistent with the metathesis of this book, Rofes advises: "Progressive heterosexual couples need to be organized by the queer community or by themselves."[25]

Rofes is not alone in demanding more from heterosexual allies. In his *Village Voice* article extolling the sacrifice of "heterosexual holdouts," Eric Baard also openly ridicules heterosexual celebrities who talk the talk of supporting gay rights but nonetheless get married.

> Can you really claim to support the rights of gays while you're buying into the institution that most painfully marginalizes gay couples? Recently married gay-icons Margaret Cho, Megan Mullally, and Madonna apparently see no hypocrisy in this. Celebrity heterosexual spokespeople for gay rights are happy to join gay marches but happier still to do the wedding march straight into government benefits and legitimization of their relationships.[26]

It seems both possible and reasonable that an increasing number of gay men and lesbians will feel some insult and hurt when heterosexual friends marry into a club that blatantly excludes them.

Indeed, a central moment for insult is the wedding invitation. If even 3 percent of the invitation list is gay or lesbian, and forty people attend the average wedding, then the majority of weddings are attended by at least one gay or lesbian person. How do gay people feel about being invited to celebrate such events?

Does Anyone Here Know of a Reason Why
These Two Should Not Be Married?

A friend of ours who is a lesbian once confided,

> You know, it's not always easy for me to sit through the weddings of my college classmates. [My partner] and I have been together longer than some of these couples, and we're committing to each other for life, too. But do we get to celebrate it in this public way? Do we get support from our families and friends for our relationship? [My partner] often hasn't even been invited along with me. Sometimes, I don't know . . . It just hurts, you know?

Even though this woman, like many gay men and lesbian women, would never think of raising the issue with her marrying heterosexual friends, she privately harbored feelings of disquiet and pain.

For others, the feelings take a decidedly more negative turn. Professor Rofes, for example, with characteristic bluntness opines,

> These days, when I receive an invitation to the marriage of heterosexual friends, family members, or students, I am filled with outrage. What nerve! Sending an invitation to me (and, often, my lover) with no reference to the fact that I am being asked to participate as an observer in an event in which I legally am not permitted to be a central participant! No note acknowledging the disparity and injustice, no sheepish apology for participating in an institution of segregation, no phone call checking-in about the politics of it all.[27]

Here we see the victim's perspective on a topic we discussed in the last chapter. In chapter 7, we suggested that progressive parishes bound to discriminate by the religious powers that be should publicly acknowledge their discrimination—and that this acknowledgment would naturally lead to apology. Professor Rofes wants invitations to acknowledge the discrimination, and this leads him naturally to expect an apology as well.

Indeed, Professor Rofes goes still further and calls on gays and straight allies to boycott *attending* discriminatory weddings.

> It may be time for queers to stop letting heterosexuals off the hook! They embrace marriage uncritically only because we let them! And they will continue to be blind to the politics of engagements, marriage, and weddings until they are forced to see them as segregated rituals and institutions that must be challenged, undermined, and transformed. Lesbian, gay, bisexual, and transgender

(LGBT) people and our allies may be ready to take direct action by refusing wedding invitations and articulating our reasons loudly.[28]

Marriage is a decision people make only once in their lifetimes (if they are lucky), but choosing whether or not to attend is something that we face repeatedly throughout our lives. Seen from this perspective, the strategy of renouncing marriage is not just a choice about whether heterosexuals themselves marry, it is a choice about whether they will participate in other people's marriages as well.

One might think that the legalization of same-sex marriage in some jurisdictions would reduce the pain and resentment that gays and lesbians feel about being invited to heterosexual marriages. But a heterosexual's choice to marry in a discriminatory state even as nondiscriminatory options become more readily available may exacerbate the negative feelings.

Of course, not all gays and lesbians harbor ambivalent feelings about heterosexual marriages. The story of Esera Tuaolo, "a 6-foot-3, 300-pound Samoan-Hawaiian former NFL defensive tackle who played for the Packers and Vikings, and ultimately played in the Super Bowl for the Falcons," is particularly poignant.[29] In his rookie season, this youngest of eight children of an impoverished family of banana-plantation workers took his newfound cash and bought his widowed mother something she'd never had: a wedding ring. He, like Cohen and Frank, expressly rejects the idea of calling upon heterosexuals not to marry. When told about examples of heterosexual couples who have declined to marry in this era of de jure discrimination, Tuaolo responded:

> That is one of the sweetest sacrifices I've ever heard of, but to ask someone to do that for you is asking too much. I wouldn't shun it away if someone came up to me and said that's what they're doing. [But we] have other ways to fight the fight and create a better world for us and everybody. I wouldn't go and ask my niece not to get married because of this.[30]

Even though Tuaolo parts company with Rofes in calling for an ally boycott, he certainly isn't offended by the idea.

The takeaway point for heterosexuals is one of simple sensitivity. Your gay and lesbian friends may not express them, but they will almost surely harbor a mixture of emotions—ranging from joy to deep ambivalence to pain and outright anger—when invited to a wedding. We can't imagine a priest's semirhetorical question, "Does anyone know a reason why these two may not be married?" actually eliciting this response: "because this rite

174

is invidiously denied same-sex couples." When asked to "speak now or forever hold your peace," most hold their peace. But that doesn't mean they aren't thinking about discrimination.

Alternatives to Renunciation

The foregoing discussion and the examples of actual refusals to marry by heterosexual couples, ministers, and government officials show that there are stronger arguments for the exit strategy than acknowledged in the "go ahead and marry" conclusions of Representative Frank and ethicist Cohen. But these stronger arguments may still not carry the day.

Strategies of renunciation can be counterproductive. Trying to promote tolerance and understanding with negative and divisive tactics can backfire. Refusing to attend a wedding can make the bride and groom intransigent. If you ask too much from your allies, they may turn on you. If the gay rights movement is going to play the "which side are you on" game, it needs to be careful that it doesn't draw a line at a place that will cause mass defection. If marrying means "you're not with us," then the movement will have precious few allies (and allies who are already married are unlikely to divorce just to make the political point).

There are some types of renunciation that no one supports. Perhaps boycotting marriage and weddings is not enough; why not also call on allies not to associate with people who are married? The renunciation strategy taken to the extreme tends toward a kind of ethical solipsism. Even Professor Rofes does not go this far.

So what, short of renouncing marriage and rejecting the wedding invitations of your friends and family, can serve as a guide to action? Our basic answer is to embrace the prior strategies of voice and pro rata sharing. Participants in marriages during this age of discrimination—whether they be heterosexual couples, celebrants, or attendees—should begin by acknowledging to themselves and others that they are choosing to participate in an institution that is invidiously closed to others. We recommend that you be particularly attuned to the personal here. Add a personal note to the invitation of your gay and lesbian friends. What should be in the note? Perhaps an apology—for marrying, when they cannot. An apology for marrying in a discriminatory church or discriminatory state, when you might have chosen nondiscriminating alternatives. Maybe an explanation as well ("We have decided to legally marry in Missouri—despite the fact that it discriminates—because we want to marry in the bedroom of Ian's bedridden mom," or, "We've decided to marry in the Catholic Church, because we want to be married by Jennifer's uncle who is a priest").

Or consider making a public statement of support—either as part of the service or as part of the surrounding festivities. One might include a prayer or toast specifically acknowledging the love and commitment of gay and lesbian couples who cannot marry. Imagine the power of giving your wedding attendants, "I support same-sex marriage" T-shirts. We know where you can buy some, cheap.[31]

You should also take seriously the duty of pro rata sharing. If you marry, you are duty bound to devote some combination of your time and money to work for change and compensate the victims of discrimination. As outlined above, the duty is not boundless. But at a minimum the value of your efforts should be no less than a pro rata share of your benefit. As Representative Frank suggested, you can begin by voting your preference. You can lobby your house of worship for change.

And as Cohen suggested, you can give money. As newlyweds, you might sign the Vacation Pledge and choose to honeymoon in whichever state is currently leading the legislative race for equality (we found that Vermont is particularly lovely in the spring). Indeed, simply asking that attendees consider making contributions to freedomtomarry.org sends a powerful positive message of support. Shouldn't at least 3 percent of wedding presents be channeled to the gay rights cause? Wedding guests can make such gifts on their own initiative, even if the bride and groom don't ask. Instead of boycotting the wedding nuptials, an invited guest might make a small contribution to the Human Rights Campaign in the couple's honor. You can still buy the couple a toaster, but it is appropriate to buy a slightly smaller gift and redistribute part of the money in the interest of people who are unfairly prohibited from marrying.

Conclusion

What started as a dichotomy, to marry or not to marry, has become an array of choices. Renunciation might mean refusing to marry or refusing to attend the marriages of others (or refusing to marry in discriminatory jurisdictions or houses of worship). Voice might mean acknowledgment, explanation, or apology. Sharing might mean contributing time and money to the cause of equality. Attendees or the marrying couple might consider charitable contributions in lieu of presents.

There are so many choices. So which is the best? The next chapter will suggest giving limited deference to the victims of discrimination in deciding between tactics. But sometimes representatives speak with different voices. Frank advised marriage; Rofes called for boycott. Connie Ress, executive director of the New York City–based gay-marriage rights group Marriage Equality, promotes strategic diversity: "I think that sometimes it's good for people to use a variety of strategies to get a point across."[32] We would be remiss if we failed to acknowledge that some theorists and activists reject marriage altogether as a hopelessly sexist and outdated institution. There may be no single best strategy. Instead, the cause of equality may be best served by different people doing different things. A movement that is relentlessly confrontational may be counterproductive, but there may be a useful role for both "bad cops" and "good cops," for Malcolm as well as Martin.

How have we personally answered these questions? We have opted for a combination of voice and sharing, rather than renunciation. After much discussion about the morality of participating in discrimination, we chose to marry in 1993. In our Church service, we prayed publicly for a time when marriage would be more inclusive. We have, throughout our marriage, donated money to various equal marriage rights organizations. We have been actively lobbying our current (Episcopal) parish and diocese to include same-sex couples in the marriage rite, and we have testified or submitted written materials to state legislatures asking for equal marriage rights.

But the question of renunciation is still very present in our lives. We are considering switching (one of us would say "poised to switch") to an Episcopal parish that has already joined two same-sex couples in holy union. But maybe we should go further. Stephen Spielberg resigned from the board of the Boy Scouts of America because of its discrimination; former CBS chief executive Thomas H. Wyman resigned from Augusta National because of its discrimination. We should at least consider whether we should resign from this discriminatory club. Professor Rofes paints a colorful picture when he writes, "Imagine if heterosexual allies publicly burned their marriage certificates?"[33] To many readers this will again seem beyond the pale. But if President George W. Bush's discriminatory preferences are written into our country's Constitution, remaining married could send an increasingly strong—and untenable—signal.

Working with Organizations Advocating Gay Rights

Before this book draws to a close, let's review the general strategies proposed here for heterosexual people who support gay rights. We've discussed both intuitive and counterintuitive steps supporters can take. On the intuitive side, we've stressed the importance of voice. In many situations (several quite close to home), there is a power in standing up specifically as a heterosexual person to say, "This is important to me, too: I support equality for LGBT people." We've discussed heterosexual privilege and the role it may play when nongay people weigh in on issues affecting the lives of gay, lesbian, and bisexual people. We've argued that the power of privilege is such that heterosexual allies should think carefully, as they participate in this larger movement, about whether they should exploit or renounce the potential influence they possess simply because they identify as heterosexual.

In some cases, renouncing privilege might require disassociation from the organizations or structures that would endow heterosexual people with rights invidiously denied to gay, lesbian, and bisexual people; to work effectively for gay rights, heterosexual people might be called upon to support or initiate boycotts of businesses, private associations, and even public institutions. The Informed Association Statute discussed in chapter 7 would be one way to spur this renunciation approach.

Implicit in most threats, however, are offers: the flip side of a boycott is buycott, and we've argued that heterosexual people can promote gay rights by rewarding entities—public and private—that act progressively with respect to sexual orientation. The Vacation Pledge and the Fair Employment Mark put this strategy into practice.

Finally, we've explored what might happen as heterosexual people begin to renounce the privilege attached to their sexual orientation. One result could be "ambiguation." Some forms of gay rights advocacy may require a willingness for heterosexual people to be perceived as gay. To implement strategies that place them in greatest solidarity with gay, lesbian, and bisexual people, heterosexual allies may have to let go of the urge, the need, quickly and constantly, to clarify their "true" sexual orientation. The clearest example of a strategy that relies in part upon heterosexual people's willingness to ambiguate is the Inclusive Command proposal in chapter 6. The success of the Inclusive Command rests on the willingness of heterosexual service members to work side by side with gays, to be part of the same team with them, and even, at times, to leave open the question about which specific members of the command are gay or nongay.

Exploiting or renouncing privilege, boycott or buycott, ambiguation. . . all may be fine strategies in theory, but how should heterosexual allies decide which to put into practice, and when? Most readers would find it dissatisfying and unhelpful to hear at this point: "OK, now, use your best judgment." At various points, we've already offered some substantive advice. Chapter 5 suggested factors that argue for ambiguation or disambiguation. And the last chapter unpacked the difficult trilemma of voice, exit, or pro rata sharing.

This chapter focuses instead on a procedural approach. Instead of relying on your own substantive judgment, you might give the victims of discrimination your proxy. Deferring to the preferences of gay rights advocacy organizations is a natural way of managing privilege—in a sense delegating the privilege to people who have good incentives to deploy the power in the most effective way. Of course, there are difficulties with implementing this strategy, and in the end we will argue for a kind of qualified deference—where allies presumptively defer to the advice of gay rights advocacy organizations unless there are sufficient reasons not to do so. To conclude this book about mobilizing nongay support, then, this chapter will consider when and to what extent heterosexual allies should look to gay rights advocacy organizations for their marching orders.

Forging a New Relationship

Supporters of gay rights who identify as heterosexual are not likely to be members of major gay rights advocacy organizations, nor are they likely to fall within the groups targeted by those organizations for representation.[1] They might be solicited at fund-raising time, but otherwise they could feel as if they are largely overlooked. In part because of this lack of attention, nongays may tend to look elsewhere for guidance on how to act to support the movement for equal rights.

We think this relationship can and should be improved on both sides. Advocacy organizations can do more to court the support of nongay allies. And heterosexuals in turn should look to gay rights organizations as a source for pragmatic, tactical advice. The tendency of each side to overlook the other robs the movement of important constituents.

Asking for Nongay Support

In recent years, a number of advocacy organizations have been reaching out to a broader constituency. PFLAG (Parents and Friends of Lesbians and Gays) is constituted in a way that embraces nongay support. Freedom to Marry is a relatively new organization that explicitly bills itself as a "gay and non-gay partnership" working to win marriage equality nationwide. On one page of Freedom to Marry's web site, photographs appear of famous civil rights advocates the public probably identifies as heterosexual (Rep. John Lewis, Coretta Scott King, and Gloria Steinem).[2] Likewise, Gender Public Advocacy Coalition's mission statement explicitly disavows identity-based politics in defining its intended constituency.

> GenderPAC is committed to achieving gender rights for all. This means we organize around the common issue of gender rights, rather than representing any single identity or constituency. We believe that all of us, at some time or another, are harassed, shamed, or made to feel afraid because of our gender. Therefore we believe gender is too basic to be left to any single group, and too fundamental to leave anyone behind.
>
> This form of organizing, sometimes called "post-identity political" or "issue-based organizing," means that while respecting how individuals identify, we work on bringing people together for the common work of achieving gender rights. GenderPAC believes this is the best way to build a strong, broad-based, and inclusive movement to secure gender civil rights.[3]

The marriage equality organization Love Makes a Family (LMF) has been particularly effective in enlisting the help of nongays. For example, in an effort to lobby Connecticut lawmakers and shift public opinion, LMF compiled a book entitled *Our Stories, Our Lives*, in which ordinary citizens expressed what equal marriage rights would mean to them. Importantly, the book includes testimonials not only from same-sex couples but also from straight allies, who are highlighted in a special section of the book.[4]

We still see a value in organizations that dominantly represent the members of discrete and insular groups—especially when these groups are continually subjected to both private and public discrimination. Indeed, the central thesis of this chapter is that groups representing the victims of injustice can play a vital role in directing the struggle for equality. But even these groups with narrower constituencies can do more to connect with heterosexual supporters. Lambda Legal and Human Rights Campaign, for example, could ask their members to provide the names and addresses of three (gay or nongay) friends who might be interested in supporting the cause of equality. When contacting these potential members, the organization might even invoke the name of the member who listed them. This could be a particularly effective way to subtly remind heterosexual people of their responsibilities to gay friends, family members, and coworkers. The organization would not attempt to represent these nongay members. The organization's proper purpose is to represent the victims of discrimination. But advocacy groups waste an important opportunity if they fail to organize and marshal the force of heterosexual allies.

The rainbow sash movement provides a vivid example of an organization that could do more to harness the power of nongay supporters. Beginning in 1997, a number of gay and lesbian Roman Catholics in Chicago, Dallas, Los Angeles, Rochester, New Orleans, and New York (as well as Australia and England) began to test whether their churches would welcome them at Holy Communion.[5] They did this by wearing a rainbow sash when approaching the altar. The sash is expressly defined by the movement's own mission statement as a marker of the wearer's LGBT orientation:

> In wearing The Rainbow Sash we proclaim that we are Gay, Lesbian, Bisexual, Transgender people who embrace and celebrate our sexuality as a Sacred Gift.[6]

The church's response has been mixed. While churches in Massachusetts and Los Angeles have allowed sash wearers to receive Communion, Chicago cardinal Francis George directed Chicago priests to withhold the Eucharist from anyone wearing one.[7] On Pentecost Sunday 2004 (one of the major holy days following Easter Sunday, on which the church celebrates the spiritual anointing of the apostles following Jesus's death), dozens of sash bearers approached the altar but were denied Communion. The sash movement creates a powerful visual image of exclusion, and highlights the ongoing discrimination practiced by the church.

But we think that the sash movement would be even stronger if there were a secondary symbol for nongay supporters to wear. This symbol—let's call it the equality sash—might only proclaim that the wearer believes that gay, lesbian, bisexual, and transgender sexuality, like heterosexuality, need not be sinful and indeed can be an expression of God's love. Would the church refuse the sacrament to wearers of this symbol? The equality sash would pose a different, difficult question for the church, because the wearers are not signaling that they engage or intend to engage in behavior the church considers sinful. But most importantly, the creation of this secondary sash might easily double or triple the number of people who are willing to wear a symbol of support.

Tip O'Neill, the longtime Speaker of the House, was fond of a simple political truth: "People like to be asked."[8] There are people of goodwill who are looking for direction. They may put proper limits on how much they are willing to do. Some may even be put off if you ask too much. But others actually appreciate being asked for their help and are more likely to give it if someone expressly asks.

Listening to the Requests of LGBT Organizations

While advocacy organizations should do more to reach out for nongay support, nongay supporters should do more to listen and respond to the requests of advocacy groups. Nongay people owe a duty of "qualified deference" to advocacy organizations. Individuals should still determine the amount of time and money they are willing to devote to the cause. Indeed, the last chapter's analysis of pro rata sharing provided guidelines on establishing minimum duties. But we believe that allies within this budget should presumptively take their marching orders from gay rights advocacy organizations. You decide how much time or money you are willing to devote this year to the cause, but then let one or more advocacy groups take the first shot at deciding what you will do or how your money will best be spent.

Deference economizes on decision making for three reasons.

1. *Research*: There are often economies of scale and scope in research. Instead of each individual wasting time trying to figure out the most effective strategy, organizations can undertake surveys and other empirical

studies to try to understand the lay of the land. They can undertake a single analysis to assess the most effective legal challenges. It is massively inefficient for each supporter to reinvent the same strategic wheel.

2. *Coordination:* There are often economies of scale in coordinated action. A mass rally on the courthouse steps next Tuesday can have a greater impact than the same number of people marching individually at locations of their own devising. Coordination of successive legal challenges that raise the most helpful issues can be more effective than helter-skelter activism.

3. *Credibility:* Some gay rights groups have worked for decades to establish relationships and reputations, especially with legislators, regulators, the media, and large employers. They can persuade decision makers in ways that individuals may be unable to do.

Most importantly, the strategy of deference is based on the idea that the victims of discrimination are well placed to figure out the best strategies to end it. Victims of discrimination have excellent incentives, and their advocacy organizations can be focal points to capitalize on the foregoing decision-making economies.

One Approach: The Loyalist

These economies of scale and the incentive effects provide a prima facie argument for loyalty. A loyalist picks an organization advocating gay rights, supports it financially, and follows that organization's strategies for policy and activism to a T. This loyalty approach has several attractions.

First, loyalty is *coherent.* Choosing a single organization, consuming the information it distributes, and following the instructions it issues can give heterosexual allies a sense of security. The organization can educate people in depth about a particular issue and provide a consistent strategy for addressing it. For example, heterosexual supporters of Lambda Legal in the 1990s learned about the importance of equal marriage rights and the usefulness of nationally coordinated litigation in state courts as a strategy for achieving those rights. One could conduct independent research and come to the same conclusions, of course, but competing views do exist. Without a strong sense of affiliation with Lambda, a person might question the importance of marriage (relative to, say, employment protections or military service). Even if one identified equal marriage rights as the single most important goal for LGBT people today, one might wonder whether litigation is the optimal means to that end. Social change can be a difficult, confusing thing; pledging and practicing loyalty to one organization can at the very least cure the paralysis that sometimes results from information overload.

A second virtue of the loyalist approach is that it permits a *concentration* of effort. Loyalists can identify the issue with which they connect most strongly and choose an organization that has worked in a focused way, perhaps with some success, on that issue. A clear victory on one front in the battle for gay rights might create momentum for changes in other areas. Loyalists could be criticized for "putting all of their eggs in one basket." By affiliating with one organization and following its instructions, however, loyalists can avoid a converse problem: spreading themselves too thin. Fighting on all fronts, but doing it weakly, may serve the cause of gay rights less effectively than concentrating one's effort in one or two important areas.

Notwithstanding these advantages, we reject the idea of unqualified loyalty. Loyalty is not risk-free, because it requires heterosexual allies to expend some effort in choosing the group or groups to which they will defer. Not all such choices will be good. When choosing a group or groups to which they will defer, allies face two challenges: the problem of representation and incomplete or conflicting instructions.

The first arises when allies cannot easily verify that organizations are sufficiently representative of victim groups. From time to time, advocacy organizations have been criticized for becoming unresponsive to the needs of their own constituencies. Instead of individually researching the best substantive strategies for equality, the strategy of deference requires the individual to assess whether particular groups are adequate representatives. To aid in the process, we suggest that allies consider the views of a variety of gay rights groups (see table 3 for a few examples).[9] Web-based resources can point potential members and donors to hundreds of LGBT organizations focused on specific issues or geographic regions.[10]

Organizations that can make a more credible claim of representing the interests of victims deserve more deference. But LGBT advocacy groups, like the communities they represent, are not monolithic. Allies need to identify the victims of discrimination that matter most to them, and perform ongoing due diligence to assure that they are deferring to an organization that truly represents those victims. Indeed, the deference perspective suggests another way in which advocacy organizations could more effectively reach out to allies: advocacy organizations could make their representative character more transparent. Whose concerns are brought to bear

TABLE 3. LGBT ADVOCACY ORGANIZATIONS

National Organizations	Regional and Issue-Specific Organizations
Lambda Legal Defense	Love Makes a Family
Human Rights Campaign	Freedom to Marry
National Gay and Lesbian Task Force	Service Members Legal Defense
ACLU's Lesbian and Gay Rights Project	Network
The Gay and Lesbian Alliance Against Defamation (GLAAD)	Gay and Lesbian Advocates and Defenders (New England)
National Lesbian Rights Center	Scouting for All
Gay Men's Health Crisis (GMHC)	Family Pride Coalition (adoption, foster parenting, and other family issues)
	AIDS Coalition to Unleash Power (Act Up) (city-based groups)
	Immigration Equality (formerly the Lesbian and Gay Immigration Rights Task Force)
	Gay, Lesbian, and Straight Education Network (GLSEN)

for that organization? Membership numbers and demographics tell some of the story. But organizations could go further by actually conducting internal referenda on policy issues within their memberships.

But even perfect representatives may give incomplete or conflicting advice. A loyalist's view of the field will almost inevitably be incomplete. Many gay rights groups choose one issue or a limited constellation of issues on which to focus, and they often choose one principal strategy to pursue their goals. So, for example, the Human Rights Campaign (HRC) has historically emphasized employment issues and stressed lobbying as the primary process for change.[11] Concentrating all of one's energy or attention on HRC might lead a person to overlook other important gay rights issues, and the promise of litigation as a vehicle for change.

Putting all of a heterosexual supporter's eggs in one basket may provide a rather incomplete view of the gay rights landscape. It could reinforce stereotypes about the race, gender, or economic status of the "typical" gay person, leading heterosexual allies to misunderstand the gay community. Heterosexual supporters' experience of the issues affecting the gay commu-

185

nity will often occur at some remove. They will encounter the issues second- or thirdhand (not personally but through friends or loved ones who are gay). For some the distance may be even greater; they may not know that any of their relatives or friends are gay, and thus must look to organizations that serve LGBT people for information. Heterosexual allies, perhaps more than activists who themselves identify as gay, lesbian, and bisexual,[12] will in a sense have higher "information costs." It seems unlikely that a single organization would be able to educate them fully.

Unqualified loyalty may not be possible if different groups give conflicting or inapposite instructions. As we noted in chapter 8, for example, some activists call upon heterosexuals to boycott wedding ceremonies, while others would never dream of making such a request. A loyalist cannot simultaneously follow conflicting commands. And loyalists cannot follow instructions when none are given. Some of the strategies suggested by gay rights advocates are simply inapposite for heterosexual allies. The rainbow sash movement is a strategy that is expressly limited to LGBT people. The point here is that gay rights groups may be so conditioned to expect *only* LGBT people as participants that they don't quite know what to do with heterosexual supporters. Loyalists who internally pledge to follow one organization and its "party line" may lose opportunities for some powerful advocacy because the organization has not designed its work to include significant, on-the-ground, nonfinancial support from heterosexual people.

A final problem with the loyalist approach is that gay rights organizations may be unwilling openly to ask heterosexual allies to pursue certain strategies, even though they secretly might hope that some allies will adopt the strategies. Let's call this the problem of "plausible deniability." The problem here does not arise from any failure on the part of gay rights organizations to contemplate or fold in heterosexual support. Indeed, the organization may have contemplated a particular kind of heterosexual support and believe that it is the most effective strategy. But the organization might not want to be seen as the entity calling the shots. It may worry that explicitly organizing the strategy will cause a backlash—either from opponents of gay rights or from potential allies who believe the movement is asking too much. In these circumstances, the advocacy organization might prefer that the impetus for a controversial strategy appear to come (indeed, that it actually come) from heterosexual supporters themselves.

For example, a major boycott of an association like the Boy Scouts of America in the wake of *Dale* is probably not something for which Lambda Legal wants to receive credit (or blame, depending on one's perspective).

The boycott is much more powerful if—as appears actually to be true—it comes from multiple, decentralized decisions by heterosexual people to cease their support for BSA and agitate for policy change. Boycotts are negative, and Lambda would probably rather not be seen as spearheading efforts to harm the BSA.[13]

At the beginning of part III, we told the story of a man who said loudly, so that others might hear, "Oh look, there are some Boy Scouts. They practice discrimination." Like chapter 7's Informed Association Statute, this confrontational strategy would create uncomfortable space, space in which parents of scouts might be forced to take a stand. Hearing someone say that the Boy Scouts practice discrimination might lead children to ask their parents some difficult questions. Being forced to answer these questions could shame parents, or even force them to admit that ongoing association with scouting is inconsistent with their values. Clearly, though, this shaming strategy is an extremely aggressive approach to the problem of the BSA's exclusionary policy. Lambda and other organizations that have fought to change these policies might approve of the accusation, but would probably not want to be seen as having "put anyone up to it."

This may be an extreme example. It suggests, however, that some strategies are high risk: potentially effective but combative in ways that could undermine the credibility of more mainstream gay rights organizations. If heterosexual allies are unwilling or unable to undertake any action independently, they may miss opportunities to pursue strategies that would not—indeed, should not—be directed by gay rights organizations.

Another Approach: The Lone Ranger

The problems of plausible deniability, representation, and incomplete, conflicting, or inapposite instructions all undermine the case for unqualified loyalty and unquestioning deference. Supporters of gay rights who are daunted by the downsides of a loyalist approach could go to the other extreme, simply setting forth on their own. These activists would work for gay rights independently, selecting issues and strategies according to their own preferences and priorities.

Such an approach has its advantages. Without the guidance of an organization, a "lone ranger" is more likely to seek information from diverse sources. A broad sampling of information might give this activist a more general view of the field of gay rights and the many issues in play. Getting information about a wider range of issues affecting gay men and lesbians would facilitate the activist's informed decision-making about where to devote his time and energy. This research could have an added benefit if it helps heterosexual allies to understand and empathize with gay people.

Furthermore, being more broadly educated about gay rights might allow an activist to decide independently whether a particular form of action (political, social, educational, legal, or economic) is likely to be effective for a specific issue. So, for example, a lone ranger might learn that Lambda has pursued litigation and public education in its work for equal marriage rights, but independently determine that an economic approach (such as chapter 3's Marriage Pledge) is also worth trying.

Moreover, lone rangers can adopt confrontational or negative strategies without implicating the major gay rights advocacy groups, since those groups can credibly disclaim any responsibility for the lone ranger's actions. Thus, lone rangers do not suffer some of the limitations that constrain loyalists. For example, lone rangers could spearhead a boycott of a discriminatory employer. Imposing economic harm on the company might be something HRC or NGLTF would support, even though they would not want to be held responsible for it. Having such action come, independently, from activists who identify as heterosexual could help gay rights advocacy groups.

Despite its strengths, this approach carries significant risks. Lone rangers can sometimes save damsels who are not really in distress. They can impart gifts (of time, money, or energy) where they are not really wanted. And while they are rushing about saving people who are perfectly safe, others who genuinely need their help may suffer. To the extent the gay rights groups devote resources to learning what matters most to the LGBT people they represent, lone rangers ignore those organizations at their peril. Lone rangers may be forgoing important sources of information about where the priorities for action should lie.

Moreover, lone rangers can be presumptuous. They run the risk of exploiting heterosexual privilege in unthinking ways, especially if they presume to speak *for* LGBT people when, in fact, they are unauthorized to do so. This may be the most insidious form of heterosexual privilege, because it masquerades as liberation even as it perpetuates social and political structures (the privilege) that are so oppressive. Better, it seems, for heterosexual allies to remember that they can speak only for themselves, or for others only when authorized to do so.

The final problem with the lone ranger approach is more subtle. Recall that one of the most important benefits heterosexual allies can bring to the gay rights movement, alluded to in chapter 6, is a *demonstration effect.* Gay-straight alliances demonstrate to bigots and skeptics that heterosexual and LGBT people can stand and work together, shoulder to shoulder, for common goals. The very process of collaborating and creating an integrated team has this educating benefit. This demonstration effect is lost, however, if heterosexual allies only act independently, never joining a team that includes LGBT people.

A Third Way: Qualified Deference

In the end, we reject the extremes of unqualified loyalty and unqualified independence. Instead, we argue for a kind of qualified deference. Nongay allies should presumptively defer to the instructions of gay rights organizations. But this deference is qualified in a number of ways to which we have already alluded.

> Less deference should be paid to groups that are less transparently representative of the LGBT community (or portions of the LGBT community that matter most to the ally).
>
> Less deference should be paid to instructions that are incomplete, inapposite or contradictory.
>
> Less deference should be paid to instructions if there are good reasons to think that the organization wants to maintain plausible deniability.
>
> As emphasized in the last chapter, less deference should be paid to instructions that go beyond the amount of time, money, and energy required by a principle of pro rata sharing.

In a sense, we are embracing a kind of feudal pledge, "Choose up to half my kingdom," where the ally chooses the proportion of her estate that she is willing to commit to the cause but empowers the beneficiary to choose within these limits the specific strategies to be followed.

It is commonplace in our social and legal system to defer to victims when the time comes to remedy the wrong that has been done to them. In civil lawsuits, plaintiffs are permitted, within some constraints, an "election of remedies." But it is striking to us how often we overlook the chance to let the victim choose.[14]

At the very least, nongay allies can use a representative group's agenda as a kind of *internal* litmus test. For example, a heterosexual ally contemplating a specific form of social or political activism might ask, "What would Lambda do?" before committing to the issue or a particular strategy. Why not just ask Lambda directly? Again, there could be some cases in which social or political action will actually be more useful to Lambda if it occurs independent of Lambda's direction. Nonetheless, the anticipation of what Lambda might want is necessary to avoid wasted or even counterproductive effort.

Reciprocal Deference?

If serving as an ally requires heterosexual activists to collaborate with and defer to gay rights organizations, are there situations in which LGBT actors should defer to heterosexual allies' judgments? This is tricky, because movements for social change have to be careful not to reproduce the conditions of oppression against which they are struggling. In some cases, however, it may be that heterosexual allies can provide a kind of litmus test for the way a policy proposal might be received by the heterosexual majority. In this way, perhaps, heterosexual allies might "speak for" heterosexual America when strategy talks take place within the movement.

For example, in 2001 in the state of Connecticut, discussions took place, quietly and informally, about legal recognition for same-sex couples. Michael Lawlor, a representative to the state general assembly and cochair of the Judiciary Committee, strongly supported some form of legal recognition. Lawlor worked with Love Makes a Family to coordinate several day-long hearings on the subject before the Judiciary Committee. Proponents of legal recognition generally avoided taking a position about whether civil union, domestic partnership, or marriage ultimately should be pursued. The short-term goal was merely to get the subject on the table within the state legislature and to begin to educate the legislators about the impact on same-sex couples of their lack of legal recognition.

After a full and successful day of testimony before the committee, and substantial informal discussions with fellow legislators, Lawlor believed that the issue was not sufficiently "ripe" to pursue in earnest in the spring of 2001. In deference to Lawlor (confirmed, no doubt, by their own research), Love Makes a Family backed off for the remainder of the legislative session, determined to work for increased public awareness of the issue rather than pushing to introduce a bill in the current legislative session. Granted, LMF's deference to Lawlor was no doubt based upon his political position and influence, not his sexual orientation (he seems to identify as a heterosexual), but to some extent his advice to delay the full assault was probably based on a judgment about what heterosexual legislators were ready to do.

In addition to the clearly authoritative voices like Lawlor's (who earlier sponsored legislation to secure second-parent adoption rights in Connecticut, and therefore won the trust and respect of many gay rights advocates in Connecticut), more lowly heterosexual allies could also bring their message to gay rights organizations, demand that space be made, and ask that a role be created for them. To riff a bit on the chant often heard at pride parades throughout the country, heterosexual supporters might demand of such organizations: "We're here, we're not queer, but give us something to do!" The gay rights organizations, in turn, need to understand that if they don't find a specific role or task for heterosexual supporters, they run the risk of losing their support. It is not that heterosexual supporters will turn around and join the Eagle Forum in disgust, but rather that they'll become inactive or apathetic, convinced that there is nothing they can do to advance gay rights. Those who remain active despite their inability to find a place within the gay rights movement might waste a great deal of time and energy, reinventing the wheel and duplicating expenditures already made by gay rights organizations. They could also waste time, energy, and money by working for legislation or litigation outcomes gay rights groups actually oppose.[15] At worst, these disaffected heterosexual allies could become loose cannons, potentially harmful to the movement if they perpetuate assumptions about heterosexual privilege.

Perhaps the greatest benefit of collaboration with gay rights organizations is that it can clarify for heterosexual allies when they might speak on behalf of LGBT people and when they can speak only for themselves. Heterosexual allies might speak on behalf of gay people (as discussed in chapter 2, for example) when LGBT people are excluded from the discussion and a heterosexual person's voice is the only vehicle to convey an LGBT perspective. When speaking on behalf of LGBT people, however, it is important that heterosexual people understand their role to be that of agents. Agents must be authorized by a principal to speak and act. "Speaking for" is legitimate only if heterosexuals are authorized by their principals—gay people and gay rights organizations.

Sometimes, heterosexual allies should simply speak for themselves. We need to recognize that heterosexual people can have an important and constructive voice on gay rights that is distinct from that of gay people or gay advocacy groups. When they choose to express that distinct perspective, however, heterosexual allies need to understand—and clearly convey to their audience—that they are speaking *only* for themselves, and not presuming to speak *for* gay people.

Something

A story is told of a young white woman at Columbia University who approached Malcolm X and told him that she supported his struggle. When she asked: "What can I do to help?" he is said to have responded coldly with a single word—"Nothing"—and walked on.[16]

Our book rejects this approach. Not only can nongays do something, but so many potentially useful things might be done, that the real problem is choosing which among the plethora of possible actions is the most appropriate. There are a host of different strategies that sometimes are complementary but at other times are mutually counterproductive. While the desired end of equality is straightforward, this book has shown that it is devilishly difficult for a righteous individual to choose how to act in a juridical world that discriminates. Because we do not individually have the power to end discrimination, we may have counterintuitive and crosscutting duties of renunciation, voice, pro rata sharing, and ambiguation.

In the course of this book, we have shown how these strategies might be deployed at some of today's most important flashpoints—employment, marriage, military service, and private associations. But the same approach could be applied to virtually any example of discrimination. Thus, in closing, it useful to sketch how the ideas of this book might be applied in yet another context. Consider the case of Florida adoption law. Florida and New Hampshire are the only states in the nation with absolute statutory bans on adoption by gay men and lesbians, regardless of whether they are single, partnered, or married.[17] Florida's law was passed in 1977 "at the height of Anita Bryant's antihomosexual crusade."[18] In 2004 the Eleventh Circuit Court of Appeals upheld the statute's constitutionality.[19]

How should heterosexual allies in Florida respond to the state's invidious disparate treatment? First and foremost, they should use their voices—by actively lobbying their legislature for repeal of the statute, voting for candidates who favor repeal, and supporting individuals and organizations challenging the statute. But there are other options as well. Heterosexuals who have been permitted to adopt in Florida might consider surrendering a portion of their gains to help compensate those who are denied the right to adopt. Or Florida residents who are planning to adopt might go further and consider the strategy of renunciation. If it is immoral to marry in a state that discriminates against gays and lesbians, it may be immoral to adopt in a state that discriminates.

At first the adoption context seems a very poor candidate for the strategy of renunciation. It is unfair to punish a child by refusing to adopt. As with marriage, however, the renunciation strategy might not require avoiding adoption all together. Rather, it would call for allies to avoid adopting in a discriminatory jurisdiction. There is nothing to stop Florida residents from adopting in other states—indeed, same-sex couples have been doing it for years to avoid the effects of adoption discrimination they suffer in some states.[20] Florida couples who adopt Massachusetts children do not sacrifice the needs of children. They just adopt different children. Refusing to adopt in Florida is more than just a symbolic "self-comforting" gesture; it has the probable effect of increasing the amount that Florida needs to spend on foster care (while reducing the cost of foster care for some other nondiscriminatory jurisdiction). While refusing to adopt in Florida at first seems ill-advised, upon closer inspection, this strategy deserves real consideration.[21]

The first and crucial step is merely to acknowledge how heterosexuals voluntarily associate with discrimination. Florida gets poor marks for acknowledgment. Its adoption web site in answering the question "Who Can Adopt?" fails to mention the ban on homosexuals.[22] But once we start to acknowledge the ways in which we participate in and benefit from explicitly discriminatory institutions, it becomes natural to ask whether there are nondiscriminatory alternatives.

Indeed, the adoption context illuminates how the strategy of renunciation may grow out of a felt need to ambiguate. Imagine that you are a single parent who is seeking to adopt in Florida. Florida requires applicants to disclose their sexual orientation on the application. It specifically asks the applicant or applicants if they are homosexual. If they check yes, the form tells them to not proceed any further.[23]

How would you answer this question? Even if you internally identify as heterosexual, the reasoning of chapters 5 and 8 suggests that you might have difficulty denying that you are gay. And this strategy of ambiguation is not limited to unmarried individuals or people who are willing to lie. A married couple might have the same effect by saying (or writing in the margin), "As far as you know, we might be bisexual." The urge to adopt in other jurisdictions can be spawned not only by the normative carrot of nondiscrimination, but by the deontological distaste of having to affirmatively claim a heterosexual dividend. As we saw in chapter 7 when we considered the informed association statute, there are some pieces of paper that people just can't bring themselves to sign.

EXPLOITING PRIVILEGE. Exercising voice. Ambiguation. Pro rata sharing. Renunciation. These strategies resist easy prioritization. Deferring, within limits, to the victims of discrimination and their representatives can be a welcomed respite to the daunting task of deciding how to live in a world that mandates discrimination. Our book has been an attempt to guide readers about how to live in such a world as we struggle to bring that discrimination to an end.

NOTES

Preface

1. "Competitive Federalism and the Legislative Incentives to Recognize Same-Sex Marriage," 68 S. Cal. L. Rev. 745 (1995); "Sweeping Reform from Small Rules? Anti-bias Canons as a Substitute for Heightened Scrutiny," 85 Minn. L. Rev. 363 (2000); "Adjudication According to Codes of Judicial Conduct," 11 Am. U. J. Gender Soc. Pol'y & L. 67 (2002); "Facilitating Boycotts of Discriminatory Organizations through an Informed Association Statute," 87 Minn. L. Rev. 481 (2002).
2. *Pervasive Prejudice? Unconventional Evidence of Race and Gender Discrimination* (2001); "When Does Private Discrimination Justify Public Affirmative Action?", 98 Colum. L. Rev. 1577 (1998) (with Frederick E. Vars).

Chapter One
Heterosexual Allies and the Gay Rights Movement

1. Bruce Ryder, "Straight Talk: Male Heterosexual Privilege," 16 Queens L.J. 287, 290 (1991).
2. Jamie Washington & Nancy J. Evans, "Becoming an Ally," at 196 *in Beyond Tolerance: Gays, Lesbians, and Bisexuals on Campus* (Nancy J. Evans & Vernon A. Wall, eds. 1991).
3. Ryder, *supra* note 1, at 287.
4. Judith Butler, *Bodies That Matter* 125–26 (1993).
5. *See* Employment Non-Discrimination Act, HR 2692 (107th Cong., July 31, 2001) for the most recent proposal of the bill.
6. A reciprocal and perhaps more radical claim would be that gay men and lesbians should also be willing to be "mistaken" for bisexuals. This claim is supported by the argument that gay and heterosexual people implicitly deal, or contract, to "erase" bisexuals and make them invisible. *See* Kenji Yoshino, "The Epistemic Contract of Bisexual Erasure," 52 Stan. L. Rev. 353 (2000).

7. See Devon Carbado, "Straight Out of the Closet," 15 Berkeley Women's L.J. 76, 115 (2000) ("Independent of any question of intentionality on the author's part, his wife functions as an identity signifier to subtextually 'out' his heterosexuality. We *read* 'wife,' we *think* heterosexual").

8. If a heterosexually identified academic writes about sexual orientation and the law from an explicitly heterosexual perspective, this can be criticized, as if the writer were saying, "Enough about you, let's talk about how all of this affects *me*, a straight person." *See, e.g.,* K. A. Lahey, "Introduction," 16 Queens L.J. 231, 232 (1991) (critiquing an essay on white male heterosexual privilege authored by a white heterosexual man, Lahey writes: "Bruce Ryder demonstrates that white heterosexual males—and, to a lesser extent, white heterosexual women—can continue to be the subject matter of their own work even while they claim to centre it on something else. Although this quality of openness is usually thought to signal a 'radical' approach to the subject matter, in fact it can become symptomatic of the author's actual privilege"). *See also* Carbado, *supra* note 7.

9. *Cf.* Janet Halley, "Sexuality Harassment: A Critique of Sex Harassment Law," Draft Essay circulated to Yale Legal Theory Workshop, March 2001, at 2: "a queer approach thinks it is fine to be 'queer in the streets, straight in the sheets'" (copy on file with author); Janet Halley, *Split Decisions* (forthcoming 2005).

10. Carmen Agra Deedy, *The Yellow Star: The Legend of King Christian X of Denmark* (2000).

11. Ultimately, of course, gentiles pursued a more helpful undertaking: they actively resisted and eventually defeated Adolph Hitler, bringing the Holocaust to an end and rendering all the hiding unnecessary. Then, as now, short-term protective goals need to be balanced with longer-term goals of liberation.

12. An anonymous reader of an earlier draft of this book read the preceding sentence as evidence of our own unexamined and perhaps unresolved homophobia. On the narrow point, we think the reader was empirically mistaken. It is not *we* who are equating parenting with heterosexuality, but the wider world. The wider world would tend to infer that a different-sexed married couple with children is likely to be heterosexual. This doesn't mean that same-sex couples cannot have children. It doesn't mean that different-sex couples without children are not heterosexual. It just means that most people in society would infer that a different-sex couple with children is likely to be heterosexual.

But the reader's larger point is valid and important. It is sobering to realize how difficult it can be to shed heterosexist and homophobic habits of thought. It may be impossible in some sense for us and others to get outside of homophobic thinking. For many of us—gay and nongay—this can prove to be a lifelong project.

13. Albert O. Hirschman, *Exit, Voice, and Loyalty: Responses to Declines in Firms, Organizations, and States* (1972)
14. Boy Scouts v. Dale, 530 U.S. 640 (2000).

Chapter Two
Parenting, Parishes, PTAs, and Places of Employment

Eleanor Roosevelt, Remarks at Presentation of Booklet on Human Rights, *In Your Hands*, to the United Nations Commission on Human Rights, United Nations, New York, March 27, 1958, United Nations typescript of statements at presentation (microfilm), http://www.bartleby.com/73/866.html (last visited July 1, 2004).

1. Judith Butler, *Bodies That Matter* 125–26 (1993).
2. *See* Devon Carbado, "Straight Out of the Closet," 15 Berkeley Women's L.J. 76, 79 (2000) ("Resistance to identity privileges may be futile, we cannot know for sure. But, to the extent that we do nothing, this much is clear: we perpetuate the systems of discrimination that our identities reflect").
3. For example, children's books, movies, and television programs uniformly present romantic love as something that happens between a man and a woman.
4. Carbado, *supra* note 2, at 117–22. *See also* Bruce Ryder, "Straight Talk: Male Heterosexual Privilege," 16 Queens L.J. 287, 292 (1991).
5. *See* J. M. Balkin, "The Constitution of Status," 106 Yale L.J. 2313 (1997).
6. And vice versa, as Professor Bruce Ryder argues: "What heterosexism gives straight men and women, what it takes away from lesbians and gays, is heterosexual privilege." Ryder, *supra* note 4, at 290.
7. In the context of negotiation, such situations are said to allow "integrative bargaining"; certain exchanges will increase the value of the transaction for both parties. Zero-sum dynamics, in contrast, give rise to "distributive bargaining," where the size of the pie is fixed and the bargaining concerns the relative sizes of the parties' pieces. *See* Roger Fisher, William Ury, and Bruce Patton, *Getting to Yes* (1997); Howard Raiffa, *The Art and Science of Negotiation* (1985).
8. Jack Balkin would disagree. In his view, walking hand in hand in public, for example, gains special value for heterosexual couples because this ability is denied to same-sex couples. The very creation of an "in" group and any number of "out" groups renders the privileges afforded the in group more valuable. Balkin, *supra* note 5.
9. *See, e.g.,* Tobias Wolff, "Compelled Affirmations, Free Speech and the U.S. Military's Don't Ask Don't Tell Policy," 63 Brook. L. Rev. 1141 (1997) (noting that for some gay and lesbian service members, the difference between *I* and *we* in a sentence can be huge).
10. Kenji Yoshino, "Covering," 111 Yale L.J. 769 (2002).

11. *See* Butler, *supra* note 1, at 123.
12. Barney Frank, "Bowers + Ten: Litigation, Legislation, and Community Activism," Address before Harvard Law School Symposium (Nov. 16, 1996) *in* 32 Harv. C.R. - C.L. L. Rev. 265, 274 (1997).
13. Cornell West, *Race Matters* xv–xvi (1994).
14. Carbado, *supra* note 2, at 123–24. One might ask, however, how truly reliable a witness she is. Her talk is very cheap, because she steps into the cab notwithstanding her acknowledgment of the injustice.
15. *Id. But see* Ian Ayres, "Is Discrimination Elusive?" 55 Stan. L. Rev. 2419, 2424 (2003) (arguing that victims' perceptions of discrimination may not be sufficient to convince biased decision-makers).
16. *See generally* Betty Fairchild & Nancy Hayward, *Now That You Know: What Every Parent Should Know about Homosexuality* (1989) (collecting "coming out" narratives by parents and gay/lesbian/bisexual children who discuss the way the child's homosexuality has affected relationships with their parents).
17. Eve Kosofsky Sedgwick, *Tendencies* 156 (1993).
18. *Id.* at 156–57 (quoting DSM-III (1980) at 265–66).
19. Indeed, it is letting go of these stories that causes many nongay parents so much pain when they learn about their child's homosexuality. *See* Fairchild & Hayward, *supra* note 16, at 51 (parent needed "a glimpse of a possible good future to replace the wonderful imagined one I had built up in my head while Larry was growing up, and which had been lost with his announcement [that he was gay]").
20. Some people feel compelled to explain to even very young children that "boys can't marry boys" and "girls can't marry girls." While such a response is, in some ways, true, it is in other ways inadequate. First, with respect to the celebration or sacrament of marriage, the statement is partially false: in several religious faiths, men *can* marry men and women *can* marry women. Second, the statement emphasizes current law rather than the law that will ultimately be most relevant to the child: it is by no means clear that by the time a three-year-old comes of age, marriage laws will continue to discriminate as they currently do. Finally, while parents might strive for accuracy in their positive statements of law (thus requiring them to make clear that civil marriage in the United States is currently limited to couples consisting of one man and one woman), they can and perhaps should complement the positive statement with a normative claim (making clear that they think current marriage laws are unfair and ought to be changed). This needn't require parents to overload their children with jargon; even a three-year-old can understand this simple statement: "Some rules say that boys can only marry girls and girls can only marry boys, but we think this is unfair and we're working to change those rules."
21. When celebrity Rosie O'Donnell came out as a lesbian, she admitted with some reluctance that she hopes her children will be heterosexual, if only because life

is easier in some ways for heterosexuals than for gay people. *See 20/20* (ABC television broadcast interview), March 15, 2002.

22. Though we do not think of our children as sexual beings, many gay and lesbian people report that they perceived themselves as "different" even from a very early age: "According to gay people, both women and men, many of them knew from a very early age (even at three or four or five years) that they were 'different.' They didn't have words for it; none could say at that tender age, 'I am homosexual,' but they sensed that somehow they did not fit the picture of what girls or boys were 'supposed to be.' Many have experienced an attraction to others of the same gender for most of their lives." Fairchild & Hayward, *supra* note 16, at 25.

23. Unfortunately, many parents do this in a negative way, wracking themselves with guilt in a search for "mistakes" they made that caused their children's homosexuality. *See, e.g., id.* at 56.

24. Fern Kupfer, "Mothering: A Child's Insight about Gay Love," Newsday, Feb. 10, 1996, at B3.

25. See, for example, an excerpt from Fred Small's lullaby, "Everything Possible":

> As the moon sets sail to carry you to sleep
> over the midnight sea
> I will sing you a song no one sang to me
> May it keep you good company
>
> You can be anybody you want to be
> You can love whomever you will
> You can travel any country where your heart leads
> And know I will love you still

Fred Small, Everything Possible (Pine Barrens Music (BMI) 1983).

26. William N. Eskridge, *Gaylaw: Challenging the Apartheid of the Closet* 224 (1999).

27. Marjorie B. Garber, *Vice Versa: Bisexuality and the Eroticism of Everyday Life* 33–34 (1995), citing Montieth M. Illingworth, "Looking for Mr. Goodbyte," *Mirabella*, December 1994, at 111.

28. We deliberately put these words in the mouth of a white man, because we recognize that the issue may play out differently for women, particularly women of color. Because this country's history has witnessed African-American women under the rule and even under the ownership of white men, an African-American woman's desire to find a nonwhite mate has a different social meaning from that created when members of an historically empowered group judge people on the basis of race.

29. *See* Anmol "Moe" Chaddha & Liz Lee, "Anti-Asian Hate Crimes in Amerikkka," at http://us_asians.tripod.com/articles-fetish.html (last visited Sept. 24, 2004) ("This exoticization seems so prevalent now that an Asian American female,

the 'object of desire,' can't even discern whether a white guy is attracted to her as an individual or because of her exotic 'Asianness.').

30. Peter Norton, the originator of the popular Norton Utilities software, is unapologetic in having a heteroracial orientation: he is white but is only attracted to African-American women. *See* Stacey E. Blau, "Honesty about That Which Disturbs Us—Discussion of the Relationships between White Men and Asian Women Needs More Truthfulness," The Tech, Nov. 18, 1997 *at* http://www-tech.mit.edu/V117/N59/blau.59c.html (last visited June 28, 2004).

31. Evolutionary psychologists have puzzled over the continued existence of homosexuality, given their assumptions about a procreative imperative. How, they have asked, could a genetic disposition toward homosexuality survive, if it was only through heterosexual sex that genes could be passed to future generations? Notwithstanding this puzzle, some have suggested that homosexuality might carry some advantages from an evolutionary standpoint. Robert Wright, for example, has posited that nonprocreating relatives (a "gay uncle" or "lesbian aunt") would have shared significant genetic material with procreating siblings. And because these gay uncles and aunts would have lacked their own children to care for, they would have had even greater resources to contribute to the survival of their nieces and nephews—by feeding, protecting, and nurturing them. Therefore, their genes (or at least something close) would have had enhanced success. Other scholars have suggested additional ways in which attraction to members of the same sex could prove sufficiently advantageous that evolution would sustain it. *See* Robert Wright, *The Moral Animal: Why We Are the Way We Are : The New Science of Evolutionary Psychology* (1995).

32. Any remaining justification for discrimination based on procreation turns on a preference for offspring who are doubly genetically related that is hard to justify. Half of bisexuals by chance will have access to traditional means of procreation, and the other half could have adopted children or have children that share the genetic traits of at least one of the partners.

33. In Spike Lee's film *Jungle Fever*, a black man's attraction to a white woman is experienced and critiqued as a racist rejection of black women.

34. *See* Andrew Koppelman, "The Miscegenation Analogy: Sodomy Law as Sex Discrimination," 98 Yale L.J. 145, 147 (1988); Sylvia Law, "Homosexuality and the Social Meaning of Gender," 1988 Wis. L. Rev. 187, 188–97, 218–22 (1988).

35. As Professor Devon Carbado explains:

> There is a tendency on the part of dominant groups (e.g., males and heterosexuals) to discount the experiences of subordinate groups (e.g., straight women, lesbians and gays) unless those experiences are authenticated or legitimized by a member of the dominant group. For example, it is one thing for me, a Black man, to say I experienced discrimination in a particular so-

cial setting; it is quite another for my white male colleague to say he witnessed that discrimination. My telling of the story is suspect because I am Black (racially interested). My white colleague's telling of the story is not suspect because he is white (racially disinterested). The racial transparency of whiteness—its "perspectivelessness"—renders my colleague's account "objective."

Carbado, *supra* note 2, at 122.

36. Karen Marie Harbeck, *Gay and Lesbian Educators: Personal Freedoms, Public Constraints* (1997).
37. Dan Woog, *Friends and Family: True Stories of Gay America's Straight Allies* 111–121 (1999).
38. One federal judge has noted that "studies show that more than ninety percent of high school students hear negative comments regarding homosexuality during the school day." Chambers v. Babbitt, 145 F.Supp.2d 1068 (D. Minn. 2001).
39. 251 F.3d 604 (7th Cir. 2001).
40. "GLSEN Celebrates 2000th Gay-Straight Alliance," http://www.glsen.org/cgi-bin/iowa/chapter/library/record/1635.html (last visited June 28, 2004).
41. Chambers v. Babbitt, 145 F.Supp.2d 1068 (D. Minn. 2001).
42. William N. Eskridge, Jr., "No Promo Homo: The Sedimentation of Antigay Discourse and the Channeling Effect of Judicial Review," 75 N.Y.U. L. Rev. 1327 (2000).
43. ACLU, "Letter to School Officials Regarding Gay/Straight Alliances" http://www.aclu.org/LesbianGayRights/LesbianGayRights.cfm?ID=9180&c=106 (last visited June 26, 2004).
44. ACLU, "Letter Urging Adoption of Safe Schools Policies" (Jan. 23, 2004), http://www.aclu.org/LesbianGayRights/LesbianGayRights.cfm?ID=9179&c=106 (last visited June 28, 2004).
45. http://www.aclu.org (last visited June 28, 2004).
46. *See* Fairchild & Hayward, *supra* note 16, at 152–82 (outlining various denominations' responses to gay clergy).
47. Joe Miksch & Colleen Van Tassell, "Priests Are Standing against the Church and Supporting Gay Unions. Quietly," New Haven Advocate, Dec. 19, 2002, http://old.newhavenadvocate.com/articles/fathercourage.html (last visited July 1, 2004).
48. http://anglicancommunionnetwork.org/theological/ (last visited June 28, 2004).
49. http://anglicancommunionnetwork.org/news/dspnews.cfm?id=24 (Apr. 16, 2004) (last visited June 28, 2004).
50. *See* Press Release, Laura Montgomery Rutt, "Soulforce Announces Direct Actions in 2001 against Antigay Policies of Southern Baptist, Lutheran, Mormon, & Catholic Churches. Urges Gay, Lesbian, Bisexual, Transgender Individuals and Allies to Stand Up against Church Teachings and Actions

That Lead to Spiritual Violence against Them" (Mar, 23, 2001) (on file with author).

51. Fr. Michael Ray & Lou Nemeth, "Memorandum to Interested Parties, Faith United: The Bishop's Fund for Humanity," June 21, 2004 (copy on file with author).

52. *Id.*

53. In chapter 7, we propose an Informed Association Statute that would require Boy Scouts to sign a written acknowledgment that they are choosing to associate with an organization that retains the right to discriminate on the basis of sexual orientation. You should ask yourself if you would be willing to sign such a document with regard to your church.

54. *See generally* Jammie Price, *Navigating Differences: Friendship between Gay and Straight Men* (1999) (study of forty-four friendships between gay and nongay men across sexual orientations).

55. M. V. Lee Badgett, "Thinking Homo/Economically," *in Overcoming Heterosexism and Homphobia: Strategies That Work* 381 (James T. Sears & Walter L. Williams, eds. 1997), citing M. V. Lee Badgett, "The Wage Effects of Sexual Orientation Discrimination," 48 Indus. & Labor Rel. Rev. 726 (1995).

56. Woog, *supra* note 37, at 216–23.

57. For a description of the Safe Spaces Program and how it fits into the larger project of being an "ally," see the Human Rights Campaign web site, http://www.hrc.org/Content/NavigationMenu/Coming_Out/Get_Informed4/Allies_and_Safe_Zones/Full_Text.htm (last visited June 28, 2004).

58. Amy Joyce, "Sexuality an Overlooked Diversity Factor: Short-Sighted Companies Might Miss Out on about 10 Percent of the Labor Pool," Washington Post, April 25, 2004, F6.

59. *Id.*; "Coverage & Access: USA Today Examines Employer Provision of Health Benefits for Domestic Partners," Kaisernetwork.org (Apr. 14, 2004), http://www.kaisernetwork.org/daily_reports/rep_index.cfm?DR_ID=23189 (last visited June 28, 2004).

60. Stephanie Armour, "Gay Marriage Debate Moves into Workplace," USA Today, April 14, 2004, at B1, http://www.usatoday.com/money/workplace/2004–04–14–gay-marriage-workers_x.htm (last visited June 28, 2004).

61. Portland, Maine, Code of Ordinances, Sect. 13.6–34 (2003), http://www.ci.portland.me.us/Chapter013_6.pdf (last visited June 28, 2004).

62. Broward, Fla., County Code of Ordinances Sec. 16 ½-157 (2003).

Chapter Three
The Vacation Pledge for Equal Marriage Rights

1. Baehr v. Lewin, 852 P.2d 44 (Haw. 1993).
2. Goodridge v. Department of Public Health, 798 N.E.2d 941 (Mass. 2003).

3. *See, e.g.,* "Oregon Attorney General: Gay Marriage Illegal," CNN.com, http://www.cnn.com/2004/LAW/03/12/oregon.gay.marriage/index.html (visited June 28, 2004).

4. 2004 N.Y. Op. Atty. Gen. No. 1 (2004).

5. George W. Bush, "President Calls for Constitutional Amendment Protecting Marriage, Remarks by the President" (Feb. 24, 2004), http://www.whitehouse.gov/news/releases/2004/02/20040224-2.html (last visited Sept. 24, 2004).

6. Jennifer Gerarda Brown, "Competitive Federalism and the Legislative Incentives to Recognize Same-Sex Marriage," 68 S. Cal. L. Rev. 745 (1995).

7. Aude Lagorce, "Same-Sex Weddings, The Gay-Marriage Windfall: $16.8 Billion," Forbes, Apr. 5, 2004, at 84.

8. These state statutes have been dubbed "mini-DOMAs" to refer to the fact that they mirror the federal Defense of Marriage Act. The goal of this statute (the constitutionality of which has yet to be tested) is to establish that the U.S. Constitution's full faith and credit clause—which generally requires states to recognize the acts and judgments of sibling states—does not apply to marriages between people of the same sex.

9. H.D. 751, 2004 Gen. Assemb., Reg. Sess. (Va. 2004).

10. Christoper Lisotta, "Study: Gay Marriage Boosts California Budget" (posted May 12, 2004), Gay.com, http://www.gay.com/news/article.html?2004/05/12/2 (last visited Sept. 24, 2004).

11. Jon Macey and Geoff Miller have pointed out that in commercial contexts, states compete not just for franchise taxes, but also for other jurisdictional rents (such as increased litigation and transactional business for members of the state bar). See Jonathan R. Macey & Geoffrey P. Miller, "Toward an Interest-Group Theory of Delaware Corporate Law," 65 Tex. L. Rev. 469 (1987).

12. *See* Roberta Romano, "Law as a Product: Some Pieces of the Incorporation Puzzle," 1 J. L. Econ. & Org. 225, 265–73 (1985).

13. Brown, *supra* note , at 785–86.

14. *See* Sam Howe Verhovek, "Texas County Retreats over Apple's Gay Policy," N.Y. Times, Dec. 8, 1993, at A18.

15. See, e.g., Macey & Miller, *supra* note 11, at 471 (complete theory of Delaware corporate law requires analysis of internal as well as external interest groups); Thomas E. Wilson, "Separation between Banking and Commerce under the Bank Holding Company Act—a Statutory Objective under Attack," 33 Cath. U. L. Rev. 163, 165 (1983) (South Dakota competed for affiliations with national banks by permitting its banks to engage directly or through subsidiaries in the insurance business).

16. Michael Wright, "Avoidance Tactics," Atlantic, Oct. 1993, at 44, 48.

17. *Id.*

18. Stuart Elliott, "A Sharper View of Gay Consumers," N.Y. Times, June 9, 1994, at D1.

19. Mary Gottschalk, "Gay Cachet: Advertisers Get Wise to the Fact That the Gay and Lesbian Community Is a $500 Billion a Year Gold Mine," San Jose Mercury News, Sept. 19, 1993, at 1H, 7H.

20. *Id.*

21. Stu Glauberman, "Gay Tourism: Island Companies Tap a Growing Market," Honolulu Advertiser, Feb. 14, 1994, at C1.

22. One could draw a humorous analogy to Ben & Jerry's ice cream, which offers consumers a socially conscious rationale (the company donates a percentage of profits to charity) for buying a fairly decadent product.

23. Elizabeth Mehren, *Legislature Moves to Bar Gay Marriages*, L.A. Times, Mar. 30, 2004, at 1A. With the departure of House Speaker Thomas M. Finneran in September 2004 and the elevation of the more liberal Salvatore F. DiMasi to the post, some legislators have voiced doubts that the constitutional amendment will even come up for a legislative vote in 2005. DiMasi supports same-sex marriage and voted against the amendment in 2004. See Frank Phillips, "Prospects Shift as DiMasi Takes Over for Finneran," Boston Globe, Sept. 28, 2004, at http://www.boston.com/news/local/articles/2004/09/28/prospects_shift_as_dimasi_takes_over_for_finneran?mode=PF (last visited Oct. 7, 2004).

24. To be sure, elected representatives, like the mayors of San Francisco and New Paltz acting in their official capacities, have sought to further the cause of equal marriage rights. But to date no legislative action has occurred.

25. *See generally* Heather Hamilton, "The Defense of Marriage Act: A Critical Analysis of Its Constitutionality under the Full Faith and Credit Clause," 47 DePaul L. Rev. 943 (1998); Paige E. Chabora, "Congress' Power under the Full Faith and Credit Clause and the Defense of Marriage Act of 1996," 76 Neb. L. Rev. 604 (1997).

26. N.M.Stat. Ann. § 40–1–4 (Michie 1978).

27. Stanley Kurtz, "The Next State to Drop: Gay Marriage Heads to New Mexico" (last modified Mar. 3, 2004), at www.nationalreview.com/kurtz/kurtz 200403030846.asp (last visited Sept. 24, 2004).

28. States that have enacted mini-DOMAs may nonetheless recognize the same-sex marriages of other states for some purposes. For example, imagine that long-term Massachusetts residents of the same sex marry in the commonwealth and then reside there permanently. On a ski vacation in Utah, one of them is severely injured. It is difficult to imagine that Utah would deny spousal privileges of hospital visitation to such a couple, even if the state would refuse to recognize the marriage in other contexts.

29. New York State Board of Elections, Election Results, http://www.elections.state.ny.us/elections/election.htm (last visited Sept. 28, 2004).

30. *See* Tom Precious & Jerry Zremski, "Marriage Bans/Same-Sex Marriage Is a 'Volatile Issue' Unlikely to Get Quick Congressional or State Legislature Action," Buffalo News, Dec. 3, 2003, at News A1.

31. For a list of laws passed since 1998 related to gay rights, see Pride Agenda, http://www.prideagenda.org/pressreleases/accomplishments.html (last visited Sept. 24, 2004).

32. Of course, it is possible that the legislature of another state such as Connecticut, in good competitive federalism fashion, would beat Massachusetts to the punch. But at this writing, the possibility of such a race seems remote.

33. In the United States, the United Church of Christ has 1.4 million members (not all of whom, it should be noted, support gay rights, despite the church's policy to let individual congregations decide whether to celebrate gay unions, hire gay clergy, or promote gay rights). *See* "About the UCC," http://www.ucc.org/aboutus/whatis.htm (last visited May 20, 2004). Other religious organizations, including the Society of Friends (Quakers), the Unity Church, the Metropolitan Community Church, and the Unitarian Universalist Church have adopted "welcoming" policies or missions toward LGBT people, and together they boast membership in excess of 300,000. In addition, several mainline Protestant churches (Episcopalians, Methodists, and Presbyterians) have debated the propriety of celebrating marriages or holy unions between people of the same sex, which suggests that within each of these denominations some significant group of people supports equal marriage rights.

34. On this list one might include *Harpers, Utne, Mother Jones,* and *Common Cause.* While *The New Republic* is also a possibility, the readership of that publication seems to have a much more diverse political outlook.

35. Paul Weyrich, "American Airlines Cuts Jobs but Sponsors Gay Events," Newsmax.com (Sept. 13, 2003) (noting Southern Baptist boycott of Disney Corp due to gay-friendly employment policies, and calling for boycott of American Airlines on same basis), http://www.newsmax.com/archives/articles/2003/9/12/174936.shtml (last visited Sept. 24, 2004).

36. For a discussion of this "tipping" problem and a prediction that it would cause little or no harm to the first-mover state, see Brown, *supra* , at 806–10.

37. Pam Belluck, "Romney Won't Let Gay Outsiders Wed in Massachusetts," N.Y. Times, Apr. 25, 2004, A1.

38. Amendment 2 in Colorado forbade any local government to pass a law granting protections or rights to people on the basis of sexual orientation. In Romer v. Evans, 517 U.S. 620 (1996), the U.S. Supreme Court struck down Amendment 2 as a violation of the equal protection clause, finding that it failed even the deferential "rational relationship" test. Organizations such as the Family Research Council and Colorado for Family Values were active in the passage and defense of Amendment 2.

39. When Hawaii debated the issue of same-sex marriage in the early and mid-1990s several organizations and religious institutions actively opposed extending marriage rights to same-sex couples. The American Family Association in Tupelo, Mississippi, threatened a boycott of the state by its "1.8 million sup-

porters." Peter Rosegg, "Gay Marriage Furor Intensifies," Honolulu Advertiser, Feb. 12, 1994 at C1. Mormon leaders called upon members of that church to oppose same-sex marriages actively. In 1997, the Southern Baptist Convention called upon its 15 million members to boycott the Walt Disney Company, citing what it called "anti-family, pro-gay" practices and policies. See "Southern Baptists Vote for Disney Boycott" (posted June 18, 1997), CNN Interactive, http://www.cnn.com/US/9706/18/baptists.disney/ (last visited Sept. 24, 2004). Compliance was reportedly spotty, however, as many church members disagreed with and disregarded the boycott. Supporters of gay rights and Disney launched a "buycott" in response. To counter pickets and protests planned by two conservative organizations for the first week in June 1998, LGBT and ally customers were encouraged to visit Walt Disney World as well as Disney retail stores on June 6, 1998 (http://www.gayday.com/stand/index.htm). Despite the lack of evidence that it has had any impact on Disney, the American Family Association continues to promote a Disney boycott (http://www.afa.net/ disney/default.asp) ("Profits from family entertainment products and theme parks are subsidizing Disney's promotion of the homosexual agenda. A boycott— including even their good products—is the only way to impact the company").

40. This is a conservative number, when one considers the cost of hotels and restaurants. But in 2000, the average American visitor to Hawaii spent $1,722 (ten days at $172.20 per day). Tourists probably spend more days, on average, in Hawaii than they do in other states, and daily spending might be higher as well. *See 2000 State of Hawaii Data Book*, table 7.11, "Length of Stay of Visitors Staying Overnight or Longer, by Points of Origin: 1999 and 2000"; *id.* at table 7.14, "Average Expenditure per Visitor Day in Constant Dollars, for Visitors from the Mainland: 1931–1932 to 2000."

41. *2000 State of Hawaii Data Book* table 7.09, "Domestic Visitors by States and Regions: 1999 and 2000."

42. We can calculate this probability by dividing the number of visitors to Hawaii in a year—3.95 million people—by the total number of Americans—285 million. *See* Population Division, U.S. Census Bureau, table US-2001EST-01, "Time Series of National Population Estimates: April 1, 2000 to July 1, 2001" (December 27, 2001).

43. We reach this number by multiplying one million people times $500 times .03.

44. If it seems impossible that all of the pledge signers will honor their promise, we can reduce this number. If only half of the signers make good on their promise, the expected revenue per year attributable to signers of the pledge holds at $83 million!

45. For a state like Hawaii, for example, addresses could be particularly valuable, as it would allow the state to target potential visitors from the central, eastern, and southern United States. These are more likely to be first-time visitors, and first-time visitors spend more in the state, on average, than repeat visitors.

46. Forty states have restricted marriage rights through DOMA legislation, a referendum, or a state constitutional amendment. These include Alabama, Alaska, Arizona, Arkansas, California, Colorado, Delaware, Florida, Georgia, Hawaii, Idaho, Illinois, Indiana, Iowa, Kansas, Kentucky, Louisiana, Maine, Michigan, Minnesota, Mississippi, Missouri, Montana, Nebraska, Nevada, New Hampshire, North Carolina, North Dakota, Ohio, Oklahoma, Oregon, Pennsylvania, South Carolina, South Dakota, Tennessee, Texas, Utah, Virginia, Washington, and West Virginia. *See* Marriage Watch, "State Defense of Marriage Acts (DOMA)," http://www.marriagewatch.org/states/doma.htm (last visited June 28, 2004).

47. This parallels the interjurisdictional effect of "Patriot Dollars" campaign contribution vouchers. *See* Bruce A. Ackerman & Ian Ayres, *Voting with Dollars: A New Paradigm for Campaign Finance* (2002); Pamela S. Karlan, "Elections and Change under Voting with Dollars," 91 Cal. L. Rev. 705 (2003).

Chapter Four
The Fair Employment Mark

1. Licensing a trademark while giving up control of the product would constitute abandonment of the mark under federal trademark law.

2. *See* 15 USC §§1054, 1064.

3. Ernest R. Spedden, Johns Hopkins University Studies in History and Political Science Series 28, no. 2, *The Trade-Union Label* (John Hopkins Press 1910), *microformed on* Primary Source Media, 1998, Fiches 34,876–77.

4. U.S. Dept. of Labor Bureau of Int'l Labor Affairs (ILAB), "By the Sweat and Toil of Children, vol. 4: Consumer Labels and Child Labor" (1997), http://www.dol.gov/ILAB/media/reports/iclp/sweat4/toc.htm (visited May 21, 2004).

5. *Id.*

6. *Id.*

7. *Id.*

8. *Id.*

9. S. 1705, 108th Cong., 1st Sess. (2003). J. Banning Jasiunas, Note, "Is ENDA the Answer? Can a 'Separate but Equal' Federal Statute Adequately Protect Gays and Lesbians from Employment Discrimination?" 61 Ohio St. L.J. 1529 (2000).

10. Representative Barney Frank, a supporter of ENDA, has stated that ENDA would result in legal protection "for gay and lesbian people" identical to the protections granted by Title VII. *See* Jasiunas, *supra* note 9, at 1545–46.

11. Jasiunas, *supra* note 9, at 1546.

12. *Id.*

13. Some employers might also want to make these benefits available to employees' different-sex domestic partners. In our view, an employer's decision *not* to cover different-sex domestic partners should not preclude use of the Fair Em-

ployment Mark. Because different-sex couples have the option of marrying and thereby gaining employment benefits, while same-sex couples cannot (except in Massachusetts), it seems fair to include unmarried same-sex couples, but not unmarried different-sex couples in the benefits package. If the employer operates in a state that extends equal marriage rights to same-sex couples, the need for domestic partner benefits might similarly dissipate; discriminating on the basis of marital status need not have a disparate impact on gay people.

14. Daryl Herrschaft & Kim I. Mills, Human Rights Campaign, "The State of the Workplace for Lesbian, Gay, Bisexual, and Transgender Americans, 2003 (2004), http://www.hrc.org/Template.cfm?Section=20042&Template=/Content Management/ContentDisplay.cfm&ContentID=18678 (last visited May 21, 2004).

15. The Human Rights Campaign is a gay rights advocacy organization based in Washington, D.C., that administers the index.

16. HRC acquired "glvindex" in 2001 and subsequently renamed it the HRC Corporate Equality Index survey. *See* http://www.hrc.org/Content/Navigation Menu/Work_Life/Get_Informed2/Corporate_Equality_Index/Non_Responders/ CEI_Non-Responders.htm (last visited Sept. 20, 2004).

17. *See* Human Rights Campaign Foundation, Search Companies with Corporate Equality Index Ratings, http://www.hrc.org/Template.cfm?Section=Corporate_ Equality_Index&Template=/CustomSource/WorkNet/WorkplacePolicySearch CEI.cfm (last visited and searched May 21, 2004).

18. Gay rights advocacy organizations continue to debate the merits of ENDA's omission of gender identity. *See, e.g.,* Adrian Brune, "HRC Vows No ENDA If No Trans Protection: Dramatic Policy Shift Follows Protests, Lobbying Effort," Washington Blade Online, Aug. 13, 2004, http://www.washblade.com/2004/ 8–13/news/national/enda.cfm (last visited Aug. 23, 2004).

19. *See generally,* Kenneth Timmerman, *Shakedown: Exposing the Real Jesse Jackson* (2002); Marc Morano, "PUSH Comes to Shove: Jesse Jackson's Empire Crumbles," CNSNews.com, Jan. 15, 2002, http://www.newsmax.com/archives/articles/ 2002/1/14/170935.shtml (last visited May 21, 2004).

20. *See* Human Rights Campaign, HRC WorkNet Employer Database, http:// www.hrc.org/Template.cfm?Section=Search_the_Database&Template=/Custom Source/WorkNet/WorkplacePolicyEmployerDetail.cfm&EmpID=1184&List Sector=1&MarketSector=PFS&ShowCEI=1 (last visited June 28, 2004).

21. *See id.*

22. Gallup Poll, Question Id: USGALLUP.0331 Q19, *see also* 2004 L.A. Times Poll, Question Id: USLAT .041104 R52 (70 percent favor . . . laws to protect gays against job discrimination).

23. FAQ, web site for the Coalition for Consumer Information on Cosmetics, http://www.leapingbunny.org/faq.htm (last visited May 21, 2004).

24. U.S. Patent Office #636,593 and #1,087891, http://www.ou.org/kosher/policy.htm (last visited May 21, 2004).
25. http://www.ou.org/about/ou.htm (last visited May 21, 2004).
26. The web site of the Orthodox Union carries a short article that illustrates the complexity of compliance. *See* "Is Your Kosher Program Running Smoothly?" http://www.ou.org/kosher/behindsymbol/kosherprog.htm (last visited May 21, 2004).
27. Havens Realty Corp. v. Coleman, 455 U.S. 363, 102 S.Ct. 1114, 71 L.Ed.2d 214 (1982) (giving standing to civil rights organization to sue as fair housing plaintiff).
28. A final consideration concerns arbitrability of these nondiscrimination claims. Again, we adhere to a model that makes the mark a privatized analog to ENDA itself. Under ENDA (as with Title VII), discrimination disputes would be arbitrable so long as the arbitration agreement was conscionable. *See* Circuit City Stores, Inc. v. Adams, 532 U.S. 105, 121 S.Ct. 1302, 149 L.Ed.2d 234 (2001) (contract requiring arbitration of all employment disputes is enforceable), *on remand* 279 F.3d 889 (9th Cir. 2001) (ordinary principles of state contract law determine validity of agreement to arbitrate; because arbitration agreement was both procedurally and substantively unconscionable under California law, it was unenforceable), *cert. denied* 535 U.S. 1112, 122 S.Ct. 2329, 153 L.Ed.2d 160 (2002). We believe the same standards should generally apply to the licensing agreement, ENDA, and Title VII. But since the licensing agreement does not include an arbitration clause, applicants would be free to litigate claims arising from it. Even employees who signed employment contracts containing arbitration clauses might be able to litigate violations of the employment mark, qua third-party beneficiaries of the licensing agreement.
29. On the one hand, this seems to be an extremely conservative assumption, since 88 percent of Americans oppose employment discrimination on the basis of sexual orientation, according to a 2003 Gallup Poll. Question Id: USGALLUP .01M010 R30. *See also* L.A. Times Poll, *supra* note 22. On the other hand, this group of Americans might not feel so strongly about the issue that they would make purchasing decisions based upon it.
30. Some of the remaining eight firms may affirmatively signal their antipathy for gays to gain some of the antigay consumers.
31. M.V. Lee Badgett, "Thinking Homo/Economically," *in Overcoming Heterosexism and Homphobia: Strategies That Work* 380 (James T. Sears & Walter L. Williams, eds. 1997).
32. The Equality Project, for example, is "an investor coalition dedicated to supporting and espousing full adoption of the Equality Principles on Sexual Orientation and Gender Expression in the workplace through shareholder activism, education and community outreach" (http://www.equalityproject .org/index.htm, last visited July 1, 2004). The HRC Equality Index also helps

investors avoid discriminatory companies and direct their money to companies that treat LGBT employees fairly.

Chapter Five
Ambiguation

1. Jamie Washington & Nancy J. Evans, "Becoming an Ally," at 199 *in Beyond Tolerance: Gays, Lesbians, and Bisexuals on Campus* (Nancy J. Evans & Vernon A. Wall, eds. 1991).
2. We are indebted to Devon Carbado for presenting so clearly the dilemma this chapter seeks to address (if not resolve).

   > On the one hand, self-identifying as a heterosexual is a way to position oneself within a discourse so as not to create the (mis) impression of gay authenticity. Moreover, revealing one's heterosexuality can help to convey the idea that "heterosexism should be as much an issue for straight people as racism should be for white people." On the other hand, "coming out" as a heterosexual can be a heteronormative move to avoid gay and lesbian stigmatization.

   Devon W. Carbado, "Straight Out of the Closet," 15 Berkeley Women's L.J. 76, 113 (2000) (quoting Bruce Ryder, "Straight Talk: Male Heterosexual Privilege," 16 Queens L.J. 287, 287 (1991)).
3. In written forums, more deliberate signaling may be necessary. *See, e.g.,* April L. Cherry, "Nurturing in the Service of White Culture: Racial Subordination, Gestational Surrogacy, and the Ideology of Motherhood," 10 Tex. J. Women & L. 83 (2001) ("It might help to know that I am African-American").
4. Lawrence Lessig, "The Regulation of Social Meaning," 62 U. Chi. L. Rev. 943, 1010 (1995).
5. Able v. United States, 968 F. Supp. 850, 860 (E.D. N.Y. 1997), *rev'd on other grounds,* 155 F.3d 628 (2d Cir. 1998) ("The argument as to privacy is without substantial merit. It assumes that, provided homosexuals stay in the closet, heterosexuals will believe there are no homosexuals present in their unit. In fact homosexuals are present and are entitled to be present. . . . Even if homosexuals keep their orientation a secret, no rational person would be deceived into believing that the facilities are heterosexual only").
6. This example is also discussed in Lessig, *supra* note 4, at 1010–11.
7. Historians have been unable to document this as having actually happened. *See* Jorgen H. Barfod, Norman L. Kleebatt, and Vivian B. Mann, eds., *Kings and Citizens: the History of the Jews in Denmark 1622–1983* (1983).
8. See Carmen Agra Deedy, *The Yellow Star: The Legend of King Christian X of Denmark* (2000) for a poetic and moving rendition of this story.

9. Lessig, *supra* note 4, at 1010–11.
10. Laurie Goodstein & Tamar Lewin, "Victims of Mistaken Identity, Sikhs Pay a Price for Turbans," N.Y. Times (Sept. 19, 2001), at A1, http://www.nytimes .com/2001/09/19/national/19HATE.html (last visited May 28, 2004).
11. *Id.*
12. *See* Ann Rostow, "Girlbriefs," Girlfriends, October 2000, at 9.
13. The differences were calculated, apparently. One city commissioner noted that the bumper sticker used a six-color rainbow, while the gay pride flag uses eight colors. In addition, she insisted, the designers of the bumper sticker chose a shade of purple different from the purple in the pride flag. Heather Van Dyke, "'Diversity' Stickers Will Be Removed," Traverse City Record-Eagle, January 3, 2001, http://www.recordeagle.com/2001/jan/03sticke.htm (last visited May 28, 2004).
14. Amber Arellano, "City's Rainbow Sticker Causes Controversy," Detroit Free Press, January 4, 2001, 1A, http://www.freep.com/news/mich/bumper4_ 20010104.htm (last visited May 29, 2004). In other interviews, however, this same city commissioner embraced the association between the rainbow and gay rights. Indeed, she conceived the sticker idea expressly to emulate the Danes' appropriation of the yellow star when she heard that gay citizens were removing rainbow flag stickers from their own cars out of fear of attack. See "Traverse City Over the Rainbow," http://www.ntac.org/news/01/01/02 city.html (last visited Oct. 13, 2004).
15. Van Dyke, *supra* note 13.
16. *Id.*
17. *See Id.* ("[City attorney W. Peter] Doren announced at Tuesday's city commis- sion meeting that city property displaying the stickers—such as city police, fire and snowplow vehicles—were made a 'public forum' by affixing a sticker that represented only one group of people. Doren said the placement of the stickers did not 'themselves violate any rights,' but if the city commission doesn't re- move the bumper sticker 'it becomes hard to refuse second, third or fourth stickers'"). One might ask attorney Doren to identify the one group repre- sented by a sticker that says, "We are Traverse City"—or why the use of a rain- bow in the design leads to the conclusion that only one group is represented there.
18. Though the pink triangle has become a symbol of pride, it originated as a sym- bol to mark homosexual prisoners in Nazi concentration camps.
19. Thomas Bevier, "Traverse City Washes Hands of Controversial Sticker, Cultural Diversity Logo Being Sold by Panel to Antibias Organization," Triangle Foun- dation, February 23, 2001, http://www.tri.org/news/010223.html (last visited Oct. 11, 2004)
20. Interestingly, no one in the movie claims to be "bisexual," though Jack's friend comes close when he says he is gay but can't resist bragging about his skill in

doing "it" with "chicks." *See* Kenji Yoshino, "The Epistemic Contract of Bisexual Erasure," 52 Stan. L. Rev. 353 (2000).

21. Association of American Law Schools, *The AALS Directory of Law Teachers, 1996–1997*. The list, of modest length when it first appeared, now fills more than two pages of the directory.

22. Michael has not responded to our efforts to discuss the list and his appearance on it (such conversations would, after all, be disambiguating). We thus obscure his identity and offer this analysis only tentatively, and decidedly not with the intent to criticize or judge him negatively.

23. Robin West, "Sex, Reason, and a Taste for the Absurd," 81 Geo. L.J. 2413, 2432 (1993) (reviewing Richard A. Posner, *Sex and Reason* (Harvard University Press 1992)).

24. Alfred C. Kinsey et al., *Sexual Behavior in the Human Male* (1948). The Kinsey Report found that 4 percent of the male respondents had been more or less exclusively homosexual all their lives, and 8% had been more or less exclusively homosexual for at least three years between the ages of sixteen and fifty-five. *Id.* at 651. *See also* Alfred C. Kinsey et al., *Sexual Behavior in the Human Female* 473–74 (1953) (between 3 percent and 8 percent of the unmarried females in the sample, and less than 1 percent of the married females, had homosexual responses or experiences more often than heterosexual responses or experiences; between 2 percent and 6 percent percent of the unmarried females in the group, but less than 1 percent of the married females, had been more or less exclusively homosexual in each of the years between twenty and thirty-five years of age).

25. *See* West, *supra* note 23, at 2433.

26. Interestingly, Posner later wrote that he was "floored" by West's statement. Richard Posner, *Overcoming Law* 573 (1995):

> It is difficult to believe that over a period of twenty years of adulthood (for West was not a child twenty years ago) one could have "no idea" whether one was exclusively attracted to members of one's own sex or almost exclusively attracted to members of the opposite sex.

27. Michael Gross, "Even Richard Gere Gets Dumped," Esquire, July 1995. at 54–63, http://www.mgross.com/profiles/gere.htm (last visited May 27, 2004).

28. *Id.*

29. Gere has also shown a sense of humor about the rumors regarding his sexual orientation. In October 1994, Gere attended a fund-raising event for a gay and lesbian lobbying group in London. There he took the stage to announce: "You've all heard some rumors about me over the years. I guess this is the moment to do it. My name is Richard Gere . . . and I am a lesbian." Gross, *supra* note 27.

30. Gere is not always so circumspect, unfortunately. When his marriage to Cindy

Crawford came under attack and was the subject of media rumor mongering, Crawford and Gere jointly placed a full-page ad in the *London Times* in which they declared, "We are heterosexual and monogamous and take our commitment to each other very seriously." Perhaps to soften the antigay tone of this declaration, the same ad resolved that "we will continue to support 'difficult' causes such as AIDS research and treatment . . . Gay and Lesbian Rights . . . and anything else we wish to support irrespective of what the tabloids try to imply." A Personal Statement by Richard Gere and Cindy Crawford, Advertisement in the Times, London, May 6, 1994, www.tibet.ca/wtnarchive/1994/5/6–2_2.html (last visited May 29, 2004).

31. Girlfriends, November 2000, at 13.

32. Jamie Washington and Nancy Evans may be suggesting something like this when they counsel allies to "model nonheterosexist behavior," including "avoiding making a point of being heterosexual." Washington & Evans, *supra* note 1, at 199. Washington and Evans are contemplating advocacy specifically in the context of conversations with other heterosexuals. It is not clear that they would prescribe such ambiguation before an audience assumed to be more gay-friendly.

33. "A Walk in His Brothers' and Sisters (*sic*) Shoes," Out & Equal Newsletter, Nov. 2002, at 6.

34. See, for example, the earnest discourse within the AALS regarding the compromise schools must strike between the AALS nondiscrimination policy—which in the ordinary course would require all member schools to deny on-campus interviewing privileges to any employer that discriminates on the basis of sexual orientation—and the "Solomon Amendment," a federal statute that threatens to cut off federal funding to any educational institution that bars military employers from campus job interviewing and recruiting (http://www.saltlaw.org/solomon.htm).

35. Professor Devon Carbado has examined and ultimately rejected the argument that heterosexual people should be closeted about their own sexuality in order to preserve the privacy of gay people or render sexual orientation irrelevant to "social and political decision-making." Carbado, *supra* note 2, at 111. Carbado appears to limit his analysis to academic discussions about sexual orientation, however; in these settings sexual orientation may be less often used to disqualify or exclude gay people.

36. Paul Brest & Miranda Oshige, "Affirmative Action for Whom?" 47 Stan. L. Rev. 855, 883 n. 148 (1995) (noting distinctions some have drawn between designations as "Latino" vs. "Hispanic").

37. Carbado, *supra* note 2.

38. The greatest risk in using words like *we, us*, and *our* is that such words might appropriate authority to speak for people who prefer to speak for themselves. In other words, before using such words, one must be careful that "we" actually

exist as an identifiable group, and that the members of the group authorize the heterosexual supporter as a sort of spokesperson.

39. Jamie Washington and Nancy Evans prescribed something like this more than a decade ago when they suggested that allies should "model nonheterosexist behaviors such as being equally physical with men and women." Washington & Evans, *supra* note 1, at 199.

Chapter Six
The Inclusive Command

This chapter substantially reprints an essay we published in the *Michigan Law Review*, October 2004, Vol. 103 No. 1. Copyright 2004 by The Michigan Law Review.

The epigraph comes from Cass R. Sunstein, "Situationism," New Republic, Mar. 13, 2000, at 42, 46 (reviewing Malcolm Gladwell, *The Tipping Point: How Little Things Can Make a Big Difference* (2000)).

1. For simplicity's sake, we will use the term *soldier* to refer to service members of all branches of the military.
2. 1993 Defense Budget House Hearing, 102d Cong., at 45 (1993).
3. Policy Concerning Homosexuality in the Armed Forces: Hearing before the S. Comm. on Armed Services, S. Hrg. No. 103-845, Ex. JX-1, vol. 3, at 707 (testimony of General Powell, Chair of the Joint Chiefs of Staff).
4. *Id.* at 612 (testimony of General Norman Schwatzkopf).
5. Melissa Wells-Petry, *Exclusion: Homosexuals and the Right to Serve* 113–19 (1993). According to Akhil Amar and Alan Hirsch, the official policy against gays in the military resulted largely from "historical accident":

   > Many soldiers returned from World War I suffering from shell shock. The emerging psychiatric profession offered to help the government minimize such problems in the future by screening soldiers to keep out the mentally ill or poorly adjusted. At the time, homosexuality was regarded as a mental illness, so the screening policy kept identified homosexuals out of the armed forces.

   Akhil Reed Amar & Alan Hirsch, *For the People: What the Constitution Really Says about Your Rights* 141 (1998). *See also* Randy Shilts, *Conduct Unbecoming* 115 (1993) (quoting psychiatrist Albert Abrams, who wrote in his 1918 essay "Homosexuality—a Military Menace," that "the homosexualist is not only dangerous but ineffective as a fighter"); Diane H. Mazur, "The Unknown Soldier: A Critique of 'Gays in the Military' Scholarship and Litigation, 29 U.C. Davis L. Rev. 223, 234 (1996).
6. *See, e.g.,* Cammermeyer v. Perry, 97 F.3d 1235, 1236 (9th Cir. 1996) ("a highly

decorated nurse" who received the Bronze Star for distinguished service in Vietnam); Steffan v. Aspin, 8 F.3d 57, 59 (D.C. Cir. 1993) ("an exceptional midshipman" who earned "the respect and praise of his superior officers" and for whom "the sky was the limit"); Watkins v. United States Army, 875 F.2d 699, 701 (9th Cir. 1989) (en banc) ("an outstanding soldier"). *See generally* Shilts, *supra* note 5 (describing the history of gay men and lesbians in the U.S. military and the occasional "purges" that would result in the revelation and termination of many gay and lesbian soldiers).

7. *See generally* Mary Ann Humphrey, *My Country, My Right to Serve: Experiences of Gay Men and Women in the Military, World War II to the Present* (1990) (hereinafter *My Right to Serve*).

8. American Psychiatric Association, *Diagnostic and Statistical Manual of Mental Disorders* 261–83, 380 (3d ed. 1980); Shilts, *supra* note 5, at 715; American Medical Association, H-160.991 Policy on the Healthcare Needs of the Homosexual Population (calling for "physician's nonjudgmental recognition of sexual orientation" and instructing physicians to "oppose[ ] . . . therapy that is based upon the assumption that homosexuality per se is a mental disorder"), http://www.ama-assn.org/ (last visited July 1, 2004).

9. U.S.C. section 654 (b)(1) (1994). The statute provides in pertinent part:

> (b) Policy.—A member of the armed forces shall be separated from the armed forces under regulations prescribed by the Secretary of Defense if one or more of the following findings is made . . .
>
> (1) That the member has engaged in, attempted to engage in, or solicited another to engage in a homosexual act or acts . . .
>
> (2) That the member has stated that he or she is homosexual or bisexual . . .
>
> (3) That the member has married or attempted to marry a person known to be of the same biological sex.

The "don't ask" portion of the policy is contained in a regulation that states that "applicants for enlistment, appointment, or induction shall not be asked or required to reveal whether they are heterosexual, homosexual, or bisexual." Dep't of Defense Directive No. 1304.26, E1.2.8.1. Thus, while the "don't tell" part of the policy is enshrined in statute, the "don't ask" portion is "strictly a regulatory creation." *See* Kenji Yoshino, "Assimilationist Bias in Equal Protection: The Visibility Presumption and the Case of 'Don't Ask, Don't Tell,'" 108 Yale L.J. 485, 539 (1998).

10. Not the least of these flaws is the fact that discharges due to homosexuality have accelerated rather than slowed since its inception. *See* Philip Shenon, "Pentagon Moving to End Abuses of 'Don't Ask, Don't Tell' Policy," N.Y. Times, Aug. 13, 1999 at A1 (noting that 67 percent more gay and lesbian troops were discharged in 1997—a total of 997 individuals—than were discharged in 1994,

the first full year the DADT policy was in effect). More recent drops in discharges are due to America's temporary involvement in war rather than any permanent shift in the practical effects of "don't ask, don't tell." *See* John Files, "Study Says Discharges Continue under 'Don't Ask, Don't Tell,' " N.Y. Times, Mar. 24, 2004, at A18 (suggesting that America's involvement in war may counteract the otherwise steady increase in discharges of homosexuals, noting that 787 were discharged in 2003, "the lowest number since 1995," compared to 906 in 2002 and 1,273 in 2001); Beth Fouhy, "Soldier Dismissed after Revealing He's Gay," FindLaw.com, June 21, 2004 (noting that 770 people were discharged for homosexuality in 2003, a reduction from 1,227 discharges in 2001, "before the invasions of Afghanistan and Iraq"), http://news.findlaw.com/ap_stories/a/w/1152/6–21–2004/20040621051504_40.html (last visited July 1, 2004).

11. *See, e.g.,* Able v. United States, 968 F.Supp. 850, 858 (1997) ("The government does not justify its discrimination by reference to some defect in the performance of homosexuals, or claim that they represent a security risk as likely targets for blackmail," but instead "says that the Act helps foster unit cohesion, promotes the privacy of heterosexuals, and reduces sexual tensions"), *rev'd on other grounds,* 155 F.3d 628 (1998).

12. *Id. See also* Yoshino, *supra* note 10, at 553 ("the justifications for 'don't ask, don't tell'—unit cohesion, privacy, and sexual tension—primarily focus not on the gay servicemember but on the straight servicemember. This can be counted as a pro-gay achievement, as it correctly traces the source of the dysfunction not to the gay servicemember, but to the straight one").

13. *See generally* Charles C. Moskos & John Sibley Butler, *All That We Can Be: Black Leadership and Racial Integration the Army Way* (1996) (suggesting the military has become the most race-egalitarian institution in American society).

14. *Able,* 968 F.Supp. at 859 (quoting Philips v. Perry, 106 F.3d 1420, 1435 (9th Cir. 1997)).

15. Closeted gay individuals often find other gays or gay allies threatening, if for different reasons than intolerant individuals find them threatening. *See* Byrne Fone, *Homophobia: A History* 6 (1998) ("Homophobia is not limited to heterosexuals, of course. It can also be found among . . . repressed homosexuals"). This might stem from a fundamental fear of being outed, either within the military, or within their personal lives, and will cause some gay soldiers to opt for the exclusive command.

16. Indeed, we perversely considered returning to the rule of total exclusion with regard to the exclusive command as a way of further bolstering the tendency of gays to choose the inclusive command. Under this alternative, the military was able to "ask" and then remove gay and lesbian soldiers from the exclusive command. Soldiers who are on the fence would arguably feel less comfortable opting into such a system, and thus choose the inclusive command. In equilib-

rium, most gay soldiers would be better off than under the current regime because they would be able to opt for a safer environment, the inclusive command, and a greater number of soldiers overall may participate. But in the end, we reject this idea. The idea of retrenchment to total exclusion, even if limited to the exclusive command, is too unpalatable to be proposed. *But see* Janet E. Halley, *Don't: A Reader's Guide to the Military's Anti-Gay Policy* 33 (1999) (noting that "don't ask, don't tell" is "much, much worse than" total exclusion since it achieves essentially the same ends, but in a way that is less offensive and less easily contestable).

17. In theory, this atmosphere should currently exist in the military. In the navy, for example, the personnel chief, Vice Admiral Daniel T. Oliver, issued a memorandum on October 28, 1999, reminding commanding officers that they "must not condone homosexual jokes, epithets or derogatory comments, and must ensure a command climate that fosters respect for all individuals." Elizabeth Becker & Katherine Seelye, "The Military Orders Spot Check of Bases on Gay Harassment," N.Y. Times, Dec. 14, 1999. Yet these policies are clearly not effective, and the military knows it. A survey of service members conducted by the Department of Defense in 1999 revealed that 80 percent of soldiers had "heard offensive speech, derogatory names, jokes, or remarks about homosexuals in the last 12 months," 85 percent "believed such comments were tolerated to some extent," and 37 percent said they had "witnessed or experienced an event or behavior toward a Service member that they considered to be harassment based on perceived homosexuality." *See* Office of the Inspector General, Department of Defense, *Report on the Military Environment with Respect to the Homosexual Conduct Policy* (2000) at ii. *See also* Francis X. Cline, "Killer's Trial Shows Gay Soldier's Anguish," N.Y. Times, Dec. 9, 1999, at A18 (noting the "months of vile name calling, rumor mongering," "harassment," and "taunting" that preceded the beating to death of Pfc. Barry Winchell "with a baseball bat as he slept in his barracks bed").

18. *See generally* Tobias Barrington Wolff, "Compelled Affirmations, Free Speech, and the U. S. Military's Don't Ask Don't Tell Policy," 63 Brook. L. Rev. 1141 (1997) (DADT implicitly requires gay and lesbian soldiers, even when silent as to their sexual orientation, falsely to affirm assumptions that they are heterosexual).

19. In theory, it should be possible to test this even now. In some military settings, gay, lesbian, or bisexual service members have been permitted to serve even after commanders and fellow service members become aware of their homosexuality. Commanders of such units could test the unit cohesion hypothesis by tracking performance levels before and after the date on which the service member's homosexuality became widely known. While theoretically possible, such studies are unlikely to occur because a commander might violate DADT if he or she fails to initiate discharge proceedings against an openly gay service

member. Thus the commander's self-interest precludes an admission that the gay service member's homosexuality is or was widely known within the unit.

20. This may be an overstatement with respect to individuals. Anecdotal evidence suggests that some openly gay service members have been permitted to serve and have even received promotions. Their success seems to turn on the tolerance of commanders and extent to which circumstances create a demand for their presence. *See, e.g., My Right to Serve, supra* note 7, at 248–57 (openly gay man served and received promotions during Vietnam War).

21. This was proposed by Miriam Ben-Shalom at the beginning of the crisis in the Persian Gulf. She wrote to President Bush suggesting the formation of a "gay command" consisting of current and former service members who are gay or lesbian. She pointed out that the government could save thousands in training costs by deploying these soldiers, who were ready and willing to serve. *See* Shilts, *supra* note 5, at 727.

22. Indeed, Representative Barney Frank (D-Mass.) heard Jennifer describe the idea at a conference and was so taken with it that he asked for a written description. Frank seems to be a great believer in pragmatic incrementalism, though, so perhaps he would take to the idea more easily than the average liberal politician.

23. *See* Akhil Reed Amar, "Second Thoughts: What the Right to Bear Arms Really Means," New Republic, July 12, 1999, at 24. Professor Amar argues for universal, "compulsory or quasi-compulsory national service, with both military and nonmilitary alternatives." *Id* at 26.

24. 163 U.S. 537, 16 S.Ct. 1138 (1896).

25. 347 U.S. 483, 74 S.Ct. 686 (1954).

26. It is important to acknowledge, however, that voluntary integration almost always followed, rather than preceded, the authoritative articulation of an overarching norm of desegregation. To succeed, voluntary integration strategies may require a prior statement, such as that in *Brown*, making clear that norms have changed.

27. *See* Constance Curry, *Silver Rights: The Story of the Carter Family's Brave Decision to Send Their Children to an All-White School and Claim Their Civil Rights* 29 (1995) (recounting the history of an African-American family who took advantage of "freedom of choice" policy and sent seven school-age children to a formerly all-white school, despite intense harassment and intimidation).

28. Green v. County School Board, 391 U.S. 430 (1968) (striking down a "freedom of choice" plan when three years after implementation no white child had chosen to go to the formerly black school, and 85 percent of county's black students remained in that school; regarding such plans generally, the Court stated, "If the means prove effective, it is acceptable, but if it fails to undo segregation, other means must be used to achieve this end"). *See also* Bronson v. Board of Educ., 604 F.Supp. 68, 75 (S.D. Ohio 1984) (Cincinnati); United States v. Board

of Educ., 554 F.Supp. 912, 917, 924–26 (N.D. Ill. 1983) (Chicago); Clark v. Board of Educ., 705 F.2d 265, 272 (8th Cir. 1983) (Little Rock); United States v. Texas Educ. Agency, 679 F.2d 1104, 1110 (5th Cir. 1982) (Port Arthur); Vaughns v. Board of Educ., No. 72-325-K (D. Md. June 30, 1985) (Prince George's County); Flax v. Potts, 567 F.Supp. 859, 874 (N.D. Tex. 1983) (Fort Worth); Arthur v. Nyquist, 514 F.Supp. 1133, 1139 (W.D.N.Y. 1981) (Buffalo); Smiley v. Vollert, 453 F.Supp. 463, 476 (S.D. Tex. 1978) (Galveston), modified sub nom. Smiley v. Blevins, 514 F.Supp. 1248, 1263 (S.D. Tex. 1981).

29. In Jennifer Brown's own hometown of Champaign, Illinois, this was the integration plan adopted by the school board in the late 1960s and early 1970s. For some black families, the asymmetry of the choice fell as a very heavy burden; while black children were riding buses all over the district, the vast majority of white children were staying put in their own neighborhood schools. Sam Fulwood III, "NAACP Policy on Integration May Face Test," L.A. Times, July 13, 1997, at A1 (quoting local activist in Champaign who says busing plan sending black children from city's center to affluent outlying areas was structured by whites "for their [own] comfort and not for fairness").

30. An en banc Eighth Circuit court approved a consent decree containing an interdistrict transfer provision in the St. Louis metropolitan area. Liddell v. Missouri, 731 F.2d 1294 (8th Cir.), cert. denied, 105 S.Ct. 82 (1984). Other courts have commented generally on the advantages of interdistrict transfer arrangements as something states and suburbs might undertake voluntarily. See, e.g., Columbus Bd. of Educ. v. Penick, 443 U.S. 449, 488 (1979) (Powell, J., dissenting); Little Rock Sch. Dist. v. Pulaski County Special Sch. Dist., 778 F.2d 404, 436 (8th Cir. 1985); Ross v. Houston Indep. Sch. Dist., 699 F.2d 218, 222–24 (5th Cir. 1983); Berry v. Sch. Dist., 698 F.2d 813, 819–20 (6th Cir. 1983); see Paul Gewirtz, "Choice in the Transition: School Desegregation and the Corrective Ideal," 86 Colum. L. Rev. 728, 781 n. 179 (1986) (emphasizing the practical impact of Liddell, noting that by 1986 approximately seven thousand black students had transferred from St. Louis schools to suburban schools, about one-fourth of the students who were attending all-black schools in St. Louis, and about 540 white suburban students had transferred to St. Louis schools).

31. Women served in the armed forces only as nurses until World War II, when they began serving in various auxiliary corps. Charles C. Moskos, "From Citizen's Army to Social Laboratory," 17 Wilson Q. 90 (Winter 1993). The auxiliary corps were sex-segregated in their barracks and for purposes of administration and promotion, but they went to work with men in regular units. In this sense they enjoyed greater integration than African-American soldiers in the time of race-segregated units. Women served primarily in administrative, clerical, and health-care positions until 1973, when the abolition of the draft created some scarcity in personnel. See William N. Eskridge Jr. & Nan D. Hunter, Sexuality, Gender, and the Law 343 (1997). In 1978, women's integration in the military

gained further ground when Congress eliminated the separate women's auxiliary corps, permitting women to join all branches of the military and fill all roles save those involved in direct combat. *See id.* at 346.

32. Like gay men and lesbians, African-Americans have always fought for this country (including the war for independence, before this country was a country). Shilts, *supra* note 5, at 7 ("Even before the armed forces of the United States were formally organized, gays were bearing arms for the yet unborn nation"). Initially, black enlistments were officially forbidden by order of the Counsel of Generals. John Sibley Butler, "Race Relations in the Military," *in The Military: More Than Just a Job?* 118 (Charles C. Moskos & Frank R. Wood, eds. 1988). The British offered the black men freedom if they would join the British ranks. In response, General George Washington told the Continental Congress that he would enlist black men notwithstanding the official prohibition, and this resulted in over five thousand black men serving the Colonial side in the Revolutionary War. *Id.* Black men were allowed to fight and die for this country's independence, but when the fighting ended, they were excluded from any ongoing participation within military institutions. *Id.*

33. Many high-ranking military officials acknowledge but explicitly refuse to entertain parallels between sexual orientation and race. Former head of the Joint Chiefs of Staff Colin Powell, a retired four star General, has said that "as an African-American," he is "well aware of the attempts to draw parallels between" the military's stance on homosexuality "and positions used years ago to deny opportunities to African-Americans." He says, however, that "[s]kin color is a benign, non-behavioral characteristic. Sexual orientation is perhaps the most profound of human behavioral characteristics. Comparison of the two is a convenient but invalid argument." *See* Letter from Colin Powell, Chairman of the Joint Chiefs of Staff, to Rep. Patricia Schroeder (May 8, 1992) (cited in 139 Cong. Rec. S 1262, S1295).

34. Kenneth L. Karst, "The Pursuit of Manhood and the Desegregation of the Armed Forces," 38 U.C.L.A.L. Rev. 499, 502 (1991).

35. *See* Eskridge & Hunter, *supra* note 31, at 332.

36. *Id.*

37. Butler, *supra* note 32, at 118. As had happened earlier with the Revolutionary War, when the fighting ended in the Civil War, black men were again excluded from ongoing participation in the military.

38. *Id.*

39. The military set a maximum quota for black soldiers to correspond with the proportion of the general population that was black. The number of African-Americans in the service never approached this maximum, reaching 5.9 percent on the eve of Pearl Harbor and, at its highest during World War II, topping out at about 10 percent of total personnel. *See* Charles C. Moskos, *The Ameri-*

can Enlisted Man: The Rank and File in Today's Military 110 (1970). The black units were usually used for heavy-duty labor and not combat. *Id.*

40. Exec. Order No. 9981, 13 Fed. Reg. 4313 (1948).

41. The history of racial integration in the other branches varied slightly from that of the army. In 1947, when the air force was established as separate from the army, it began its own movements toward racial integration, and by 1950 the air force was largely integrated. In the navy, black sailors served during the Civil War, but in the early twentieth century restrictions were imposed on their service, and by 1920 all black men were barred from enlisting. In 1932, black men were permitted to join the navy as stewards in the messman's branch, and in 1942, some general service openings were allowed in segregated harbor and shore assignments. In 1944, the navy took initial steps toward integration by assigning a small number of black men to general service to an oceangoing vessel. After World War II, the navy took major steps toward integration, but even in 1970, African-Americans accounted for only 4 to 5 percent of total navy personnel. *See* Moskos, *supra* note 39, at 112–13. By 1995, African-Americans constituted roughly 17 percent of navy personnel. U.S. Census Bureau, *Statistical Abstract of the United States* §11 at 374 (1999) (table 587: Department of Defense Manpower: 1950 to 1997"). In the Marine Corps, policy evolved from total exclusion of African-Americans before World War II, to segregated units of "heavy-duty laborers, ammunition handlers, and anti-aircraft gunners" in 1942, to full integration in 1949–50. *See* Moskos, *supra* note 39, at 112–13.

42. As Kenji Yoshino has argued, however, in the military context this invisibility option is disempowering rather than helpful to gay and lesbian soldiers. *See* Yoshino, *supra* note 9, at 544 ("[DADT] simultaneously dampens the empowering aspects and amplifies the disempowering aspects of gay invisibility").

43. Perhaps the closest analog to segregated inclusion applicable to sexual orientation is the DADT policy currently in force. Just as segregated inclusion permitted the military to insulate white soldiers from the perceived threat or disruption of racial integration, so too DADT allows the military to include gay men and lesbians while at the same time shielding heterosexual soldiers from the knowledge that any given individual is gay.

44. *Id.* at 554.

45. Maj. Gen. Jeanne Holm, USAF (Ret.), *Women in the Military: An Unfinished Revolution* 258 (1982); Eskridge & Hunter, *supra* note 31, at 345–46.

46. In a 1991 study by Overlooked Opinions designed to discover the percentage of gay men who had tested HIV positive, researchers used both direct techniques (direct questions with promises of anonymity) and randomized response techniques. Of the respondents who were surveyed using direct methods, 4 percent said they were HIV positive. Of those surveyed using randomized response techniques, 11 percent said they were HIV positive.

Overlooked Opinions, Inc., Apples and Oranges (undated media release) (hereinafter Apples and Oranges).

47. Unfortunately, some researchers have found that respondents' aversion to homosexuality is so strong that they will even *disobey instructions* in order to avoid answering "yes" to a question about homosexual activity. In one study, the coin flip was actually observed by hidden camera, and 26 percent of respondents instructed to answer "yes" to the question, "Have you ever had a homosexual experience" disregarded the coin flip and answered "no." Edgar Edgell et al., *Urban Power and Social Welfare* (1982). *See generally* Apples and Oranges, *supra* note 46 (discussing survey methodologies and the variations in reported numbers of homosexuals). Such disregard for the instructions would cause the survey to underreport the number of respondents who were gay. A second problem with such a survey is that it might violate both the "don't ask" and "don't tell" portions of DADT. But to our minds, the randomization of the coin-flipping mechanism avoids a legal problem because the military does not solicit identifiable information about individual service members' sexual orientation.

48. In stage 2, the military might try to manage tipping more directly by imposing a quota on the number of openly gay soldiers that were assigned to particular inclusive commands. But quotas are unlikely to be effective, because gay and lesbian soldiers could closet themselves in order to gain admission to the inclusive unit. And quotas would expose gay and lesbian soldiers to a new type of discrimination that ultimately rests on the discriminatory preferences of their colleagues, partially negating the goal of the inclusive command.

49. Clark Freshman, "Whatever Happened to Anti-Semitism? How Social Science Theories Identify Discrimination and Promote Coalitions between 'Different' Minorities," 85 Cornell L. Rev. 313 (2000).

50. The term *fragging* was popularized during the Vietnam War, when enlisted men would occasionally fire on their own junior officers.

51. Wells-Petry, *supra* note 5, at 169–70.

52. Cal Anderson, Specialist-6 in U.S. Army, recounts, "We were situated about a mile from the Viet Cong. Being that close to possible death, I think the people were a lot more tolerant of each other, and most people kind of looked out for each other. There wasn't a lot of fear of getting caught, exposed, or kicked out of the Army for any particular infraction." *My Right to Serve, supra* note 7, at 64. J. W. "Skip" Godsey, army (1967–70), navy (1970–86), an enlisted man and officer, says, "in combat you didn't really give a fuck what men did and what men didn't do. . . . It didn't make a . . . difference whether he was black, white, queer, or straight"). *Id.*

53. *See* Shilts, *supra* note 5, at 726–27 (noting that as part of "Stop/Loss" policy designed to reduce discharges from armed forces to ensure adequate manpower, admittedly homosexual reservists were told by commanders "they did not care—the reservists would be mobilized like any other soldier"). *But see* Lou

Chibbaro Jr., "Navy 'Stop-Loss' Order Bars Gays," Washington Blade Online, Oct. 5, 2001 (U.S. Air Force and Navy institute "stop-loss" policy to limit discharges in wake of September 11 terrorist attacks, but discharges for violations of DADT will continue).

54. National Defense Research Institute, *Sexual Orientation and U.S. Military Personnel Policy: Options and Assessment* ch. 3 at 11–12 (1993).

55. Lustig-Prean & Beckett v. United Kingdom, App. Nos. 31417/96 & 32377/96, 29 Eur. H.R. Rep. 548 (1999); Smith & Grady v. United Kingdom, App. Nos. 33985/96 & 33986/96, 29 Eur. H.R. Rep. 493 (1999). *See also* Philip Britton, "Gay and Lesbian Rights in the United Kingdom: The Story Continued," 10 Ind. Int'l & Comp. L. Rev. 207, 233 (2000) (detailing the court decisions that led to the new British policy of "don't ask, can tell"); Alexander Nicoll, Military's Sexual Orientation Rules Set to Change, Fin. Times, Jan. 12, 2000, at 3. Early reports indicate that the change has not been difficult to implement. *See* Sarah Lyall, "Gays in the British Military: Ask, Tell and Then Move On," N.Y. Times, Feb. 10, 2001, at A1.

56. Geoffrey Bateman & Sameera Dalvi, U.C. Santa Barbara Center for the Study of Sexual Minorities in the Military, "Multinational Military Units and Homosexual Personnel" (Feb. 2004), http://www.gaymilitary.ucsb.edu/Publications/2004_02_BatemanSameera.htm (last visited July 1, 2004).

57. Shilts, *supra* note 5, at 732.

58. *Id.*

59. Joseph Steffan, *Honor Bound: A Gay American Fights for the Right to Serve His Country* 157 (1992).

60. *Id.* As Shilts writes:

> That young men like Greg Teran had taken up the cause indicated that among a segment of the young heterosexual population was the dawning awareness that something was wrong in the way society treated gays, and that they must help to do something about it. It was surely not a social phenomenon, but it suggested a future in which homosexuals would not be altogether alone in their fight for social acceptance.

Shilts, *supra* note 5, at 732–33.

61. *See* Diane Mazur, "A Call to Arms," 22 Harv. Women's L.J. 39, 69 (1999) ("those who choose not to participate can have a more powerful effect in creating an unrepresentative military than specific policies that limit or exclude").

62. Associated Press, "Polls Show Reduction of Soldiers' Opposition to Gays," Atlanta J. & Const., Aug. 7, 2001 (citing study conducted by Major John W. Bicknell of the Naval Postgraduate School in Monterey, Calif.).

63. Paul Johnson, "Massive Support for Gays in Military, Poll Shows," 365, Gay.com Newscenter, Dec. 24, 2003, http://www.365gay.com/newscontent/122403militaryPoll.htm (last visited June 30, 2004).

64. *See, e.g.*, Karst, *supra* note 34.
65. 139 Cong. Rec. S11157–04, *S11188.
66. Able v. United States, 968 F.Supp. 850, 864 (1997).

Chapter Seven
The Informed Association Statute and the Boys Scouts of America

This chapter is based upon an essay Jennifer published in the *Minnesota Law Review*. See "Facilitating Boycotts of Discriminatory Organizations through an Informed Association Statute," 87 Minn. L. Rev. 481 (2002).

The epigraph comes from Kenji Yoshino, "Scout Loophole," http://writ.news .findlaw.com/commentary/20000630_yoshino.html (last visited June 30, 2004).

1. 120 S.Ct. 2446 (2000).
2. *See, e.g.,* David E. Bernstein, "Antidiscrimination Laws and the First Amendment," 66 Mo. L. Rev. 83, 90 (2001) (*Dale* "affirmed what should be obvious under our constitutional system: free speech and associated rights protected by the First Amendment trump statutory antidiscrimination provisions"). *But see* Andrew Koppelman, "Should Noncommercial Associations Have an Absolute Right to Discriminate?" L. & Contemp. Problems (forthcoming 2004) (responding to Bernstein and others, Koppelman argues against the right to discriminate).
3. For example, Exxon rescinded Mobile Oil's gay-friendly employee policies when the two companies merged. The Human Rights Campaign fund, a gay rights advocacy organization, has been working to persuade Exxon/Mobile that it should reinstate the employment policies deemed more fair to gay, lesbian, and bisexual employees. *See* Coalition Packet, http://www.hrc.org/ Content/NavigationMenu/ExxonMobil_Home2/Information_and_Action/ Coalition_Packet1/Equality_Principles.htm (last visited June 30, 2004). A nationwide boycott is one of the persuasive strategies HRC is using. *See* Press Release, HRC Calls For Nationwide Boycott against ExxonMobil for Anti-gay Policies; "Exercise Your Power at the Pump," Says *HRC* (June 13, 2001), http:// www.hrc.org/equalityatexxon/newsreleases/2001/010613action.asp (last visited June 30, 2004).
4. The Informed Association Statute thus seeks to change the social meaning of Boy Scout membership through a process Professor Larry Lessig has called "tying." *See* Larry Lessig, "The Regulation of Social Meaning," 62 U. Chi. L. Rev. 943, 1009 (1995). By promoting disclosure of discriminatory membership policies, the Informed Association Statute would more closely tie the decision to join such an organization to discriminatory activity. "Tying," Lessig writes, "changes the cost [of an activity] by making it more clear just what meaning an action has." Larry Lessig, "Social Meaning and Social Norms," 144 U. Pa. L. Rev.

2181, 2189 (1996). Tying is the flip side or "nested opposition" of ambiguation, because it clarifies or highlights a particular character of some activity, while ambiguation blurs categories. *See* Lessig, "Regulation of Social Meaning," at 1010 n. 224.

5. *See* Clayborn Carson & Martin Luther King Jr., *The Autobiography of Martin Luther King, Jr.* 232–38 (1998). Dr. King explains:

> President Kennedy was a strongly contrasted personality. There were in fact two John Kennedys. One presided in the first two years under pressure of the uncertainty caused by his razor-thin margin of victory. He vacillated, trying to sense the direction his leadership could travel while retaining and building support for his administration. However, in 1963, a new Kennedy had emerged. He had found that public opinion was not in a rigid mold. American political thought was not committed to conservatism, nor radicalism, nor moderation. It was above all fluid. As such it contained trends rather than hard lines, and affirmative leadership could guide it into constructive channels.

6. 120 S.Ct. at 2449.

7. The public accommodations statute prohibited discrimination on the basis of sexual orientation in places of public accommodation. N.J. Stat. Ann. §10:5–4 (West Supp. 2000).

8. 120 S.Ct. at 2449.

9. No. MON-C-330-92 (N.J. Super. Ct. Ch. Div. Nov. 3, 1995) (on file with author). For an analysis of the trial court's opinion, see Jennifer Gerarda Brown, "Sweeping Reform from Small Rules? Anti-bias Canons as Substitute for Heightened Scrutiny," 85 Minn. L. Rev. 363 (2000).

10. In describing the basis for Dale's exclusion from the BSA, Justice Rehnquist again refers to Dale's "avowed" homosexuality (rather than "admitted," "acknowledged" or "open"). Rehnquist's decision to use a word that suggests a sort of vow-taking related to homosexuality is particularly powerful in a case examining Dale's ability to fulfill another vow—the Scout Oath. *See* 120 S.Ct. at 2450.

11. 160 N.J. 562, 605, 734 A.2d 1196, 1219 (1999) quoting Board of Directors of Rotary Int'l v. Rotary Club of Duarte, 481 U.S. 537, 544, 107 S.Ct. 1940, 95 L.Ed.2d 474 (1987).

12. 160 N.J. at 613, 734 A.2d at 1223.

13. 160 N.J. at 613, 734 A.2d at 1223–24. The U.S. Supreme Court later clarified that such a central purpose is not required in order to gain First Amendment protection. *See* 120 S.Ct. at 2454 ("associations do not have to associate for the 'purpose' of disseminating a certain message in order to be entitled to the protections of the First Amendment"). A five-year-old boy we know expressed incredulity similar to the New Jersey Supreme Court's, however. When he over-

heard some adults discussing the *Dale* case on the day the U.S. Supreme Court issued its opinion, he exclaimed in shock and indignation, "The purpose of the Boy Scouts is to *exclude?*"

14. 160 N.J. at 615, 734 A.2d at 1225 (quoting *Duarte*, 107 S.Ct. at 548).

15. Indeed, as Kenji Yoshino has noted, "the Scout Handbook defines 'morally straight' to include the following prescriptions: '[G]uide your life with honesty, purity, and justice,' 'Respect and defend the rights of all people,' 'Your relationships with others should be honest and open.'" Kenji Yoshino, "Scout Loophole," http://writ.news.findlaw/commentary/20000630_yoshino.html (last visited June 30, 2004).

16. "The Boy Scouts asserts that it 'teach[es] that homosexual conduct is not morally straight,' and that it does 'not want to promote homosexual conduct as a legitimate form of behavior.' We accept the Boy Scouts' assertion. We need not inquire further to determine the nature of the Boy Scouts' expression with respect to homosexuality." 120 S.Ct. at 2453 (citations omitted).

17. *Id.* at 2455.

18. Actually, this movement can be traced to earlier challenges to the BSA's discriminatory policy. Eight local United Way chapters adopted antidiscrimination policies affecting their relationship with the Boy Scouts prior to the *Dale* decision. *See* "United Way Funding of Boy Scouts" http://national.unitedway.org/aboutuwa/pos_bsa.cfm (last visited June 30, 2004).

19. Dave Wedge, "Taunton Church Drops Scout Program over Ban on Gays," Boston Herald, Nov. 24, 2000, at 12.

20. *Id.* ("We have a big, red and white banner out front that says, 'All Are Welcome.' . . . Jesus never said anything about homosexuality. We're taking this stance because of how we believe in Christianity").

21. Lisa Black, "Oak Park Church Is Denied Cub Scout Pack after Rejecting Gay Policy; Several Units Homeless after Refusal to Comply with Group's Stand," Chicago Tribune, Mar. 8, 2001, at L5.

22. Elizabeth Benjamin, "Scouts Facing Criticism over Ban on Gay Leaders," Albany Times Union, Nov. 7, 2000, at B1.

23. Board of Education of the City of New York, Press Release, Schools Chancellor and Board President Announce Decision to Prohibit Boy Scouts from Bidding on Future Contracts Unless Scouts' Discriminatory Policies Change, Dec. 1, 2000 (on file with author).

24. *Id. See also* Rose Arce, "New York Schools Cut Ties with Boy Scouts: Education Board Objects to Anti-gay Policy," CNN.com, Dec. 1, 2000, http://www.cnn.com/2000/US/12/01/ny.schools.boyscouts/ (last visited June 30, 2004).

25. Boy Scouts of America v. Till, 136 F.Supp.2d 1295, 1302 (S.D. Fla. 2001).

26. *Id.*

27. *See* Arthur S. Leonard, "Boy Scouts Win Preliminary Injunction against Exclu-

sion from Broward County Schools," Lesbian/Gay Law Notes, April 2001, at 56, http://www.qrd.org/qrd/usa/legal/lgln/2000/12.00 (last visited June 30, 2004).

28. 136 F.Supp.2d at 1308.

29. *See* Lou Chibbaro Jr., "Helms Measure Passes," Washington Blade Online, June 15, 2001, http://www.washblade.com/national/010615b.htm (last visited June 30, 2004).

30. Human Rights Campaign Press Release, "Schools Not Required to Sponsor Boy Scout Troops, HRC Says," Nov. 6, 2001, http://www.hrc.org/newsreleases/ 2001/011106troops.asp (last visited June 30, 2004).

31. PL 110, 115 Stat. 1425, Sec. 9525 (b)(2) (Jan. 08, 2002). Sponsored by Senator Jesse Helms, the version of the amendment approved by the Senate did not include this language. *See also supra* text accompanying note 29.

32. Bill Hirschman and Toni Marshall, "County School Board Votes to Lock Doors on Boy Scouts," South Florida Sun-Sentinel, Nov. 15, 2000, at 1A; "Florida School Board Boots Scouts over Gays," Washington Times, Nov. 18, 2000, at A1.

33. Peter Freiberg, "Rallies Target Boy Scouts Policy Banning Gays," Washington Blade Online, Aug. 24, 2001, http://www.washblade.com/national/010824g .htm (last visited June 30, 2004). Scouting for All, "List of United Ways That Have Withdrawn Their Funding of the BSA," http://www.scoutingforall .org/aaic/unitedway2/shtml (last visited June 30, 2004).

34. It is possible that the recall was also sparked by the fact that Giuliano is openly gay. *See* "Backlash to the Backlash," Advocate, Mar. 27, 2001, http:// articles.findarticles.com/p/articles/mi_m1589/is_2001_March_27/ai_7205058 3 (last visited June 30, 2004); Kim Krisberg, "Giuliano Wins: Mayoral Recall Effort Fails," Washington Blade Online, Sept. 14, 2001, http://www.washblade .com/national/010824g.htm (last visited June 30, 2004). Interestingly, the recall election went forward on September 11, 2001, even after news of the terrorist attacks in New York and Washington.

35. Associated Press, "Three Communities to Vote on Mayors," Arizona Daily Wildcat Online, http://wildcat.arizona.edu/papers/95/16/05.html (last visited June 30, 2004).

36. Tempe workers donated $42,794 in the fall of 2000, less than half of the $89,400 they contributed in the fall of 1999. "Scouts Hurt United Way," Freethought Today, Dec. 2000, http://www.ffrf.org/fttoday/2000/december2000/state_ church.html (last visited June 30, 2004). *See also* Bruce Navarro, "Tempe United Way Cash Down, Worker Gifts Down 52% from Last Year," Arizona Republic, Dec. 6, 2001, at 1.

37. Bob Mims, "Novell Halts Boy Scout Contributions," Salt Lake Tribune, Nov. 11, 2000, at A1.

38. Bob Mims, "Novell Changes Donations Policy Again," Salt Lake Tribune, Nov.

16, 2000, at A1. Although employees are free to exclude the BSA from recipients of their United Way contribution, the United Way in most places has continued to fund local Boy Scout troops. The United Way of the Great Salt Lake, for example, donated $188,000 to the Boy Scouts in 1999. *Id.*

39. David Austin, "Wells Fargo and PGE Divert Funds from Scouts; Both Companies, Who Donate to the United Way, Say They Have Strict Non-discrimination Policies That Steer Donations," Oregonian, Dec. 11, 2000, at B01. The BSA's "Learning for Life" program in city schools will continue to get Wells Fargo funding, however, since it is separately run and does not exclude gay students from participation.

40. Short of such defiance, other heads of area Scout councils have asked the BSA to revoke its ban on gay Scout leaders. *See* Laura Parker, "Big Cities' Scout Leaders Pushing for Inclusion of Gays," USA Today, June 15, 2001, at A1. *See also* Freiberg, *supra* note 33.

41. Jennifer Levitz, "Six Scout Leaders Reject Ban on Gays," Providence Journal, Nov. 7, 2000, at A1; Jennifer Levitz, "Second Group of Scouts Vows to Defy Ban on Gays," Providence Journal, Nov. 25, 2000, at A3.

42. Anemona Hartocollis, "Levy Limits Scout Events in the Schools," N.Y. Times, Dec. 2, 2000, at B1.

43. *See supra* notes 21 & 41 and accompanying text.

44. "Spielberg Quits Scout Post over Anti-gay Policy," L.A. Times, Apr. 17, 2001, at B2.

45. Young men who achieve the rank of Eagle Scout are eligible to join the elite National Eagle Scout Association as men. *See* "National Eagle Scout Association," at the Boy Scouts of America homepage, http://www.scouting.org/nav/ enter.jsp?s=ba&c=ne (last visited June 30, 2004).

46. David France, "Scouts Divided," Newsweek, Aug. 6, 2001 at 44; Freiberg, *supra* note 33 (Girl Scouts, Boys and Girls Clubs experiencing increase in membership rates). This trend may be continuing, as some data suggests an overall decline in BSA membership for 2002–3 as well. "Year in Review: 2003," http:// www.scouting.org (last visited June 30, 2004) (reached through a link that erroneously refers to 2002; contained under the "facts and figures" tab of the site's navigation bar).

47. Press Release, BSA Board Affirms Traditional Leadership Standards, and "Boy Scouts of America Resolution, February 6, 2002," http://www.scouting.org (last visited June 30, 2004). The resolution also makes clear that "duty to God is not a mere ideal for those choosing to associate with the Boy Scouts of America; it is an obligation."

48. *See, e.g.,* Boy Scouts of America v. Till, 136 F.Supp. 1295, 1302 (S.D. Fla. 2001) (quoting affidavit of Paul Eichner).

49. 120 S.Ct. at 2457.

50. Ian Ayres & Robert Gertner, "Filling Gaps in Incomplete Contracts: An Eco-

nomic Theory of Default Rules," 99 Yale L.J. 87 (1989); Randy E. Barnett, "The Sound of Silence: Default Rules and Contractual Consent," 78 Va. L. Rev. 821, 857–60 (1992).

51. *Dale*, 120 S.Ct. at 2456 ("We recognized in cases such as Roberts and Duarte that States have a compelling interest in eliminating discrimination against women in public accommodations. But in each of these cases we went on to conclude that the enforcement of these statutes would not materially interfere with the ideas that the organization sought to express").

52. A model statute might read:

(1) Unless otherwise indicated by the procedures outlined in section (2), an organization that engages in broad public solicitation implicitly promises as part of its solicitation that it will not discriminate in any accommodations, advantages, facilities, and privileges of any place of public accommodation, because of race, creed, color, national origin, ancestry, age, marital status, affectional or sexual orientation, familial status, or sex.

(2) When necessary to preserve a right of expressive association in an organization subject to this Act, an organization may, notwithstanding section (1), retain the right to discriminate in admission if it (a) makes a good faith effort to obtain signed acknowledgments from potential members before they are allowed to join the organization, and (b) maintains these acknowledgments on file for potential in camera review. To be effective, an acknowledgment must:

(a) state that the organization reserves the right to discriminate in admission to or terms of membership;

(b) list the characteristic(s) enumerated in section 1 of this Act on which the discrimination would be based; and

(c) affirms that the undersigned member chooses to associate with the organization with knowledge that the organization reserves the right to discriminate.

The acknowledgment must be signed by any person before becoming a member of the organization.

(3) Any organization failing to comply with the requirements set forth in subsection (2) is subject to the full force and effect of this Act.N.J. Stat. Ann. §10:5–4 (West Supp. 2000).

A definitions section in the statute could list in detail the sorts of facilities and organizations covered by the act. *See, e.g.,* N.J. Stat. Ann. §10:5–5 (West Supp. 2000).

53. *See Dale,* 120 S.Ct. at 2455 ("the First Amendment simply does not require that every member of a group agree on every issue in order for the group's policy to be "expressive association").

54. In this way, the discriminatory policy is analogous to a latent or hidden defect

in a commercial product: a seller must disclose the danger in order to avoid liability. 1 *Madden & Owen on Prod. Liab.* § 2:8 (3d ed. 2000) ("The maker's obligation to warn of hidden dangers in its products is an ancient one. Its roots reach back into early Roman sales law, early English civil law, and the ecclesiastical (but not the secular) law of medieval England").

55. Because our proposed statute is limited to organizations that "engage[] in broad public solicitation," we believe that it would be constitutional to require an "opt out" filing with the secretary of state. But our analysis suggests that our signed acknowledgment mechanism would be constitutional if applied to organizations that did not solicit the public generally. The state has a constitutional interest in promoting informed association—that is promoted in a targeted way by signed acknowledgments.

56. Under our proposal, if an organization were ever sued under the public accommodation statute, in order for it to invoke the "opt out" exemption, it would be required to prove to the court that it made a "a good faith effort to obtain signed acknowledgments from potential members before they are allowed to join the organization." The organization might offer signed acknowledgments of its members for confidential review by the court, and either side might offer testimony of current or former members about whether they did or did not sign the requisite acknowledgments. If an organization did succeed in opting out of the statute, members who had not signed the acknowledgment would be granted a statutory right to reimbursement of all their dues plus one hundreds dollars per year of their membership as a means of compensating them for inducing their association without sufficient information.

This review of membership acknowledgments by state actors could impermissibly infringe on the organizations' right to keep its membership lists secret. In NAACP v. Patterson, the Supreme Court recognized that compelled disclosure of member lists could burden individuals' associational opportunities, "because of fear of exposure of their beliefs shown through their associations and of the consequences of this exposure." NAACP v. Patterson, 357 U.S. 449, 463 (1958). Under *Patterson*, then, if the procedures for opting out of our informed association statute would at any point require the organization to make public the identity of its members, the statute might violate the First Amendment. But a process that turns on judicial in camera review of membership acknowledgments does not pose the same concerns as public disclosure—where censure from both state and private actors becomes more of a threat.

57. Yoshino, *supra* note 15.

58. *Id.*

59. Erving Goffman, *Relations in Public* 113 (1971) ("apology is a process through which a person symbolically splits into two parts, the part that is guilty of an offense and the part that dissociates itself from the delict and affirms a belief in the offended rule"). In this case, the "offense" would actually be compliance

with an official policy of discrimination, and the "offended rule" would be a norm of nondiscrimination.

60. 120 S.Ct. at 2458 (emphasis supplied), quoting Whitney v. California, 274 U.S. 357, 375 (Brandeis, J., concurring).

61. Whitney, 274 U.S. at 375 (Brandeis, J., concurring) (the Founders of the United States "believed that freedom to think as you will and to speak as you think are means indispensable to the discovery and spread of political truth").

62. Derrick Bell, *Faces at the Bottom of the Well* (1992); *See also* Derrick Bell, "The Racial Preference Licensing Act: A Fable about the Politics of Hate," 78 A.B.A. J. 50 (Sept. 1992).

63. *See* Yoshino, *supra* note 15.

64. Something similar occurred when President Clinton's announced intention to lift the ban on gay and lesbian military service members triggered legislation in Congress converting what had been a Department of Defense regulation excluding openly gay or lesbian service members into a federal statute.

Chapter Eight
Renounce of Share?

1. Albert O. Hirschman, *Exit, Voice, and Loyalty: Responses to Declines in Firms, Organizations, and States* (1972).

2. Our discussion emphasizes de jure discrimination, but we should be clear that analogous ethical concerns can be raised by both de facto discrimination and unjustified disparate impact. Being the recipient of an undeserved benefit is problematic. But there is a clarity and transparency to outright exclusion that causes an independent expressive harm and simply as an evidentiary matter demands a response.

3. Kant, for example, argues that even good character traits can be exploited for evil. He thus rejects the notion that there is any "end" to achieve beyond good action itself. Good action must be justified in its own right, not by the ends it achieves. As Professor Linda Meyer cautions, however:

> that is not to say that cost/benefit analysis may never be used. Indeed, one has duties of prudence and foresight. But the action is never justified only because it produced or could produce good results. It is justified because it was taken for *all* the right reasons (even if the results expected don't pan out), and always with respect for others.

E-mail from Linda Meyer, Professor of Law, Quinnipiac University, to Jennifer Brown, Professor of Law, Quinnipiac University (Sept. 19, 2001) (on file with author).

4. We can imagine deontological arguments for voice over exit. Some might argue

that there is a moral imperative not to waste resources and it is better to take the benefit and redistribute the rightful part to the victims while simultaneously working for an end to the discrimination. Or there may be contexts in which one owes a duty of loyalty to an institution that counterbalances the duty to oppose discrimination. Imagine, for example, that you learn that your spouse somehow profits from making discriminatory hiring decisions.

5. Aristotle, for example, thought that ethics—the development of "excellent" character—can be formed not by utilitarian (or cost-benefit) thinking, but by acting courageously, generously, etc., regardless of the costs and benefits of each decision. Aristotle, *The Nicomachean Ethics,* Book 3: *Moral Virtue,* ch. 6. *See also* Aristotle, *The Nicomachean Ethics,* Book 4: *Moral Virtue,* ch. 1. Utilitarianism encompasses diverse approaches.

6. The pro rata sharing principle also resonates with a kind of Rawlsianism. John Rawls, A Theory of Justice (1972). While Rawls was more interested in *social* systems of justice, the idea of pro-rata sharing attempts to imagine what duties *individuals* behind a veil of ignorance would agree were owed to each other.

7. Make a one-time or monthly contribution at https://www.digitopia.com/lambda/membership.html or http://www.lmfamily.org/about/donate.html.

8. Bruce Ackerman & Ian Ayres, *Voting with Dollars: A New Paradigm for Campaign Finance* (2002).

9. Estimates vary regarding the proportion of the population that is not heterosexual. *See, e.g.,* Richard A. Posner, *Sex & Reason* 293 (1992); Emilio Guerra, "2000 Census Information on Gay and Lesbian Couples: Total LGBT Population," http://www.gaydemographics.org/USA/2000_Census_Total.htm (visited June 28, 2004). A conservative number supports a minimum characterization of the duty to share—and even this might seem excessive to some allies.

10. Randy Cohen, "Speaking in Codes," New York Times Magazine, Apr. 25, 2004 at 26.

11. Erik Baard, "A Rites Issue: Straight Couples Who Refuse to Marry Because Gays Can't Standing on Ceremony," Village Voice, Dec. 10–16, 2003, at 283. http://www.villagevoice.com/issues/0350/baard.php (visited June 26, 2004).

12. *Id.*

13. *Id.*

14. Indeed, home rule may be another incremental strategy toward legalization that could garner support from legislators who don't want same-sex marriage in their backyard but don't want to stop other parts of the state from opting for it.

15. Currently Vermont civil union is only available to same-sex couples (as civil unions would be in Massachusetts' proposed constitutional amendment). Vt. Stat. Ann. Tit. 15 § 1202 (2000).

16. Couples might still want marriage ceremonies for religious purposes, but this sacramental layer is separate from the couple's legal status, and could easily rest on a civil union rather a civil marriage.

17. Even today gay and nongay couples can re-create many of the legal benefits of marriage via private contracting. "Living Together Contracts," http://www.nolo.com/lawcenter/ency/article.cfm/ObjectID/E354BF5F-A357–40DA-BAF2A0F4093A8BE8/catID/64C2C325–5DAF-4BC8–B4761409BA0187C3, (last visited June 28, 2004). But this contractual simulacrum still falls short with respect to governmental recognition, e.g., taxes, social security, and immigration.

18. "Conn., Mass. Clergy Refuse to Sign Marriage Licenses in Pro-gay Protest," Oct. 24, 2003, http://www.washblade.com/2003/10–24/news/religion.ribs.cfm (last visited Oct. 12, 2004). *See also* "Northampton Minister Won't Sign Marriage Licenses," Feb. 27, 2003, http://www.baywindows.com/main.cfm?include=detail&storyid=381524 (last visited Sept. 25, 2004).

19. Baard, *supra* note 11.

20. "Ore. County Halts Issuance of All Marriage Licenses," Mar. 24, 2004, http://www.bpnews.net/bpnews.asp?ID=17916 (last visited Sept. 25, 2004).

21. *Id.*

22. Judith Butler has described the "queering" effect of resisting marriage, and her discussion seems applicable to different-sex couples who eschew marriage, as well as same-sex couples:

    To what extent, then, has the performative "queer" operated alongside, as a deformation of, the "I pronounce you . . ." of the marriage ceremony? If the performative ["I pronounce you . . ."] operates as the sanction that performs the heterosexualization of the social bond, perhaps it also comes into play as the shaming taboo which "queers" those who resist or oppose that social form as well as those who occupy it without hegemonic social sanction.

    Judith Butler, *Bodies That Matter* 226 (1993).

23. Eric Rofes, "Life after Knight: A Call for Direct Action and Civil Disobedience," http://www.bandia.net/moonstone/Marriage.html (visited June 26, 2004).

24. *Id.*

25. Baard, *supra* note 11.

26. *Id.*

27. Rofes, *supra* note 23.

28. *Id.*

29. Baard, *supra* note 11.

30. *Id.*

31. http://www.yale.edu/lgblsa/ (last visited Sept. 25, 2004).

32. Baard, *supra* note 11.

33. *Id.*

Chapter Nine
Working with Organizations Advocating Gay Rights

1. A major exception is PFLAG, which specifically targets a predominantly heterosexual population for membership (http://www.pflag.org, last visited Jun. 25, 2004). More typical of gay rights advocacy organizations is the Human Rights Campaign (HRC), which calls itself "America's largest gay and lesbian organization" (www.hrc.org, (last visited June 25, 2004).

2. http://www.freedomtomarry.org/marriage_resolution.asp (last visited June 25, 2004).

3. Riki Wilchins, "GenderPAC At-a-Glance," http://www.gpac.org/gpac/index.html (last visited June 25, 2004).

4. http://www.lmfct.org/ (last visited June 25, 2004).

5. http://www.rainbowsashmovement.org/RSM%20History.html (last visited June 25, 2004).

6. "The Rainbow Sash Movement: Our Core Statement," http://www.rainbowsashmovement.org/ms.html (last visited June 25, 2004).

7. Virginia Soto, "Chicago Priests Deny Communion to Rainbow Sash Gays" (May 30, 2004), http://chicago.about.com/od/glbt/a/053104_gays.htm (last visited June 29, 2004).

8. Tim Novak, *Man of the House: The Life and Political Memoirs of Speaker Tip O'Neill* 25 (1987); *See also* Evan Wolfson, "Crossing the Threshold: Equal Marriage Rights for Lesbians and Gay Men and the Intra-community Critique" 21 N.Y.U. Rev. L. & Soc. Change 567, 612 & n. 195 (1995) (invoking the O'Neill anecdote to emphasize the importance of "asking" for community support in the quest for equal marriage rights).

9. A fuller list of organizations can be found at http://www.looksmart.com (last visited June 29, 2004).

10. *See, e.g.,* the LGBT Organizations Database, which permits visitors to sort organizations by state, issue, and/or population served, http://www.lgbtfunders.org/lgbtfunders/database.htm (last visited June 29, 2004).

11. Although the organization identifies its causes broadly ("ending workplace discrimination, combating hate crimes, fighting HIV/AIDS, protecting our families and working for better lesbian health"; *see* http://www.hrc.org/Content/NavigationMenu/About_HRC/What_We_Do_HRC.htm [last visited June 29, 2004]), for many years HRC focused on the first item—employment discrimination. More recently, and particularly with the accelerated pace of legal change on marriage, HRC has turned increased attention and resources to this issue.

12. We say "perhaps" here because it would be wrong to assume that individuals are necessarily endowed with useful information about the issues simply by virtue of being gay, lesbian, or bisexual. Indeed, their own experiences may be-

come so salient to them that they have difficulty absorbing contrary information about the experience of others within the gay community.

13. Indeed, Lambda's client, James Dale, *affirmed* the value of scouting by seeking admission as an openly gay man. If Lambda "harmed" the BSA by imposing litigation costs on the organization, such effects were unavoidable in pursuit of the principles at stake in the case.

14. When George H. Bush faced the difficult decision of whether to lift sanctions on South Africa, he took the lone ranger approach—deciding what he thought would best serve the cause of equality. But to our minds deferring to the people of color in South Africa would have been a superior method. Bush should have deferred to Mandela or better yet told DeClerq (who was desperate for sanctions to be lifted) that the U.S. would lift sanctions if a majority of the black population so voted.

15. On some issues, intense disagreement can emerge over the optimal strategy. For example, in Irizarry v. Board of Education, 251 F.3d 604 (7th Cir. 2001), a heterosexual woman challenged the Chicago Board of Education policy extending domestic partnership benefits to same-sex, but not different-sex, domestic partners of employees. Some thought that the best way to promote gay rights would have been to defend the board's policy, and vigorously. *See, e.g.,* Chris Cain, "Lambda Picks Strange Bedfellow," Washington Blade, June 22, 2001. Lambda Legal, however, filed an amicus brief supporting the plaintiff's challenge, arguing that the board shouldn't be conferring rights based upon marriage—and that this is true whether the unmarried couples are same-sex or different-sex. Without consultation and collaboration, many supporters of gay rights might have missed Lambda's somewhat counterintuitive take on the issue.

16. The incident is depicted in Spike Lee's film *Malcolm X. See* Roger Ebert, "Malcom X," Chicago Sun Times, Nov. 18, 1992, http://www.suntimes.com/ebert/ebert_reviews/1992/11/790018.html (last visited June 29, 2004).

17. Fla. Stat. ch. 63.042(3) (2004); N.H. Rev. Stat. Ann. § 170–B:4 (2004). A Mississippi statute forbids adoption by same-sex couples. Miss. Code Ann § 93–17–3(2) (2004). And a Utah statute forbids adoption by any unmarried couple in a sexual relationship. Utah Code Ann. § 78–30–1(b) (2004). Other states have not codified their hostility to adoption by LGBT persons but have nonetheless blocked gay adoptions by regulation or department policy. *See* Diane Riggs, "Two Steps Forward, One Step Back: Single and Gay Adoption in North America," Adoptalk, summer 1999, http://www.nacac.org/adoptalk_articles/two_steps.html (last visited June 29, 2004).

18. "Gays Lose Challenge to Florida Adoption Ban," CNN.Com, Jan. 28, 2004, http://www.cnn.com/2004/LAW/01/28/gay.adoption.ap/ (last visited June 29, 2004).

19. Lofton v. Secretary of Dept. of Children and Family Services, 358 F.3d 804 (11th Cir. 2004).

20. Amy Fagan, "Oklahoma Abides by Out-of-State Adoptions by Gays," Washington Times, Apr. 14, 2004, at A07, http://www.washtimes.com/national/20040414-010324-3795r.htm (last visited June 29, 2004).

21. Children, of course, are not fungible, and the special needs of the children or the adopting parents might still counsel toward a Florida adoption notwithstanding the state's discrimination. Many adoptions grow out of foster parenting, which gay people are permitted to do in Florida. Once this relationship is established, a child can become irreplaceable to a loving gay parent.

22. *See* Florida Department of Children and Families, "Who Can Adopt," http://www.myflorida.com/cf_web/myflorida2/healthhuman/adoption/faq.shtml (last visited June 29, 2004) ("Most adults who can provide a stable, loving home to a child can adopt. Married couples, single parents, working mothers, parents who already have children, people who live in apartments, and people of any religious faith, race, and education level will be considered").

23. Jeremy Jones, "Plaintiffs in Florida Gay Adoption Case Speak Out: 'Model Parents' Say It's All about the Children," Weekly News (May 20, 2004).

Lawlor, Michael, 190–91
Leckie, Bonnie, 53
Lee, Liz, 199n.29
Lee, Spike, 200n.33
legalization, democratizing *vs.* judicial, 68–71
lesbians, 17–18, 37, 102–3, 108, 111, 173, 198n.21
Lessig, Lawrence, 97–99, 110, 224n.4
Levi Strauss corporation, 109
Levy, Harold O., 150
LGBT groups: in churches, 52; in schools, 41, 45; in workplace, 56, 84
LGBT Organizations Database, 234n.9
liberation principle, 34
libraries, 46
licensing, and Fair Employment Mark, 89
licensor monitoring, and Fair Employment Mark, 89
litigation, and Fair Employment Mark, 88
Littleton, Massachusetts, 169
lone ranger approach to advocacy organizations, 187–89
Love Makes a Family (LMF), 166, 180–81, 190–91
loyalty approach to advocacy organizations, 183–87
Lucent Technologies, Safe Space Program, 53–54

Macey, Jon, 203n.11
Madison, Wisconsin, 102–3, 111
"Madison Affirmation," 52
Manford, Jeanne, 23
Manford, Morton, 23
marketing: of Fair Employment Mark, 91–93; of Vacation Pledge for Equal Marriage Rights, 72–73
marketing, corporate, and Fair Employment Mark, 88
market research, 16
marriage, 25–26, 162, 167–70. *See also* nonmarriage movement; same-sex marriage
interracial, 63–64, 168
Marriage Equality, 177

Massachusetts, 5, 61, 63–64, 68–72, 168–71; Supreme Judicial Court, 61
McCutchin, Mame, 168
membership issues, 10–12, 38. *See also* Boy Scouts of America; Informed Association Statute
Meyer, Linda, 231n.3
"Michael" (law professor), 105–6, 109, 212n.22
military, U.S: African Americans in, 220n.32, 220n.33, 220n.39, 221n.41; and "buddy system," 121; and "don't ask, don't tell" (DADT) policy, 57, 98, 117–18, 120, 123–24, 134, 141–42, 158, 215n.9, 221n.43, 231n.64; and dual-command system, 138–40; exclusion of homosexuals from, 116, 214n.5; and "gay command," 137–38, 218n.21; and goal of nondiscrimination, 125–30; and integration of sexual minorities, 117–18; and racial integration, 119, 127–30; and "Stop/Loss" policy, 222n.53; and unit cohesion hypothesis, 116–19, 122–23, 136, 140, 217n.19; use of quotas by, 220n.39, 222n.48; women in, 219n.31. *See also* exclusive command; inclusive command
military discharge, for homosexuality, 215n.10
military service, benefits of, 141–42
military training, 131–32, 135
Miller, Geoff, 203n.11
mini-DOMA statutes. *See* antirecognition statutes
mission statements, churches and, 48–49
morality, issue of, 32–34, 163–64, 167–70. *See also* pro rata sharing
Mormon church, 206n.39
Morrison, Douglas, 109
Mossin, Kyril, 168
Muslims, in United States, 99–100

NAACP v. Patterson, 230n.56
National Center for Lesbian Rights, 73
National Coming Out Day, 101–2
National Eagle Scout Association, 228n.45